Solutions Manual

to accompany

Paul Krugman and Robin Wells
macroeconomics

Robin Wells
Princeton University

Andreas Bentz
Dartmouth College

Martha Olney (consultant)
California State University, Berkeley

WORTH PUBLISHERS

Solutions Manual
to accompany
Krugman/Wells: *Macroeconomics*

© 2006 by Worth Publishers

All rights reserved.

Printed in the United States of America

ISBN: 0-7167-7964-1 (EAN: 978-0-7167-7964-3)

"Third Printing"

Worth Publishers
41 Madison Avenue
New York, NY 10010
www.worthpublishers.com

CONTENTS

First Principles

1. In each of the following situations, identify which of the nine principles is at work.

   a. You choose to shop at the local discount store rather than paying a higher price for the same merchandise at the local department store.

   b. On your spring vacation trip, your budget is limited to $35 a day.

   c. The student union provides a website on which departing students can sell items such as used books, appliances, and furniture rather than giving them away to their roommates as they formerly did.

   d. You decide how many cups of coffee to have when studying the night before an exam by considering how much more work you can do by having another cup versus how jittery it will make you feel.

   e. There is limited lab space available to do the project required in Chemistry 101. The lab supervisor assigns lab time to each student based on when that student is able to come.

   f. You realize that you can graduate a semester early by forgoing a semester of study abroad.

   g. At the student union, there is a bulletin board on which people advertise used items for sale, such as bicycles. Once you have adjusted for differences in quality, all the bikes sell for about the same price.

   h. You are better at performing lab experiments, and your lab partner is better at writing lab reports. So the two of you agree that you will do all the experiments, and she will write up all the reports.

   i. State governments mandate that it is illegal to drive without passing a driving exam.

1. a. People usually exploit opportunities to make themselves better off. In this case, you make yourself better off by buying merchandise at a lower price.

   b. Resources are scarce. Since you have only $35 a day, your resources are limited (scarce).

   c. Markets usually lead to efficiency. The market here is represented by the buyers and sellers who use the student union website to trade goods, in contrast to the "non-market" of simply giving items away to one's roommate. The market is efficient because it enables people who want to sell items to find those who want to buy those items. This is in contrast to a system in which items are simply left with a roommate, who may have little or no desire to have them.

   d. "How much?" is a decision at the margin. Your decision is one of "how much" coffee to consume, and you evaluate the trade-off between keeping yourself awake and becoming more jittery from one more cup of coffee.

   e. Resources should be used as efficiently as possible to achieve society's goals. Allocating scarce lab space according to when each student can use that space is efficient.

   f. The real cost of something is what you must give up to get it. The real cost of a semester abroad is giving up the opportunity to graduate early.

   g. Markets move toward equilibrium. Any bicycle a buyer chooses will leave him or her equally well off. That is, a buyer who chooses a particular bicycle cannot change actions and find another bicycle that makes him or her better off. Also, no seller can take a different action that makes him or her better off: no seller can charge a higher price for a bicycle of similar quality, since no one would buy that bicycle.

h. There are gains from trade. If each person specializes in what he or she is good at (that is, in comparison with others that person has an advantage in producing that good), then there will be gains from specialization and trade.

i. When markets don't achieve efficiency, government intervention can improve society's welfare. Unsafe drivers don't take into account the dangers they impose on others and often on themselves. So when unsafe drivers are allowed to drive, everyone is made worse off. Government intervention improves society's welfare by assuring a minimum level of competence in driving.

2. Describe some of the opportunity costs when you decide to do the following.

    a. Attend college instead of taking a job

    b. Watch a movie instead of studying for an exam

    c. Ride the bus instead of driving your car

2. a. One of the opportunity costs of going to college is not being able to take a job. By choosing to go to college, you give up the income you would have earned on the job and the valuable on-the-job experience you would have acquired. Another opportunity cost of going to college is the cost of tuition, books, supplies, and so on. On the other hand, the benefit of going to college is being able to find a better, more highly paid job after graduation in addition to the joy of learning.

b. Watching the movie gives you a certain benefit, but allocating your time (a scarce resource) to watching the movie also involves the opportunity cost of not being able to study for the exam. As a result, you will likely get a lower grade on the exam—and all that that implies.

c. Riding the bus gets you where you need to go more cheaply, but probably not as conveniently, as driving your car. That is, some of the opportunity costs of taking the bus involve having to walk from the bus stop to where you need to go rather than parking your car right outside the building, waiting for the bus, and probably a slower journey. If the opportunity cost of your time is high (your time is valuable), these costs may be prohibitive.

3. Liza needs to buy a textbook for the next economics class. The price at the college bookstore is $65. One online site offers it for $55 and another site for $57. All prices include sales tax. The accompanying table indicates the typical shipping and handling charges for the textbook ordered online.

    a. What is the opportunity cost of buying online?

    b. Show the relevant choices for this student. What determines which of these options the student will choose?

Shipping method	Delivery time	Charge
Standard shipping	3–7 days	$3.99
Second-day air	2 business days	$8.98
Next-day air	1 business day	$13.98

3. a. The opportunity cost of buying online is whatever you must give up to do so. That is, you give up the money for the shipping charges, and there is also an opportunity cost of your time: You have to wait for the book to be delivered (at the bookstore you get the book right away). But, of course, you save the difference in the price of the book between the bookstore and the online retailer.

b. Below is a list of all of Liza's options and their purely monetary costs:

Buy from bookstore	$65
Buy from first site (price $55), 1-day delivery	$55 + $13.98 = $68.98
Buy from first site (price $55), 2-day delivery	$55 + $ 8.98 = $63.98
Buy from first site (price $55), 3- to 7-day delivery	$55 + $ 3.99 = $58.99
Buy from second site (price $57), 1-day delivery	$57 + $13.98 = $70.98
Buy from second site (price $57), 2-day delivery	$57 + $ 8.98 = $65.98
Buy from second site (price $57), 3- to 7-day delivery	$57 + $ 3.99 = $60.99

It is clear that Liza would never buy from the second site, where the book costs $57: For each delivery time, she is better off buying the book from the first site, where the book costs $55. It is also clear that she would never buy the book from the first site and have it delivered the next business day: it costs more that way ($68.98) than getting it from the bookstore (assuming that it is costless to get to and from the bookstore). But it is not clear whether she will buy the book from the bookstore or the first site with delivery times of 2 or 3–7 days: This depends on her opportunity cost of time. The higher the cost of waiting, the more likely she is to buy the book from the bookstore, where she does not need to wait.

4. Use the concept of opportunity cost to explain the following.

  a. More people choose to get graduate degrees when the job market is poor.

  b. More people choose to do their own home repairs when the economy is slow.

  c. There are more parks in suburban areas than in urban areas.

  d. Convenience stores, which have higher prices than supermarkets, cater to busy people.

  e. Fewer students enroll in classes that meet before 10:00 A.M.

4. **a.** The worse the job market, the lower the opportunity cost of getting a graduate degree. One of the opportunity costs of going to graduate school is not being able to work. But if the job market is bad, the salary you can expect to earn is low or you might be unemployed—so the opportunity cost of going to school is also low.

  b. When the economy is slow, the opportunity cost of people's time is also lower: the salary they could earn by working longer hours is lower than when the economy is booming. As a result, the opportunity cost of spending time doing your own repairs is lower—so more people will decide to do their own repairs.

  c. The opportunity cost of parkland is lower in suburban areas. The price per square foot of land is much higher in urban than in suburban areas. By creating parkland, you therefore give up the opportunity to make much more money in cities than in the suburbs.

  d. The opportunity cost of time is higher for busy people. Driving long distances to supermarkets takes time that could be spent doing other things. Therefore busy people are more likely to use a nearby convenience store.

  e. Before 10:00 A.M. the opportunity cost of time for many students is very high—it means giving up an extra hour's sleep. That extra hour is much more valuable before 10:00 A.M. than later in the day.

5. In the following examples, state how you would use the principle of marginal analysis to make a decision.

    a. Deciding how many days to wait before doing your laundry

    b. Deciding how much library research to do before writing your term paper

    c. Deciding how many bags of chips to eat

    d. Deciding how many lectures of a class to skip

5. a. Each day that you wait to do your laundry imposes a cost: You have fewer clean clothes to choose from. But each day that you wait also confers a benefit: You can spend your time doing other things. You will wait another day to do your laundry if the benefit of waiting to do the laundry that day is greater than the cost.

    b. The more research you do, the better your paper will be. But there is also an opportunity cost: every additional hour you spend doing research means you cannot do other things. You will weigh the opportunity cost of doing one more hour of research against the benefit gained (in terms of an improved paper) from doing research. You will do one more hour of research if the benefit of that hour outweighs the cost.

    c. Each bag of chips you eat gives you a benefit: it satisfies your hunger. But it also has a cost: the money spent for each bag (and if you are weight-conscious, the additional calories). You will weigh the cost against the benefit of eating one more bag. If the cost is less than the benefit, you will eat that one more bag of chips.

    d. Each lecture that you skip implies a cost: getting further behind with the material and having to teach it to yourself just before the exam. But each skipped lecture also means you can spend the time doing other things. You will continue to skip lectures if the cost of skipping is lower than the benefit of spending that time doing other things.

6. This morning you made the following individual choices: you bought a bagel and coffee at the local café, you drove to school in your car during rush hour, and you typed your roommate's term paper because you are a fast typist—in return for which she will do your laundry for a month. In each of these actions, describe how your individual choices interacted with the individual choices made by others. Were other people left better off or worse off by your choices in each case?

6. When you bought the bagel and coffee, you paid a price for them. You would not have bought that breakfast if your enjoyment of it (your welfare) had not been greater than the price you paid. Similarly, the café owner would not have sold you the bagel and coffee if the price he received from you were less than the cost to him of making them. This is an example of how everybody gains from trade: both you and the café owner are better off.

    When you chose to drive your car during the rush hour, you added to the congestion on the road. Your choice had a side effect for other motorists: your driving slowed everybody else down just a little bit more. Your choice made other motorists worse off.

    Typing your roommate's term paper in exchange for her doing your laundry is another example of the gains that come from trade. Both of you voluntarily agreed to specialize in a task that each is comparatively better at because you expected to gain from this interaction. Your choice made both you and your roommate better off.

7. On the east side of the Hatatoochie River lives the Hatfield family, while the McCoy family lives on the west side. Each family's diet consists of fried chicken and corn-on-the-cob, and each is self-sufficient, raising their own chickens and growing their own corn. Explain the conditions under which each of the following would be true.

    a. The two families are made better off when the Hatfields specialize in raising chickens, the McCoys specialize in raising corn, and the two families trade.

    b. The two families are made better off when the McCoys specialize in raising chickens, the Hatfields specialize in raising corn, and the two families trade.

7. **a.** Gains from trade usually arise from specialization. If (compared to the McCoys) the Hatfields are better at raising chickens and (compared to the Hatfields) the McCoys are better at growing corn, then there will be gains from specialization and trade.

    b. Similar to the answer to part a, if (compared to the Hatfields) the McCoys are better at raising chickens and (compared to the McCoys) the Hatfields are better at growing corn, then there will be gains from specialization and trade.

8. Which of the following situations describes an equilibrium? Which does not? If the situation does not describe an equilibrium, what would an equilibrium look like?

    a. Many people regularly commute from the suburbs to downtown Pleasantville. Due to traffic congestion, the trip takes 30 minutes when you travel by highway, but only 15 minutes when you go by side streets.

    b. At the intersection of Main and Broadway are two gas stations. One station charges $3.00 per gallon for regular gas and the other charges $2.85 per gallon. Customers can get service immediately at the first station, but must wait in a long line at the second.

    c. Every student enrolled in Economics 101 must also attend a weekly tutorial. This year there are two sections offered: section A and section B, which meet at the same time in adjoining classrooms and are taught by equally competent instructors. Section A is overcrowded, with people sitting on the floor and often unable to see the chalkboard. Section B has many empty seats.

8. **a.** This is not an equilibrium. Assume that all that people care about is the travel time to work (not, for instance, how many turns they need to make or what the scenery is like). Some people could be better off using the side streets, which would cut down their travel time. Eventually, as the situation moves to equilibrium (that is, as more people use the side streets), travel times on the highway and along the side streets should equalize.

    b. This might be an equilibrium. Those who buy gas at the first station would be worse off by buying gas at the second if the value of their time spent waiting exceeded the savings at the pump: they would save 15 cents per gallon but would incur the opportunity cost of waiting in a long line. You should expect very busy people (a high opportunity cost of time) to buy gas at the first station. Those who buy gas at the second station might be worse off by buying gas at the first: they would not have to wait in line but would pay 15 cents more per gallon. You should expect people with a lot of free time (a low opportunity cost of time) to buy gas at the second station.

    c. This is not an equilibrium. If students from section A attended section B instead, they would be better off: they could get seats and see the chalkboard without incurring any cost (since the section meets at the same time and is taught by an equally competent instructor). Over time, you should expect students to switch from section A to section B until equilibrium is established.

9. In each of the following cases, explain whether you think the situation is efficient or not. If it is not efficient, why not? What actions would make the situation efficient?

    a. Electricity is included in the rent at your dorm. Some residents in your dorm leave lights, computers, and appliances on when they are not in their rooms.

    b. Although they cost the same amount to prepare, the cafeteria in your dorm consistently provides too many dishes that diners don't like, such as tofu casserole, and too few dishes that diners do like, such as roast turkey with dressing.

    c. The enrollment for a particular course exceeds the spaces available. Some students who need to take this course to complete their major are unable to get a space while others who are taking it as an elective do get a space.

9. **a.** This is not efficient. If the lights were turned off, many students could be made better off without making anyone else worse off because the college would save money on electricity that it could spend on student programs. By leaving lights and appliances on when leaving their rooms, residents do not take into account the negative side effect they impose on their college—the higher cost of electricity. If students were forced to pay their own individual electricity costs (that is, if they fully took into account the cost of their actions), then they would turn the lights and appliances off when leaving their rooms. This situation would be efficient.

    b. This is not efficient. Instead of serving dishes that many diners do not like, the cafeteria should serve more of the dishes that diners do like at the same cost. That way, some students could be made better off without others being made worse off.

    c. This is not efficient. In an efficient scheme, spaces would be allocated to those students who value them most. In this case, however, some spaces are allocated to students who value them less (those who take the course as an elective) than other students (those who need the course to graduate). Efficiency could be improved as follows: if a student who is not currently enrolled in the course values it more than a student who is enrolled, then the unenrolled student should be willing to pay the enrolled student to give up his or her space. At some price, this trade would make both students better off and the outcome would be efficient.

10. Discuss the efficiency and equity implications of each of the following policies. How would you go about balancing the concerns of equity and efficiency in these areas?

    a. The government pays the full tuition for every college student to study whatever subject he or she wishes.

    b. When people lose their jobs, the government provides unemployment benefits until they find new ones.

10. **a.** Although this policy is equitable, it may not be efficient, depending on the beneficial side effects of education. It does allow everyone, regardless of ability to pay, to attend college. But it may not be efficient: subsidizing the full cost of tuition for everyone lowers the opportunity cost of going to college, and this might lead some people to go to college when they could more productively follow a career that does not require a college education. And since resources (including government money) are scarce, paying tuition for these people has an opportunity cost: some other (possibly more worthwhile) government projects cannot be undertaken. One way of getting around this problem is to award scholarships based on academic ability.

b. Although this policy may be equitable (it guarantees everyone a certain amount of income), it may not be efficient. People respond to incentives. If unemployment becomes more attractive because of the unemployment benefit, some unemployed people may no longer try to find a job or may not try to find one as quickly as they would without the benefit. Ways to get around this problem are to provide unemployment benefits only for a limited time or to require recipients to prove that they are actively searching for a new job.

11. Governments often adopt certain policies in order to promote desired behavior among their citizens. For each of the following policies, determine what the incentive is and what behavior the government wishes to promote. In each case, why do you think that the government might wish to change people's behavior, rather than allow their actions to be solely determined by individual choice?

a. A tax of $5 per pack is imposed on cigarettes.

b. The government pays parents $100 when their child is vaccinated for measles.

c. The government pays college students to tutor children from low-income families.

d. The government imposes a tax on the amount of air pollution that a company discharges.

11. **a.** This policy creates an incentive to smoke less by making a pack of cigarettes more costly. This is exactly what policy makers wish to promote. Cigarettes have undesirable side effects on other people, which smokers do not (or only insufficiently) take into account. One is that other people have to breathe in second-hand smoke. Another is the cost of health care: when smokers who need treatment for lung cancer are covered by Medicare or Medicaid, the rest of society has to foot the bill. Since individuals do not take these costs (costs that arise for other people) into account in deciding whether or not (or how much) to smoke, the amount of cigarettes smoked will be inefficiently high. The tax is a way to make people take these costs into account in deciding whether or not to smoke.

b. This policy creates an incentive to have children vaccinated: it increases the benefit to parents from vaccination of their children. Getting vaccinated means not only that a child will not contract the measles but also that he or she cannot pass the measles on to other children. That is, there is a side effect on other people (their children get sick less often) that parents do not take into account in their decision of whether or not to have their own child vaccinated. The subsidy is a way to make individuals take into account in their decisions the benefit they can create for other people.

c. This policy creates incentives for low-income families to get college students to tutor their children, since getting a tutor is now cheaper or free. This results in better performance in school by these children and higher levels of educational attainment. This has positive side effects for the rest of society: the better children do in school, the more productive, happier, and healthier citizens they will be.

d. This tax creates the incentive to emit fewer air pollutants. Pollution has a negative side effect on others: it decreases air quality (for instance, it contributes to the formation of ozone smog) and results in a variety of health complications (for instance, asthma). In deciding how much pollution to discharge, a company does not take these negative side effects sufficiently into account. The tax is a way to make pollution more expensive, that is, to make the company face the cost it imposes on others.

12. In each of the following situations, explain how government intervention could improve society's welfare by changing people's incentives. In what sense is the market going wrong?

   a. Pollution from auto emissions has reached unhealthy levels.

   b. Everyone in Woodville would be better off if streetlights were installed in the town. But no individual resident is willing to pay for installation of a streetlight in front of his or her house because it is impossible to recoup the cost by charging other residents for the benefit they receive from it.

12. a. In deciding how much to drive, each driver does not take into account the cost of auto emissions he or she imposes on others. That is, the market will lead to there being too much pollution. One way for governments to intervene would be to tax fuel or to tax cars that get low gas mileage. Or governments could subsidize new and cleaner fuels or technologies, such as hybrid cars. This would create incentives for people to switch to cars that use less polluting gas or to drive less.

   b. The market in this situation leads to too few (or no) streetlights in Woodville. Government could improve residents' welfare by paying for streetlight installation from the taxes paid by residents.

chapter 2

Economic Models: Trade-offs and Trade

1. Atlantis is a small, isolated island in the South Atlantic. The inhabitants grow potatoes and catch fresh fish. The accompanying table shows the maximum annual output combinations of potatoes and fish that can be produced. Obviously, given their limited resources and available technology, as they use more of their resources for potato production, there are fewer resources available for catching fish.

Maximum annual output options	Quantity of potatoes (pounds)	Quantity of fish (pounds)
A	1,000	0
B	800	300
C	600	500
D	400	600
E	200	650
F	0	675

a. Draw a production possibility frontier with potatoes on the horizontal axis and fish on the vertical axis illustrating these options, showing points A–F.

b. Can Atlantis produce 500 pounds of fish and 800 pounds of potatoes? Explain. Where would this point lie relative to the production possibility frontier?

c. What is the opportunity cost of increasing the annual output of potatoes from 600 to 800 pounds?

d. What is the opportunity cost of increasing the annual output of potatoes from 200 to 400 pounds?

e. Can you explain why the answers to parts c and d are not the same? What does this imply about the slope of the production possibility frontier?

1. **a.** The accompanying diagram shows the production possibility frontier for Atlantis.

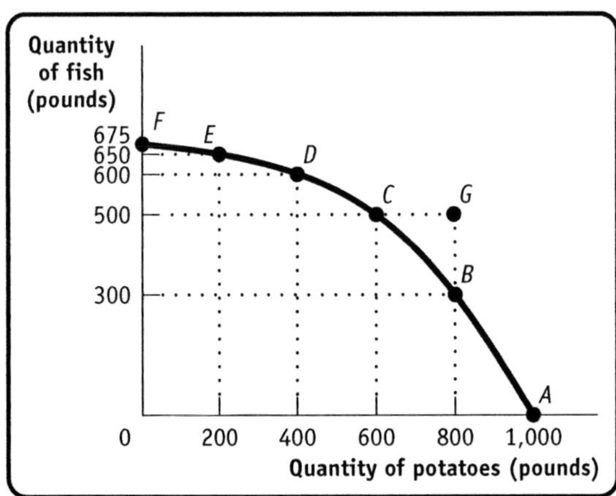

b. No, Atlantis cannot produce 500 pounds of fish and 800 pounds of potatoes. If it produces 500 pounds of fish, the most potatoes it can produce is 600 pounds. This point would lie outside the production possibility frontier, at point G on the diagram.

c. The opportunity cost of increasing output from 600 to 800 pounds of potatoes is 200 pounds of fish. If Atlantis increases output from 600 to 800 pounds of potatoes, it has to cut fish production from 500 pounds to 300 pounds, that is, by 200 pounds.

d. The opportunity cost of increasing output from 200 to 400 pounds of potatoes is 50 pounds of fish. If Atlantis increases output from 200 to 400 pounds of potatoes, it has to cut fish production from 650 pounds to 600 pounds, that is, by 50 pounds.

e. The answers to parts c and d imply that the more potatoes Atlantis produces, the higher the opportunity cost becomes. For instance, as you grow more and more potatoes, you have to use less and less suitable land to do so. As a result, you have to divert increasingly more resources away from fishing as you grow more potatoes, meaning that you can produce increasingly less fish. This implies, of course, that the production possibility frontier becomes steeper the farther you move along it to the right; that is, the production possibility frontier is bowed out. (Mathematicians call this shape *concave*.)

2. In the ancient country of Roma, only two goods, spaghetti and meatballs, are produced. There are two tribes in Roma, the Tivoli and the Frivoli. By themselves, the Tivoli each month can produce either 30 pounds of spaghetti and no meatballs, or 50 pounds of meatballs and no spaghetti, or any combination in between. The Frivoli, by themselves, each month can produce 40 pounds of spaghetti and no meatballs, or 30 pounds of meatballs and no spaghetti, or any combination in between.

a. Assume that all production possibility frontiers are straight lines. Draw one diagram showing the monthly production possibility frontier for the Tivoli and another showing the monthly production possibility frontier for the Frivoli. Show how you calculated them.

b. Which tribe has the comparative advantage in spaghetti production? In meatball production?

In A.D. 100 the Frivoli discover a new technique for making meatballs that doubles the quantity of meatballs they can produce each month.

c. Draw the new monthly production possibility frontier for the Frivoli.

d. After the innovation, which tribe now has the absolute advantage in producing meatballs? In producing spaghetti? Which has the comparative advantage in meatball production? In spaghetti production?

2. a. The accompanying diagram shows the production possibility frontier for the Tivoli in panel (a) and for the Frivoli as the line labeled "Original Frivoli *PPF*" in panel (b).

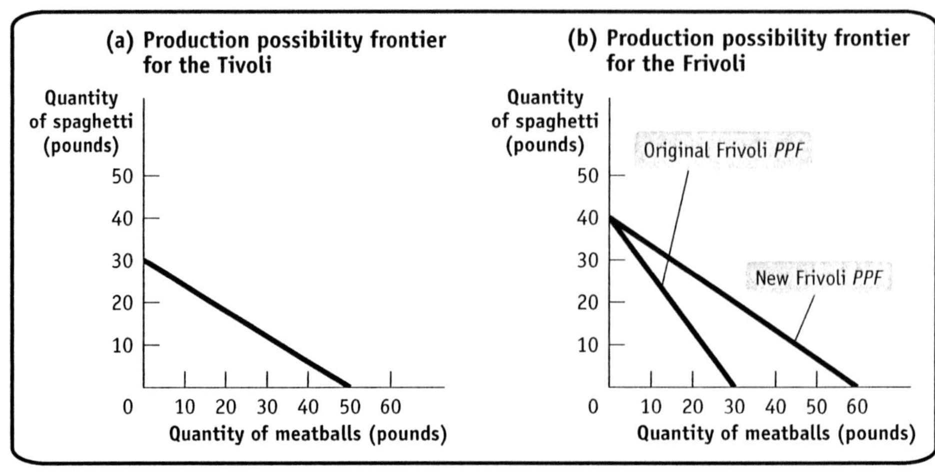

The production possibility frontier for the Tivoli was calculated as follows: The Tivoli can produce either 30 pounds of spaghetti and no meatballs, or they can produce no spaghetti but 50 pounds of meatballs. That is, the opportunity cost of 1 pound of meatballs is ⅗ of a pound of spaghetti: in order to produce 1 more pound of meatballs, the Tivoli have to give up ⅗ of a pound of spaghetti. This means that the slope of their production possibility frontier is −⅗. A similar argument for the Frivoli shows that their production possibility frontier has a slope of −⅓.

b. For the Tivoli, the opportunity cost of 1 pound of meatballs is ⅗ of a pound of spaghetti. For the Frivoli, the opportunity cost of 1 pound of meatballs is ⅓ pounds of spaghetti. That is, the Tivoli have the comparative advantage in meatball production because their opportunity cost is lower. For the Tivoli, the opportunity cost of 1 pound of spaghetti is 5⁄3 pounds of meatballs. For the Frivoli, the opportunity cost of 1 pound of spaghetti is ¾ pound of meatballs. That is, the Frivoli have the comparative advantage in spaghetti production because their opportunity cost is lower.

c. The Frivoli's new production possibility frontier is the line labeled "New Frivoli *PPF*" in panel (b) of the diagram. Instead of producing 30 pounds of meatballs (if they produce no spaghetti), they can now produce 60 pounds.

d. Now the Frivoli have the absolute advantage in both meatball production and spaghetti production. The Frivoli's opportunity cost of meatballs has now fallen to 4⁄6 = ⅔; that is, for each pound of meatballs that the Frivoli now produce, they have to give up producing ⅔ of a pound of spaghetti. Since the Frivoli's opportunity cost of meatballs (⅔) is still higher than the Tivoli's (⅗), the Tivoli still have the comparative advantage in meatball production. The Frivoli's opportunity cost of spaghetti is 3⁄2 pounds of meatballs and the Tivoli's is 5⁄3 pounds of meatballs, so the Frivoli have the comparative advantage in spaghetti production.

3. Peter Pundit, an economics reporter, states that the European Union (EU) is increasing its productivity very rapidly in all industries. He claims that this productivity advance is so rapid that output from the EU in these industries will soon exceed that of the United States and, as a result, the United States will no longer benefit from trade with the EU.

a. Do you think Peter Pundit is correct or not? If not, what do you think is the source of his mistake?

b. If the EU and the United States continue to trade, what do you think will characterize the goods that the EU exports to the United States and the goods that the United States exports to the EU?

3. **a.** Peter Pundit is not correct. He confuses absolute and comparative advantage. Even if the EU were to have an absolute advantage over the United States in every product it produces, the United States will still have a comparative advantage in some products. And the United States should continue to produce those products: trade will make both the EU and the United States better off.

b. You should expect to see the EU export those goods in which it has the comparative advantage and the United States export those goods in which it has the comparative advantage.

4. You are in charge of allocating residents to your dormitory's baseball and basketball teams. You are down to the last four people, two of whom must be allocated to baseball and two to basketball. The accompanying table gives each person's batting average and free-throw average. Explain how you would use the concept of comparative advantage to allocate the players. Begin by establishing each player's opportunity cost of free throws in terms of batting average.

Name	Batting average	Free-throw average
Kelley	70%	60%
Jackie	50%	50%
Curt	10%	30%
Gerry	80%	70%

Why is it likely that the other basketball players will be unhappy about this arrangement but the other baseball players will be satisfied? Nonetheless, why would an economist say that this is an efficient way to allocate players for your dormitory's sports teams?

4. Let's begin by establishing the opportunity cost of free throws for each player. If you allocate Kelley to the basketball team, the team gains a player with a 60 percent free-throw average and the baseball team loses a player with a 70 percent batting average. That is, the opportunity cost of allocating Kelley to the basketball team is 7/6. Similarly, Jackie's opportunity cost of playing basketball is 1; Curt's opportunity cost of playing basketball is 1/3, and Gerry's opportunity cost of playing basketball is 8/7. Jackie and Curt have the lowest opportunity costs of playing basketball; that is, they have the comparative advantage in basketball. Therefore they should be allocated to the basketball team. Kelley and Gerry have the comparative advantage in baseball and should therefore play on the baseball team.

It is likely that the basketball team will be unhappy with this arrangement. Both Jackie and Curt have an absolute disadvantage at playing basketball, compared to the other two players. (They also have an absolute disadvantage at playing baseball, but they are comparatively less bad at basketball than at baseball.) The baseball team is likely to be happy about this allocation because both Kelley and Gerry have an absolute advantage at playing baseball. However, if you are concerned with the total number of wins for the dormitory (as an economist who would be concerned about efficiency), this allocation is the best one: it maximizes the overall chances of the dormitory winning at any sport.

5. The economy of Atlantis has developed, and the inhabitants now use money in the form of cowry shells. Draw a circular-flow diagram showing households and firms. Firms produce potatoes and fish, and households buy potatoes and fish. Households also provide the land and labor to firms. Identify where in the flows of cowry shells or physical things (goods and services, or resources) each of the following impacts would occur. Describe how this impact spreads around the circle.

a. A devastating hurricane floods many of the potato fields.

b. A very productive fishing season yields a very large number of fish caught.

c. The inhabitants of Atlantis discover the Macarena and spend several days a month at dancing festivals.

5. The accompanying diagram illustrates the circular flow for Atlantis.

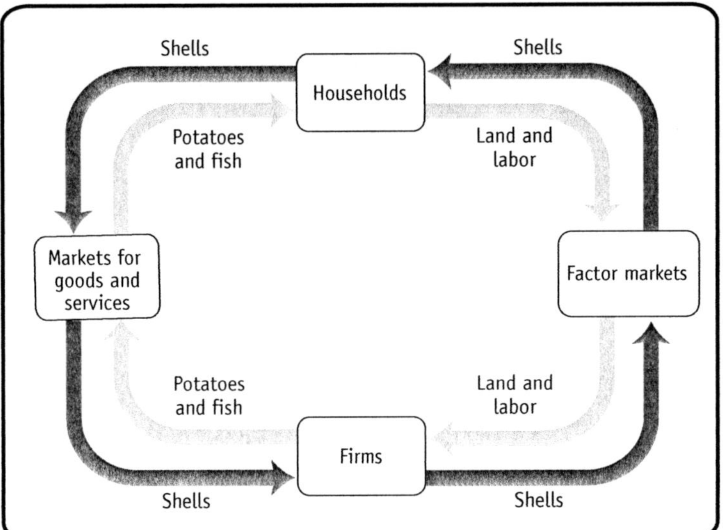

a. The flooding of the fields will destroy the potato crop. Destruction of the potato crop reduces the flow of goods from firms to households: fewer potatoes produced by firms now are sold to households. An implication, of course, is that fewer cowry shells flow from households to firms as payment for the potatoes in the market for goods and services. Since firms now earn fewer shells, they have fewer shells to pay to households in the factor market. As a result, the amount of factors flowing from households to firms is also reduced.

b. The productive fishing season leads to greater quantity of fish produced in firms to flow to households. An implication is that more money flows from households to firms through the market for goods and services. As a result, firms will want to buy more factors from households (the flow of shells from firms to households increases) and, in return, the flow of factors from households to firms increases.

c. Time spent at dancing festivals reduces the flow of labor from households to firms and therefore reduces the number of shells flowing from firms to households through the factor market. In return, households now have fewer shells to buy goods with (the flow of shells from households to firms in the goods market is reduced), implying that fewer goods flow from firms to households.

6. An economist might say that colleges and universities "produce" education, using faculty members and students as inputs. According to this line of reasoning, education is then "consumed" by households. Construct a circular-flow diagram like the one found in this chapter to represent the sector of the economy devoted to college education: colleges and universities represent firms, and households both consume education and provide faculty and students to universities. What are the relevant markets in this model? What is being bought and sold in each direction? What would happen in the model if the government decided to subsidize 50 percent of all college students' tuition?

6. The accompanying diagram shows the circular flow for the education sector.

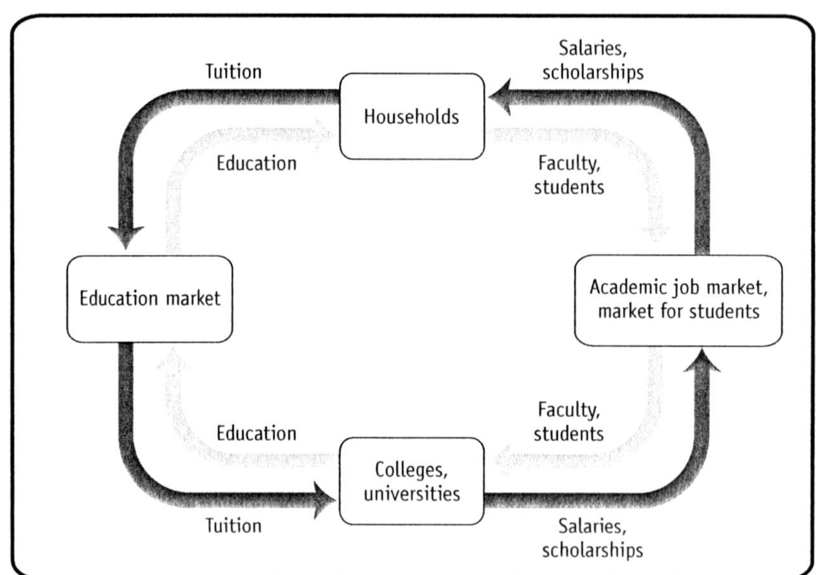

Colleges and universities buy faculty on the academic job market and attract students from the market for students. (Many colleges and universities actively try to attract good students by offering scholarships and the like.) They sell education to households in the market for education, and households buy education in that market from one (or sometimes several) of the sellers.

If the government subsidized half of all students' tuition, households would demand more education. As a result, colleges and universities would hire more faculty, and accept more students, and more money in terms of salaries and scholarships would flow from universities and colleges to the households.

7. Your dormitory roommate plays loud music most of the time; you, however, would prefer more peace and quiet. You suggest that she buy some earphones. She responds that although she would be happy to use earphones, she has many other things that she would prefer to spend her money on right now. You discuss this situation with a friend who is an economics major. The following exchange takes place:

He: How much would it cost to buy earphones?

You: $15.

He: How much do you value having some peace and quiet for the rest of the semester?

You: $30.

He: It is efficient for you to buy the earphones and give them to your roommate. You gain more than you lose; the benefit exceeds the cost. You should do that.

You: It just isn't fair that I have to pay for the earphones when I'm not the one making the noise.

a. Which parts of this conversation contain positive statements and which parts contain normative statements?

b. Compose an argument supporting your viewpoint that your roommate should be the one to change her behavior. Similarly, compose an argument from the viewpoint of your roommate that you should be the one to buy the earphones. If your dormitory has a policy that gives residents the unlimited right to play music, whose argument is likely to win? If your dormitory has a rule that a person must stop playing music whenever a roommate complains, whose argument is likely to win?

7. **a.** The statement "It is efficient for you to buy the earphones" is a positive statement (it is either right or wrong); that is, it is about description. The statement "You should do that" (that is, buy the earphones) is strictly speaking a normative statement; that is, it is about prescription (although you would find all economists agree that all trades that improve efficiency should be made). The statement "It just isn't fair" is a normative statement—that is, it is about prescription—and you would likely find much disagreement about the fairness of the proposed trade.

b. One argument that your roommate should buy the earphones is that everyone has the right to peace and quiet. If your roommate therefore wants to listen to music, she should have to be responsible for making sure that others' peace and quiet is not disturbed. Your roommate might argue that since she has the right to play as much music as she wants, it is your responsibility to make sure that you are not disturbed—for instance, by buying her earphones. If the dormitory has a policy that establishes the right to unlimited music, your roommate's argument wins. If the rule is that there is a right to peace and quiet, your argument wins.

8. A representative of the American clothing industry recently made the following statement: "Workers in Asia often work in sweatshop conditions earning only pennies an hour. American workers are more productive and as a result earn higher wages. In order to preserve the dignity of the American workplace, the government should enact legislation banning imports of low-wage Asian clothing."

a. Which parts of this quote are positive statements? Which parts are normative statements?

b. Is the policy that is being advocated consistent with the preceding statements about the wages and productivities of American and Asian workers?

c. Would such a policy make some Americans better off without making any other Americans worse off? That is, would this policy be efficient from the viewpoint of all Americans?

d. Would low-wage Asian workers benefit from or be hurt by such a policy?

8. **a.** The positive statements are:

- workers in Asia . . . [are] earning only pennies an hour

- American workers are more productive

- American workers are more productive and as a result earn higher wages

The normative statement is:

- the government should enact legislation banning imports of low-wage Asian clothing

b. It is not. The statement about the productivity of American and Asian workers is about the absolute advantage that American workers have over Asian workers. However, Asian workers may still have a comparative advantage. And if that is the case, then banning imports would result in inefficiency.

c. If America channeled more of its productive resources into producing clothing, it would have to give up producing other goods. As a result, America would be able to consume less of all goods. And this would make some Americans clearly worse off. This policy would therefore not be efficient.

d. Low-wage Asian workers would also be hurt by this policy. The Asian country would channel its resources away from producing clothing toward producing other goods that it previously imported from America. But since it does not have the comparative advantage in those other goods, the Asian country would be able to consume less of all goods.

9. Are the following statements true or false? Explain your answers.

a. "When people must pay higher taxes on their wage earnings, it reduces their incentive to work" is a positive statement.

b. "We should lower taxes to encourage more work" is a positive statement.

c. Economics cannot always be used to completely decide what society ought to do.

d. "The system of public education in this country generates greater benefits to society than the cost of running the system" is a normative statement.

e. All disagreements among economists are generated by the media.

9. **a.** True. This is a positive statement. It has a factual answer; that is, it is either right or wrong. There has been some debate about whether the statement is actually true or false, but in principle there is only one answer.

b. False. This is a statement about what we should do, and this statement has no clearly right or wrong answer. Your view will depend on whether you think encouraging more work is a good or a bad idea.

c. True. Economics is best at giving positive answers, for instance, answers about what the most efficient way is of achieving a certain aim. The question of how society ought to be organized is mostly decided in the realm of politics.

d. False. This is a positive statement. In principle, it has an answer that is either right or wrong.

e. False. Some disagreements among economists arise from the fact that in building a model, one economist thinks that a certain abstraction from reality is admissible but another economist may think that that abstraction is not admissible. Some disagreements arise from the fact that economists sometimes disagree about values.

10. Evaluate the following statement: "It is easier to build an economic model that accurately reflects events that have already occurred than to build an economic model to forecast future events." Do you think that this is true or not? Why? What does this imply about the difficulties of building good economic models?

10. True. With hindsight it is easier to see what the important features of the situation were that a model should have captured. For predictive purposes, a model needs to anticipate what the important features of reality are and which are the unimportant features that can therefore be ignored. This is why the British economist John Maynard Keynes referred to economics as an art as well as a science.

11. Economists who work for the government are often called on to make policy recommendations. Why do you think it is important for the public to be able to differentiate normative statements from positive statements in these recommendations?

11. Positive statements are those based on fact—or at least on our best estimate of what the facts are. These statements are also therefore those that do not depend on which political views the economist may have. Normative statements may sometimes be influenced by the economist's own values. Whether someone agrees with an economist's normative statement may depend upon whether they share values. It is therefore important that the public be able to distinguish normative from positive statements.

12. The mayor of Gotham City, worried about a potential epidemic of deadly influenza this winter, asks an economic adviser the following series of questions. Does each question require the economic adviser to make a positive assessment or a normative assessment?

    a. How much vaccine will be in stock in the city by the end of November?

    b. If we offer to pay 10 percent more per dose to the pharmaceutical companies providing the vaccines, will they provide additional doses?

    c. If there is a shortage of vaccine in the city, whom should we vaccinate first—the elderly or the very young? (Assume that a person from one group has an equal likelihood of dying from influenza as a person from the other group.)

    d. If the city charges $25 per shot, how many people will pay?

    e. If the city charges $25 per shot, it will make a profit of $10 per shot, money that can go to pay for inoculating poor people. Should the city engage in such a scheme?

12.   **a.** Positive

    b. Positive

    c. Normative

    d. Positive

    e. Normative

13. Assess the following statement: "If economists just had enough data, they could solve all policy questions in a way that maximizes the social good. There would be no need for divisive political debates, such as whether the government should provide free medical care for all."

13. What is true is that if economists had enough data, they could predict precisely what the outcome would be of any proposed policy (such as free medical care). That is, economists can answer positive questions. But no amount of data can lead to a determination about what a society should do—that is a normative question. An economist can predict how much it will cost to provide free medical care and what effects different ways of raising taxes will have on people's behavior (for instance, a sales tax will reduce consumption behavior; an income tax may discourage workers from working as much as before). But whether this is a trade-off worth making is a question that can be answered only in political discourse.

Appendix: Graphs in Economics

1. Study the four accompanying diagrams. Consider the following statements and indicate which diagram matches each statement. Which variable would appear on the horizontal and which on the vertical axis? In each of these statements, is the slope positive, negative, zero, or infinity?

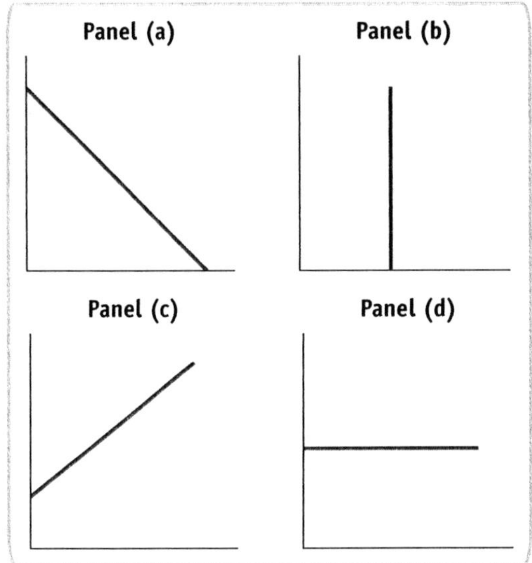

a. If the price of movies increases, fewer consumers go to see movies.

b. More experienced workers typically have higher incomes than less experienced workers.

c. Whatever the temperature outside, Americans consume the same number of hot dogs per day.

d. Consumers buy more frozen yogurt when the price of ice cream goes up.

e. Research finds no relationship between the number of diet books purchased and the number of pounds lost by the average dieter.

f. Regardless of its price, Americans buy the same quantity of salt.

1. a. Panel (a) illustrates this relationship. The higher price of movies causes consumers to see fewer movies. The relationship is negative, and the slope is therefore negative. The price of movies is the independent variable and the number of movies seen is the dependent variable. However, there is a convention in economics that, if price is a variable, it is measured on the vertical axis. So the quantity of movies is measured on the horizontal axis.

b. Panel (c) illustrates this relationship. Since it is likely that their greater experience causes firms to pay workers more, years of experience is the independent variable and would go on the horizontal axis and the resulting income, the dependent variable, on the vertical axis. The slope is positive.

c. Panel (d) illustrates this relationship. With the temperature on the horizontal axis as the independent variable, and the consumption of hot dogs on the vertical axis as the dependent variable, we see there is no change in hot dog consumption whatever the temperature. The slope is zero.

"""

d. Panel (c) illustrates this relationship. When the price of ice cream goes up, this would cause consumers to choose a close alternative, frozen yogurt. The price of ice cream is the independent variable and the consumption of frozen yogurt is the dependent variable. However, there is a convention in economics that, if price is a variable, it is measured on the vertical axis. The quantity that consumers buy of frozen yogurt is on the horizontal axis. The slope is positive.

e. Panel (d) illustrates this relationship. The fact that there is no discernable relationship between the number of diet books purchased and the weight loss of the average dieter results in a horizontal curve; the slope is zero.

f. Panel (b) illustrates this relationship. Although price is the independent variable and salt consumption the dependent variable, by convention the price appears on the vertical axis and the quantity of salt on the horizontal axis. Since salt consumption does not change whatever the price, the curve is a vertical line; the slope is infinity.

2. During the Reagan administration, economist Arthur Laffer argued in favor of lowering income tax rates in order to increase tax revenues. Like most economists, he believed that at tax rates above a certain level, tax revenue would fall because high taxes would discourage some people from working and that people would refuse to work at all if they received no income after paying taxes. This relationship between tax rates and tax revenue is graphically summarized in what is widely known as the Laffer curve. Plot the Laffer curve relationship assuming that it has the shape of a nonlinear curve. The following questions will help you construct the graph.

a. Which is the independent variable? Which is the dependent variable? On which axis do you therefore measure the income tax rate? On which axis do you measure income tax revenue?

b. What would tax revenue be at a 0% income tax rate?

c. The maximum possible income tax rate is 100%. What would tax revenue be at a 100% income tax rate?

d. Estimates now show that the maximum point on the Laffer curve is (approximately) at a tax rate of 80%. For tax rates less than 80%, how would you describe the relationship between the tax rate and tax revenue, and how is this relationship reflected in the slope? For tax rates higher than 80%, how would you describe the relationship between the tax rate and tax revenue, and how is this relationship reflected in the slope?

2. **a.** The income tax rate is the independent variable and so is measured on the horizontal axis. Income tax revenue is the dependent variable and so is measured on the vertical axis.

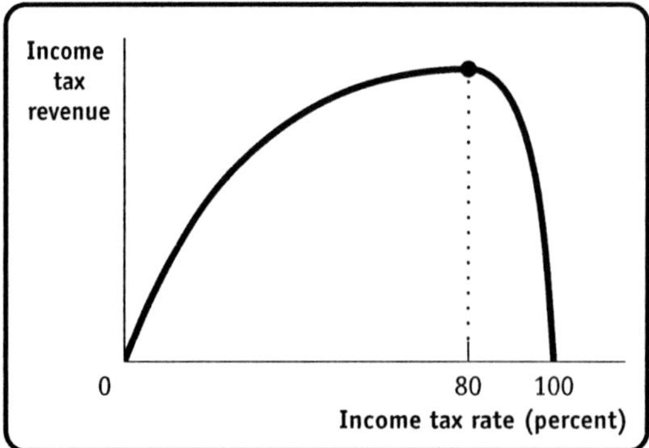

b. If the income tax rate is zero (there is no tax), tax revenue is obviously zero.

c. If the income tax rate is 100% (all your income is taxed away), you will have zero income left after tax. Since people are unwilling to work if they receive no income after tax, no income will be earned. As a result, there is no income tax revenue.

d. For tax rates less than 80%, tax rate and tax revenue are positively related and so the Laffer curve has a positive slope. For tax rates higher than 80%, the relationship between tax rate and tax revenue is negative and so the Laffer curve has a negative slope. The Laffer curve therefore looks like the diagram on page 20 with a maximum point at a tax rate of 80%.

3. In the accompanying figures, the numbers on the axes have been lost. All you know is that the units shown on the vertical axis are the same as the units on the horizontal axis.

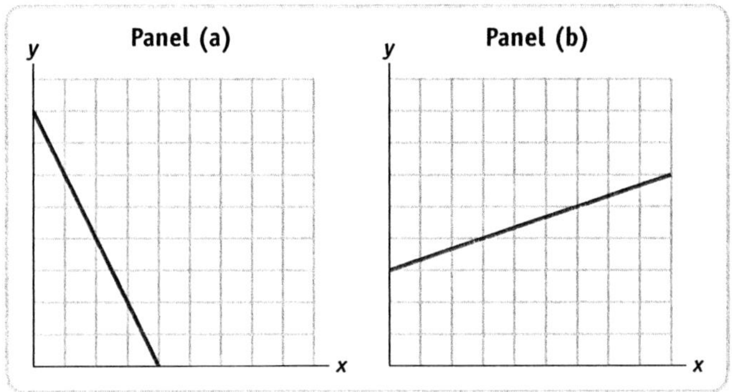

a. In panel (a), what is the slope of the line? Show that the slope is constant along the line.

b. In panel (b), what is the slope of the line? Show that the slope is constant along the line.

3. **a.** In panel (a), the slope is –2. From any point on the line, moving one unit to the right along the horizontal axis requires moving down two units along the vertical axis in order to remain on the line. The slope is the "rise" (–2) over the "run" (+1); that is, the slope is $^{-2}/_1 = -2$. The same is true starting at *any* point along the line, so the slope at every point is the same. The slope is constant.

b. In panel (b), the slope is ⅓. From any point on the line, moving three units to the right along the horizontal axis requires moving up one unit along the vertical axis in order to remain on the line. The slope is the "rise" (+1) over the "run" (+3); that is, the slope is ⅓. The same is true starting at *any* point along the line, so the slope at every point is the same. The slope is constant.

4. Answer each of the following questions by drawing a schematic diagram.

a. Taking measurements of the slope of a curve at three points farther and farther to the right along the horizontal axis, the slope of the curve changes from –0.3, to –0.8, to –2.5, measured by the point method. Draw a schematic diagram of this curve. How would you describe the relationship illustrated in your diagram?

b. Taking measurements of the slope of a curve at five points farther and farther to the right along the horizontal axis, the slope of the curve changes from 1.5, to 0.5, to 0, to –0.5, to –1.5, measured by the point method. Draw a schematic diagram of this curve. Does it have a maximum or a minimum?

4. a. The accompanying diagram schematically shows this curve. The slope is negative throughout. That means that the curve is downward sloping. Because the absolute value of the slope is increasing, the curve becomes steeper. The slope is negative increasing.

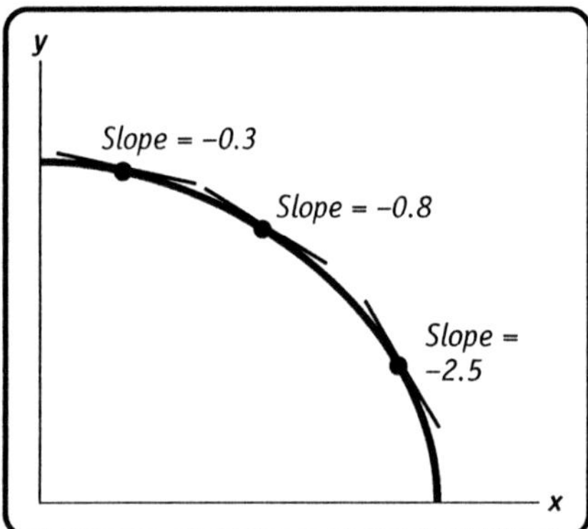

b. The accompanying diagram schematically shows this curve. The slope is positive and decreasing at first. Then it becomes negative and increasing. The curve therefore has a maximum just at the point where the slope is equal to zero.

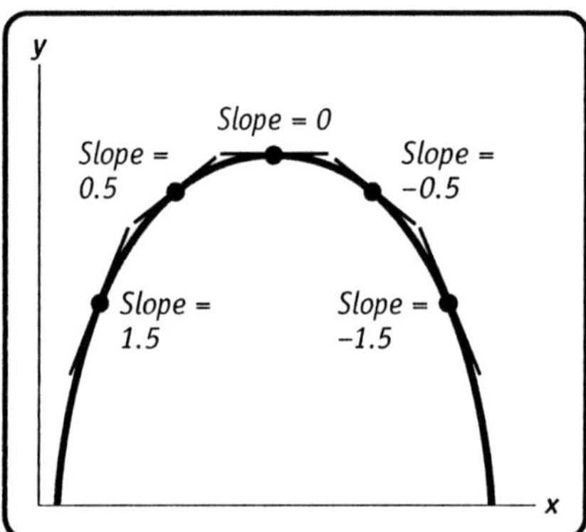

5. The accompanying table shows the relationship between workers' hours of work per week and their hourly wage rate. Apart from the fact that they receive a different hourly wage rate and work different hours, these five workers are otherwise identical.

Name	Quantity of labor (hours per week)	Wage rate (per hour)
Athena	30	$15
Boris	35	30
Curt	37	45
Diego	36	60
Emily	32	75

a. Which variable is the independent variable? Which is the dependent variable?

b. Draw a scatter diagram illustrating this relationship. Draw a (nonlinear) curve that connects the points. Put the hourly wage rate on the vertical axis.

c. As the wage rate increases from $15 to $30, how does the number of hours worked respond according to the relationship depicted here? What is the average slope of the curve between Athena's and Boris's data points?

d. As the wage rate increases from \$60 to \$75, how does the number of hours worked respond according to the relationship depicted here? What is the average slope of the curve between Diego's and Emily's data points?

5. a. If the wage rate is greater than your opportunity cost of time, you will choose to work. So the wage rate is the independent variable and the number of hours worked is the dependent variable.

b. The accompanying diagram illustrates the relationship between the hourly wage rate and the number of hours worked. Since the hourly wage rate is the price paid for labor, economists place wages on the vertical axis—just as in the case of other types of prices.

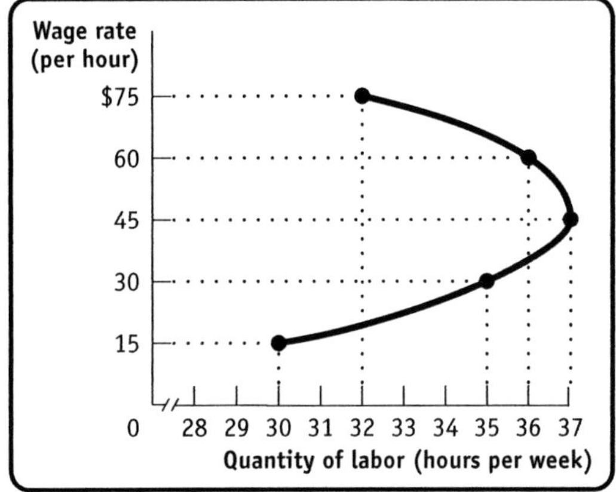

c. As the wage rate increases from \$15 to \$30, the number of hours worked increases by 5. The average slope of the curve between the two points is therefore $^{15}\!/_5 = 3$.

d. As the wage rate increases from \$60 to \$75, the number of hours worked decreases by 4. The average slope of the curve between the two points is therefore $^{15}\!/_{-4} = -3.75$.

6. Studies have found a relationship between a country's yearly rate of economic growth and the yearly rate of increase in airborne pollutants. It is believed that a higher rate of economic growth allows a country's residents to have more cars and travel more, thereby releasing more airborne pollutants.

a. Which variable is the independent variable? Which is the dependent variable?

b. Suppose that in the country of Sudland, when the yearly rate of economic growth fell from 3.0% to 1.5%, the yearly rate of increase in airborne pollutants fell from 6% to 5%. What is the average slope of a nonlinear curve between these points using the arc method?

c. Now suppose that when the yearly rate of economic growth rose from 3.5% to 4.5%, the yearly rate of increase in airborne pollutants rose from 5.5% to 7.5%. What is the average slope of a nonlinear curve between these two points using the arc method?

d. How would you describe the relationship between the two variables here?

6. a. According to the question, economic growth causes the increase in airborne pollutants. That is, the growth rate is the independent variable and the rate of increase in airborne pollutants is the dependent variable. So the rate of increase in airborne pollutants is measured on the vertical axis and the growth rate is measured on the horizontal axis.

b. The change in the growth rate is −1.5. The change in the rate of increase in airborne pollutants is −1. The slope is therefore $^-1/_{-1.5} = {}^2/_3$.

c. The change in the growth rate is +1. The change in the rate of increase in airborne pollutants is +2. The slope is therefore $^2/_1 = 2$.

d. The slope is positive and, as can be seen from the answers to parts b and c, increasing.

7. An insurance company has found that the severity of property damage in a fire is positively related to the number of firefighters arriving at the scene.

    a. Draw a diagram that depicts this finding with number of firefighters on the horizontal axis and amount of property damage on the vertical axis. What is the argument made by this diagram? Suppose you reverse what is measured on the two axes. What is the argument made then?

    b. In order to reduce its payouts to policyholders, should the insurance company therefore ask the city to send fewer firefighters to any fire?

7. a. By drawing the diagram with number of firefighters on the horizontal axis and amount of property damage on the vertical axis, you are assuming that the number of firefighters is the independent variable and amount of property damage is the dependent variable. That graph is shown here. It makes the argument that as the number of firefighters on the scene increases, the amount of damage increases. You could also have drawn the graph with amount of property damage as the independent variable (on the horizontal axis) and the number of firefighters as the dependent variable (on the vertical axis). In this case the diagram implies that more and more firefighters come to the scene as the amount of property damage increases. (But be aware that any diagram shows only a relationship between two variables and does not imply causation.)

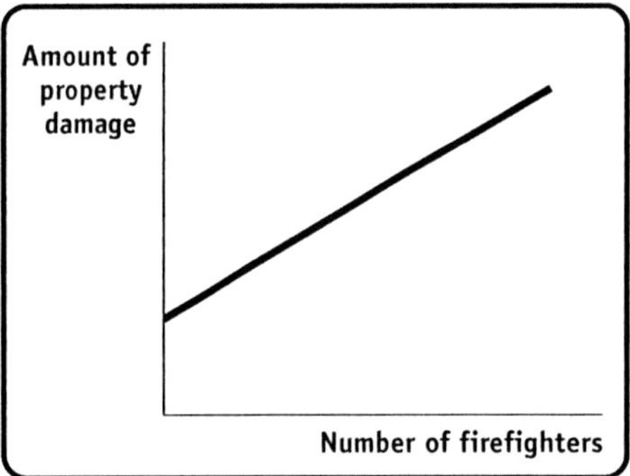

b. The statement implies that there is a causal link between the number of firefighters and the amount of property damage, and this is likely not the case. It is instead likely that there is a third, omitted, variable that is related to both the number of firefighters and the amount of property damage. This variable is the severity of the fire: more severe fires cause both greater property damage and a greater number of firefighters to be sent to the fire.

8. The accompanying table illustrates annual salaries and income tax owed by five individuals. Apart from the fact that they receive different salaries and owe different amounts of income tax, these five individuals are otherwise identical.

Name	Annual salary	Annual income tax owed
Susan	$22,000	$3,304
Bill	63,000	14,317
John	3,000	454
Mary	94,000	23,927
Peter	37,000	7,020

a. If you were to plot these points on a graph, what would be the average slope of the curve between the points for Bill's and Mary's salaries and taxes using the arc method? How would you interpret this value for slope?

b. What is the average slope of the curve between the points for John's and Susan's salaries and taxes using the arc method? How would you interpret that value for slope?

c. What happens to the slope as salary increases? What does this relationship imply about how the level of income taxes affects a person's incentive to earn a higher salary?

8. a. Annual salary is the independent variable and so is measured on the horizontal axis. Annual income tax owed is the dependent variable and so is measured on the vertical axis. As salary increases by $31,000 from Bill's $63,000 to Mary's $94,000, income tax owed increases by $9,610. That is, the slope of the curve is $9,610/31,000 = 0.31$. The interpretation is that in this income bracket, each additional dollar of income implies a tax of $0.31.

b. As salary increases by $19,000 from John's $3,000 to Susan's $22,000, income tax owed increases by $2,850. That is, the slope of the curve is $2,850/19,000 = 0.15$. The interpretation is that in this income bracket, each additional dollar of income implies a tax of $0.15.

c. The slope is positive and increasing. This implies that the tax scheme is "progressive": the higher the annual salary, the greater the amount of income tax owed per dollar of income. Therefore, the incentive to earn more and more income becomes weaker and weaker, since more of the additional income earned is owed as income taxes.

Supply and Demand

1. A survey indicated that chocolate ice cream is America's favorite ice-cream flavor. For each of the following, indicate the possible effects on demand and/or supply and equilibrium price and quantity of chocolate ice cream.

   a. A severe drought in the Midwest causes dairy farmers to reduce the number of milk-producing cattle in their herds by a third. These dairy farmers supply cream that is used to manufacture chocolate ice cream.

   b. A new report by the American Medical Association reveals that chocolate does, in fact, have significant health benefits.

   c. The discovery of cheaper synthetic vanilla flavoring lowers the price of vanilla ice cream.

   d. New technology for mixing and freezing ice cream lowers manufacturers' costs of producing chocolate ice cream.

1. **a.** By reducing their herds, dairy farmers cause the supply of cream to decrease—a leftward shift of the supply curve for cream. As a result, the market price of cream rises, which means that a unit of chocolate ice cream is more expensive to produce. This results in a leftward shift of the supply curve for chocolate ice cream as ice-cream producers reduce the quantity of chocolate ice cream supplied at any given price. This leads to a rise in the equilibrium price and a fall in the equilibrium quantity.

   b. Consumers will now demand more chocolate ice cream at any given price, representing a rightward shift of the demand curve. As a result, both equilibrium price and quantity rise.

   c. The price of a substitute (vanilla ice cream) has fallen, and consumers will tend to substitute it for chocolate ice cream. The demand for chocolate ice cream decreases, representing a leftward shift of the demand curve. Both equilibrium price and quantity fall.

   d. Because the cost of producing ice cream falls, manufacturers are willing to supply more units of chocolate ice cream at any given price. This is represented by a rightward shift of the supply curve and results in a fall in the equilibrium price and a rise in the equilibrium quantity.

2. In a supply and demand diagram, draw the shift in demand for hamburgers in your hometown due to the following events. In each case show the effect on equilibrium price and quantity.

   a. The price of tacos increases.

   b. All hamburger sellers raise the price of their french fries.

   c. Income falls in town. Assume that hamburgers are a normal good for most people.

   d. Income falls in town. Assume that hamburgers are an inferior good for most people.

   e. Hot dog stands cut the price of hot dogs.

2. **a.** A rise in the price of a substitute (tacos) causes the demand for hamburgers to increase. This represents a rightward shift of the demand curve from D_1 to D_2 and results in a rise in the equilibrium price and quantity as the equilibrium changes from E_1 to E_2.

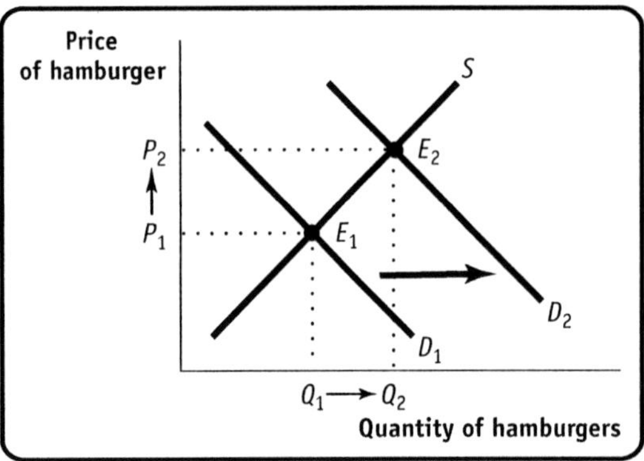

b. A rise in the price of a complement (french fries) causes the demand for hamburgers to decrease. This represents a leftward shift of the demand curve from D_1 to D_2 and results in a fall in the equilibrium price and quantity as the equilibrium changes from E_1 to E_2.

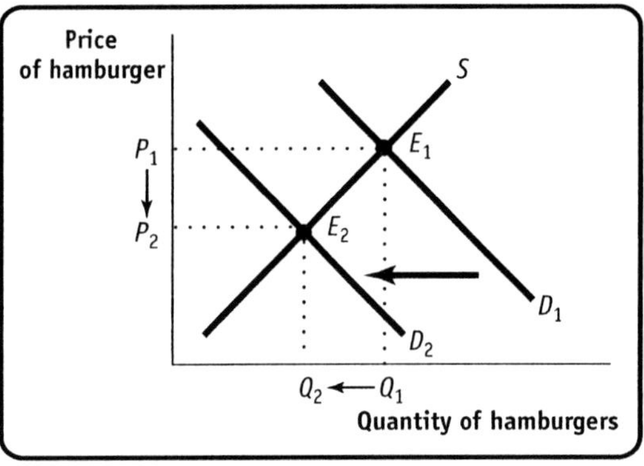

c. A fall in income causes the demand for a normal good (hamburgers) to decrease. This represents a leftward shift of the demand curve from D_1 to D_2 and results in a fall in the equilibrium price and quantity as the equilibrium changes from E_1 to E_2.

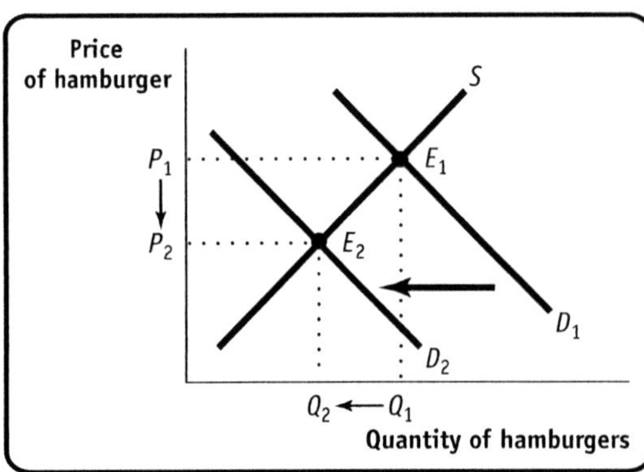

d. A fall in income causes the demand for an inferior good (hamburgers) to increase. This represents a rightward shift of the demand curve from D_1 to D_2 and results in a rise in the equilibrium price and quantity as the equilibrium changes from E_1 to E_2.

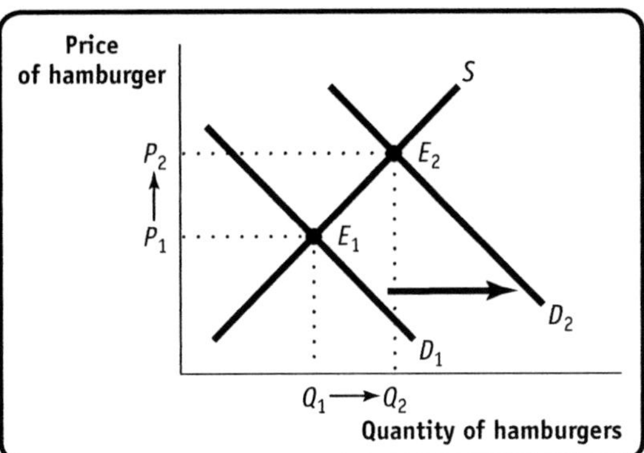

e. A fall in the price of a substitute (hot dogs) causes demand for hamburgers to decrease. This is represented by a leftward shift of the demand curve from D_1 to D_2 and results in a fall in the equilibrium price and quantity as the equilibrium changes from E_1 to E_2.

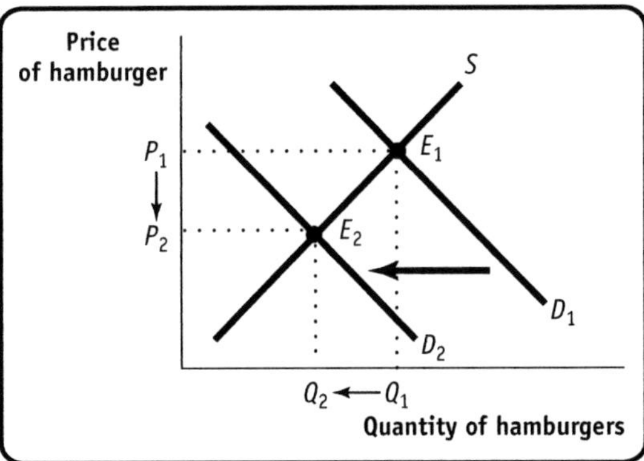

3. The market for many goods changes in predictable ways according to the time of year, in response to events such as holidays, vacation times, seasonal changes in production, and so on. Using supply and demand, explain the change in price in each of the following cases. Note that supply and demand may shift simultaneously.

a. Lobster prices usually fall during the summer peak harvest season, despite the fact that people like to eat lobster during the summer months more than during any other time of year.

b. The price of a Christmas tree is lower after Christmas than before and fewer trees are sold.

c. The price of a round-trip ticket to Paris on Air France falls by more than $200 after the end of school vacation in September. This happens despite the fact that generally worsening weather increases the cost of operating flights to Paris, and Air France therefore reduces the number of flights to Paris at any given price.

3. **a.** There is a rightward shift of the demand curve from D_1 to D_2 during the summer months, as consumers prefer to eat more lobster during the summer than during other times of the year. Other things equal, this leads to a rise in the price of lobster. Simultaneously, lobster fishermen produce more lobster during the summer peak harvest time, when it is cheaper to harvest lobster, representing a rightward shift of the supply curve of lobster from S_1 to S_2. Other things equal, this leads to a fall in the price of lobster. Given the simultaneous rightward shifts of both the demand and supply curves, the equilibrium changes from E_1 to E_2. The fall in price indicates that the rightward shift of the supply curve exceeds the rightward shift of the demand curve.

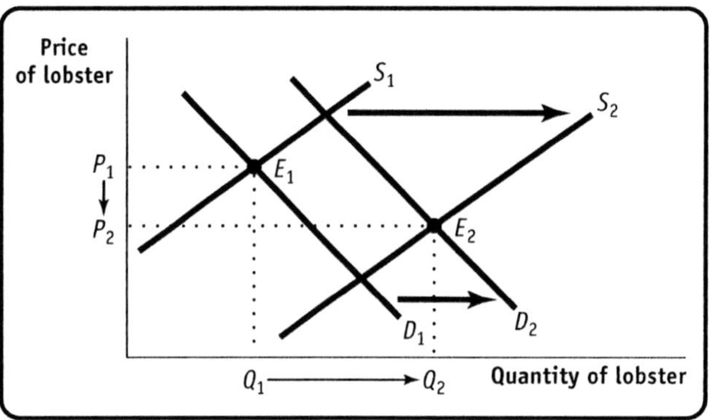

b. There is a leftward shift of the demand curve for Christmas trees after Christmas from D_1 to D_2, as fewer consumers want Christmas trees at any given price. The supply curve does not shift; the reduction in the quantity of trees supplied is a movement along the supply curve. This leads to a fall in the equilibrium price and quantity, as the equilibrium changes from E_1 to E_2.

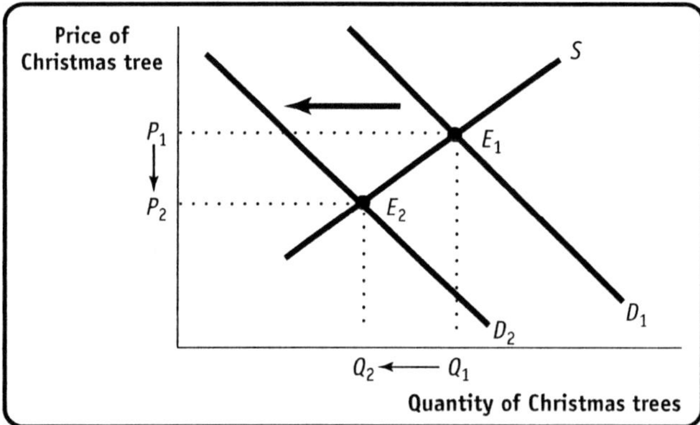

c. There is a leftward shift of the demand curve for tickets to Paris in September, after the end of school vacation, from D_1 to D_2. Other things equal, this leads to a fall in the price of tickets. At the same time, as the cost of operating flights increases, Air France decreases the number of flights, shifting the supply curve leftward from S_1 to S_2. Other things equal, this leads to a rise in price. Given the simultaneous leftward shifts of both the demand and supply curves, the equilibrium changes from E_1 to E_2. The fall in price indicates that the leftward shift of the demand curve exceeds the leftward shift of the supply curve.

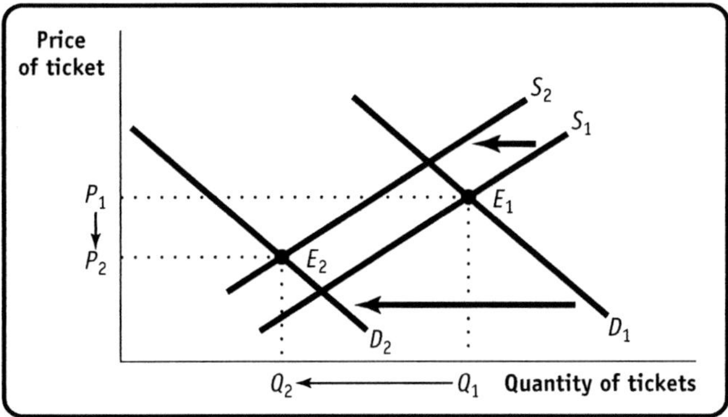

4. Show in a diagram the effect on the demand curve, the supply curve, the equilibrium price, and the equilibrium quantity of each of the following events.

a. The market for newspapers in your town.

Case 1:   The salaries of journalists go up.

Case 2:   There is a big news event in your town, which is reported in the newspapers.

b. The market for St. Louis Rams cotton T-shirts.

Case 1:   The Rams win the national championship.

Case 2:   The price of cotton increases.

c. The market for bagels.

Case 1:   People realize how fattening bagels are.

Case 2:   People have less time to make themselves a cooked breakfast.

d. The market for the Krugman and Wells economics textbook.

Case 1:   Your professor makes it required reading for all of his or her students.

Case 2:   Printing costs for textbooks are lowered by the use of synthetic paper.

4. **a. Case 1:** Journalists are an input in the production of newspapers; an increase in their salaries will cause newspaper publishers to reduce the quantity supplied at any given price. This represents a leftward shift of the supply curve from S_1 to S_2 and results in a rise in the equilibrium price and a fall in the equilibrium quantity as the equilibrium changes from E_1 to E_2.

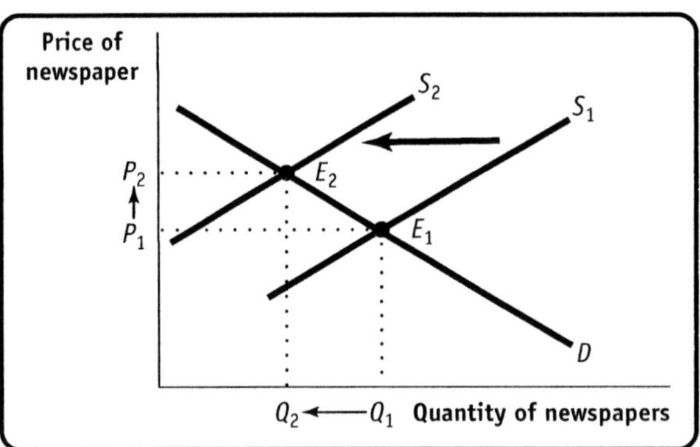

Case 2: Townspeople will wish to purchase more newspapers at any given price. This represents a rightward shift of the demand curve from D_1 to D_2 and leads to a rise in both the equilibrium price and quantity as the equilibrium changes from E_1 to E_2.

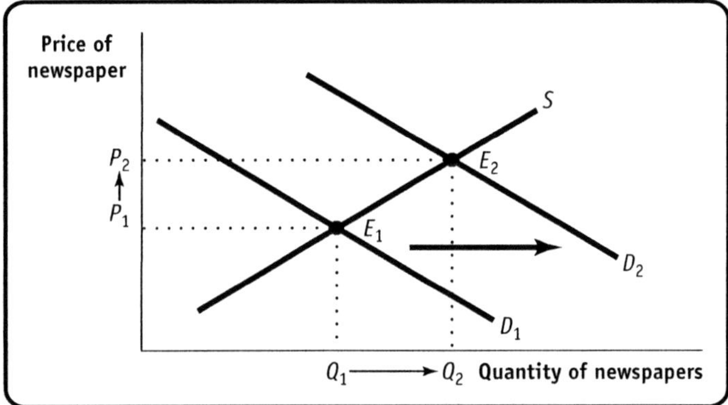

b. Case 1: Fans will demand more St. Louis Rams memorabilia at any given price. This represents a rightward shift of the demand curve from D_1 to D_2 and leads to a rise in both the equilibrium price and quantity as the equilibrium changes from E_1 to E_2.

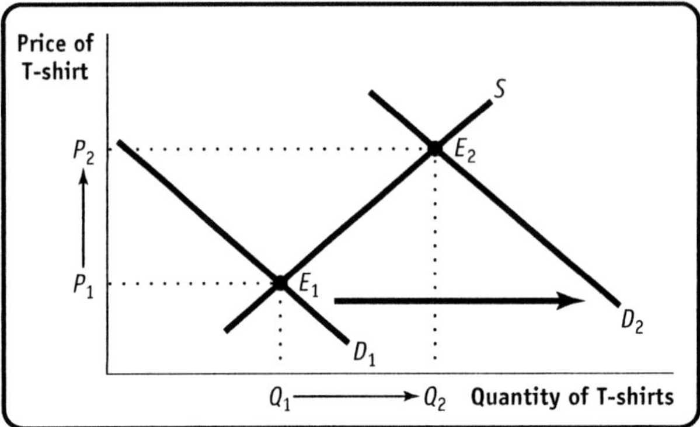

Case 2: Cotton is an input into T-shirts; an increase in its price will cause T-shirt manufacturers to reduce the quantity supplied at any given price, representing a leftward shift of the supply curve from S_1 to S_2. This leads to a rise in the equilibrium price and a fall in the equilibrium quantity as the equilibrium changes from E_1 to E_2.

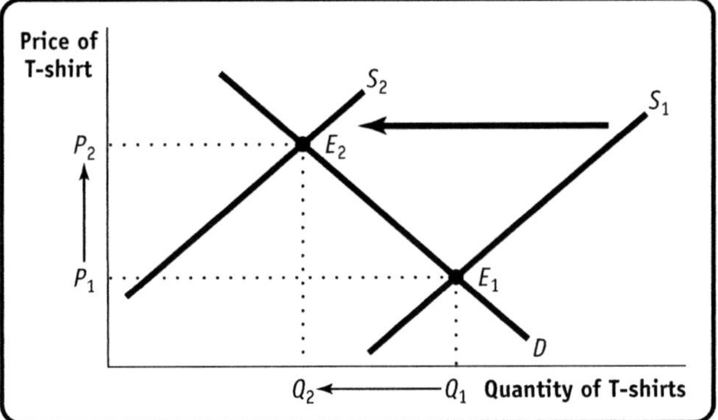

c. **Case 1:** Consumers will demand fewer bagels at any given price. This represents a leftward shift of the demand curve from D_1 to D_2 and leads to a fall in both the equilibrium price and quantity as the equilibrium changes from E_1 to E_2.

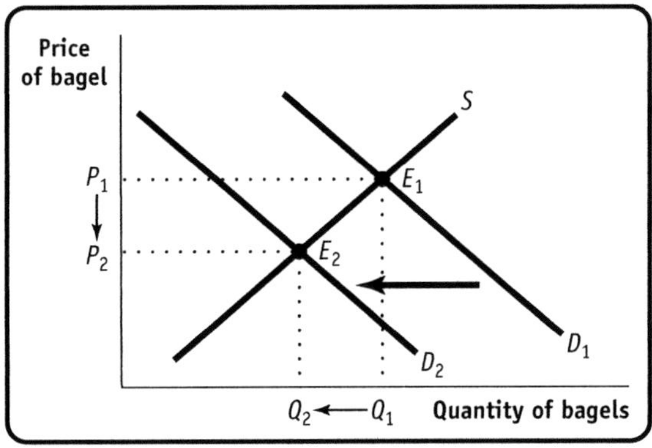

Case 2: Consumers will demand more bagels (a substitute for cooked breakfasts) at any given price. This represents a rightward shift of the demand curve from D_1 to D_2 and leads to a rise in both the equilibrium price and quantity as the equilibrium changes from E_1 to E_2.

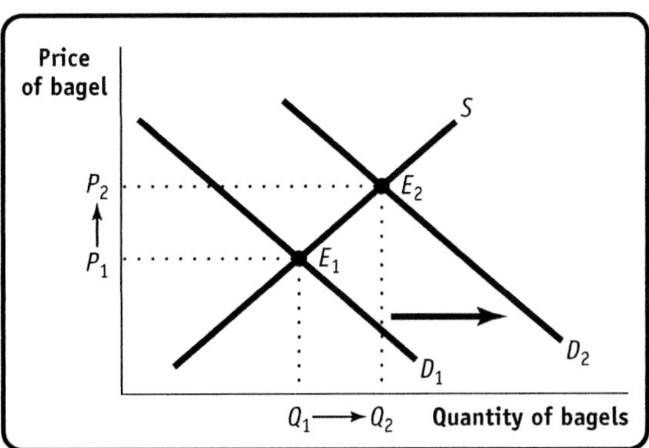

d. **Case 1:** A greater quantity of textbooks will be demanded at any given price, representing a rightward shift of the demand curve from D_1 to D_2. Equilibrium price and quantity will rise as the equilibrium changes from E_1 to E_2.

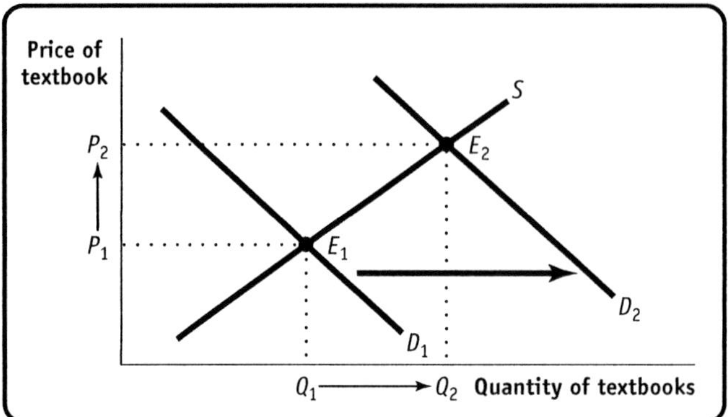

Case 2: The textbook publisher will offer more textbooks for sale at any given price, representing a rightward shift of the supply curve from S_1 to S_2. Equilibrium price will fall and equilibrium quantity will rise as the equilibrium changes from E_1 to E_2.

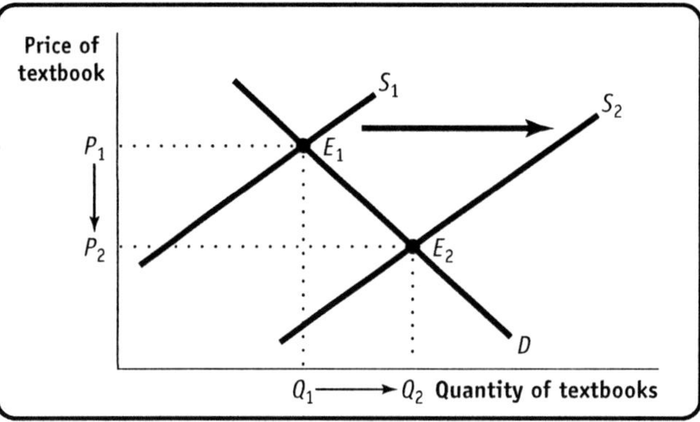

5. Suppose that the supply schedule of Maine lobsters is as follows:

Price of lobster (per pound)	Quantity of lobster supplied (pounds)
$25	800
20	700
15	600
10	500
5	400

Suppose that Maine lobsters can be sold only in the United States. The U.S. demand schedule for Maine lobsters is as follows:

Price of lobster (per pound)	Quantity of lobster demanded (pounds)
$25	200
20	400
15	600
10	800
5	1,000

a. Draw the demand curve and the supply curve for Maine lobsters. What is the equilibrium price and quantity of lobsters?

Now suppose that Maine lobsters can be sold in France. The French demand schedule for Maine lobsters is as follows:

Price of lobster (per pound)	Quantity of lobster demanded (pounds)
$25	100
20	300
15	500
10	700
5	900

b. What is the demand schedule for Maine lobsters now that French consumers can also buy them? Draw a supply and demand diagram that illustrates the new equilibrium price and quantity of lobsters. What will happen to the price at which fishermen can sell lobster? What will happen to the price paid by U.S. consumers? What will happen to the quantity consumed by U.S. consumers?

5. a. The equilibrium price of lobster is $15 per pound and the equilibrium quantity is 600 pounds, point E in the accompanying diagram.

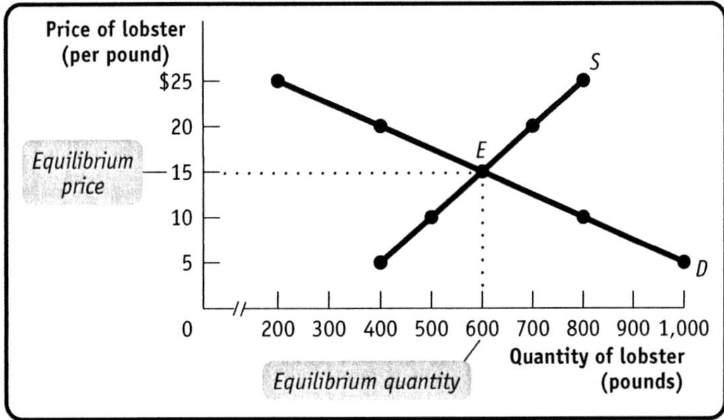

b. The new demand schedule is obtained by adding together, at any given price, the quantity demanded by American consumers and the quantity demanded by French consumers, as shown in the following table.

Price of lobster (per pound)	Quantity of lobster supplied (U.S. pounds plus French pounds)
$25	300
20	700
15	1,100
10	1,500
5	1,900

The new equilibrium price of lobster is $20 per pound and the new equilibrium quantity is 700 pounds, point E in the accompanying diagram. The opportunity to sell to French consumers makes Maine fishermen better off: they sell more lobster and at a higher price than before. U.S. consumers, however, are made worse off: they must pay a higher price for lobster ($20 versus $15 per pound), and as a result consume less lobster (400 versus 600 pounds).

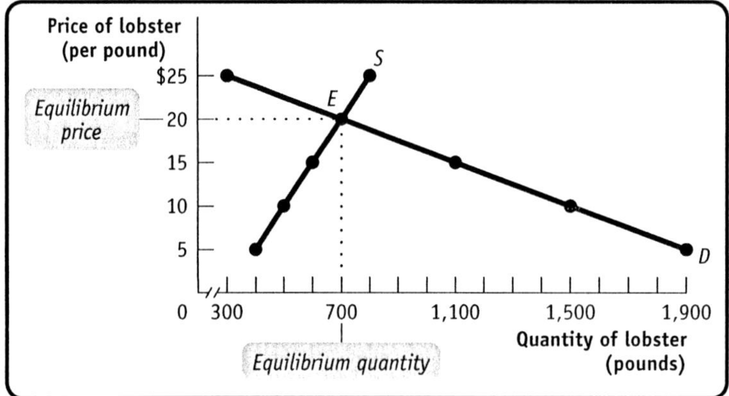

6. Find the flaws in reasoning in the following statements, paying particular attention to the distinction between shifts of and movements along the supply and demand curves. Draw a diagram to illustrate what actually happens in each situation.

a. "A technological innovation that lowers the cost of producing a good might seem at first to result in a reduction in the price of the good to consumers. But a fall in price will increase demand for the good, and higher demand will send the price up again. It is not certain, therefore, that an innovation will really reduce price in the end."

b. "A study shows that eating a clove of garlic a day can help prevent heart disease, causing many consumers to demand more garlic. This increase in demand results in a rise in the price of garlic. Consumers, seeing that the price of garlic has gone up, reduce their demand for garlic. This causes the demand for garlic to decrease and the price of garlic to fall. Therefore, the ultimate effect of the study on the price of garlic is uncertain."

6. **a.** This statement confuses a shift of a curve with a movement along a curve. A technological innovation lowers the cost of producing the good; as a result, producers will offer more of the good at any given price. This is represented by a rightward shift of the supply curve from S_1 to S_2. As a result, the equilibrium price falls and the equilibrium quantity rises, as shown by the change from E_1 to E_2. The statement "but a fall in price will increase demand for the good, and higher demand will send the price up again" is wrong for the following reasons. A fall in price does increase the quantity demanded and leads to an increase in the equilibrium quantity as one moves down along the demand curve. But it does not lead to an increase in demand—a rightward shift of the demand curve—and therefore does not cause the price to go up again.

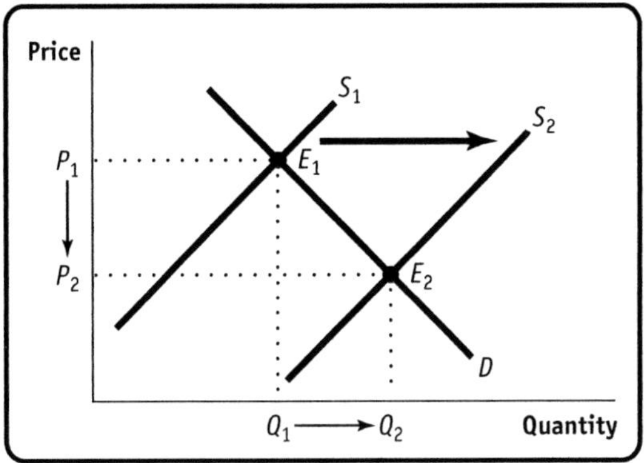

b. This statement also confuses a shift of a curve with a movement along a curve. The health report generates an increase in demand—a rightward shift of the demand curve from D_1 to D_2. This leads to a higher equilibrium price and quantity as we move up along the supply curve, and the equilibrium changes from E_1 to E_2. The following statements are wrong: "Consumers, seeing that the price of garlic has gone up, reduce their demand for garlic. This causes the demand for garlic to decrease and the price of garlic to fall." They are wrong because they imply that the rise in the equilibrium price causes the demand for garlic to decrease—a leftward shift of the demand curve. But a rise in the equilibrium price via a movement along the supply curve does not cause the demand curve to shift leftward.

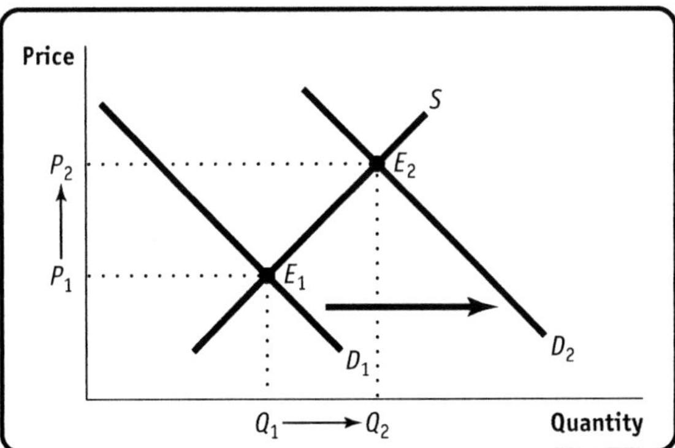

7. Some points on a demand curve for a normal good are given here:

Price	Quantity demanded
$23	70
21	90
19	110
17	130

Do you think that the increase in quantity demanded (from 90 to 110 in the table) when price decreases (from 21 to 19) is due to a rise in consumers' income? Explain clearly (and briefly) why or why not.

7. The increase in quantity demanded from 90 to 110 when the price declines from 21 to 19 is not due to a rise in consumers' income. Rather, it represents a movement along the demand curve as the price falls. In contrast, a rise in consumers' income causes the demand curve to shift rightward for a normal good; as a result, the quantity demanded will increase at any given price.

8. Aaron Hank is a star hitter for the Bay City baseball team. He is close to breaking the major league record for home runs hit during one season, and it is widely anticipated that in the next game he will break that record. As a result, tickets for the team's next game have been a hot commodity. But today it is announced that, due to a knee injury, he will not in fact play in the team's next game. Assume that season ticketholders are able to resell their tickets if they wish. Use supply and demand diagrams to explain the following.

a. Show the case in which this announcement results in a lower equilibrium price and a lower equilibrium quantity than before the announcement.

b. Show the case in which this announcement results in a lower equilibrium price and a higher equilibrium quantity than before the announcement.

c. What accounts for whether case a or case b occurs?

d. Suppose that a scalper had secretly learned before the announcement that Aaron Hank would not play in the next game. What actions do you think he would take?

8. **a.** Fewer fans want to attend the next game after the announcement is made. As a result, the demand curve will shift leftward from D_1 to D_2, as fewer tickets are demanded at any given price; other things equal, this results in a fall in both equilibrium price and quantity. In addition, the supply curve will shift rightward from S_1 to S_2, as more season ticket-holders are willing to sell tickets at any given price; other things equal, this results in a fall in equilibrium price and a rise in equilibrium quantity. In this case, the leftward shift of the demand curve exceeds the rightward shift of the supply curve; as a result, equilibrium quantity falls, shown by the change of the equilibrium from E_1 to E_2.

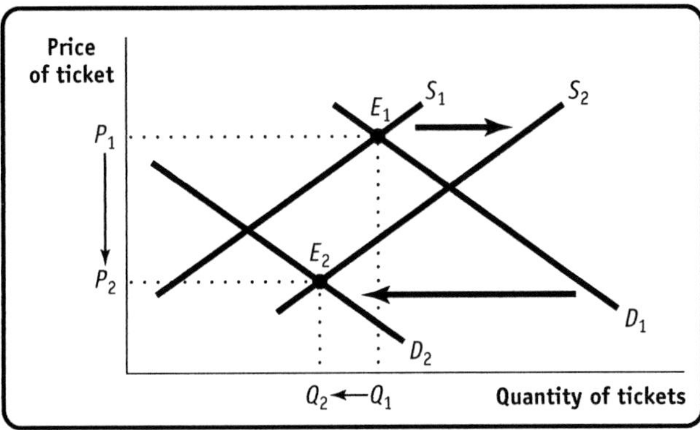

b. The supply and demand curves shift in the same manner as in part a, but in this case the rightward shift of the supply curve exceeds the leftward shift of the demand curve. Consequently, equilibrium quantity rises, shown by the change of the equilibrium from E_1 to E_2.

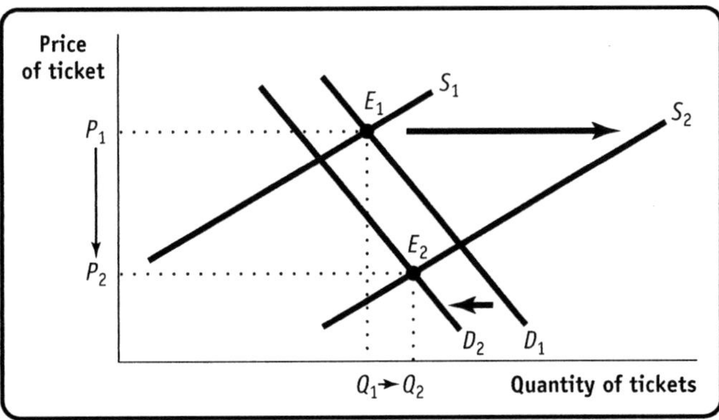

c. Case a (equilibrium quantity falls) occurs because the decrease in demand exceeds the increase in supply. Case b (equilibrium quantity rises) occurs because the increase in supply exceeds the decrease in demand.

d. A scalper who learns about the announcement secretly should take actions—such as lowering price somewhat—that ensure that he will sell all of his tickets before the announcement is made. He will do this because he knows a ticket will command a much lower price after the announcement. An expectation that the price will be lower in the future causes supply to increase today.

9. In *Rolling Stone* magazine, several fans and rock stars, including Pearl Jam, were bemoaning the high price of concert tickets. One superstar argued, "It just isn't worth $75 to see me play. No one should have to pay that much to go to a concert." Assume this star sold out arenas around the country at an average ticket price of $75.

   a. How would you evaluate the arguments that ticket prices are too high?

   b. Suppose that due to this star's protests, ticket prices were lowered to $50. In what sense is this price too low? Draw a diagram using supply and demand curves to support your argument.

   c. Suppose Pearl Jam really wanted to bring down ticket prices. Since the band controls the supply of its services, what do you recommend they do? Explain using a supply and demand diagram.

   d. Suppose the band's next CD was a total dud. Do you think they would still have to worry about ticket prices being too high? Why or why not? Draw a supply and demand diagram to support your argument.

   e. Suppose the group announced their next tour was going to be their last. What effect would this likely have on the demand for and price of tickets? Illustrate with a supply and demand diagram.

9. **a.** If markets are competitive, the ticket price is simply the equilibrium price: the price at which quantity supplied is equal to quantity demanded. No one is "made" to pay $75 to go to a concert: a potential concert-goer will pay $75 if going to the concert seems worth that amount and will choose to do something else if it isn't.

   b. At $50 each, the quantity of tickets demanded exceeds the quantity of tickets supplied. There is a shortage of tickets at this price as shown by the difference between the quantity demanded at this price, Q_D, and the quantity supplied at this price, Q_S.

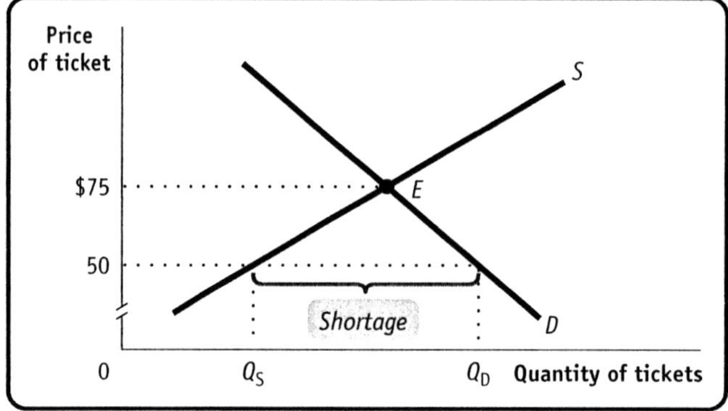

c. The band can lower the average price of a ticket by increasing supply: give more concerts. This is shown as a rightward shift of the supply curve from S_1 to S_2, resulting in a lower equilibrium price and a higher equilibrium quantity, shown by the change of the equilibrium from E_1 to E_2.

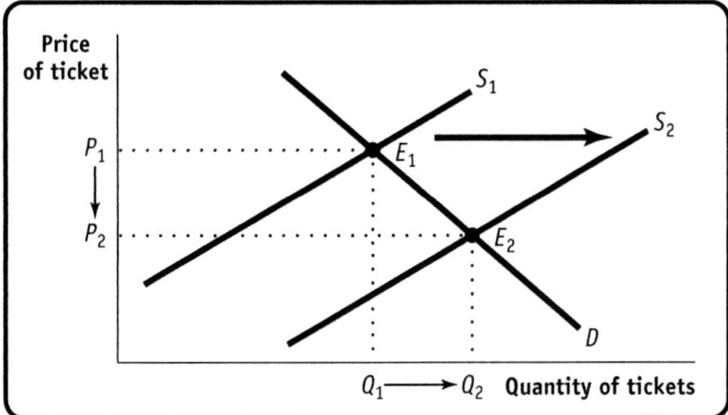

d. If the band's CD is a total dud, the demand for concert tickets is likely to decrease. This represents a leftward shift of the demand curve from D_1 to D_2, resulting in a lower equilibrium price and quantity as the equilibrium changes from E_1 to E_2. This is likely to eliminate the worry that ticket prices are "too high."

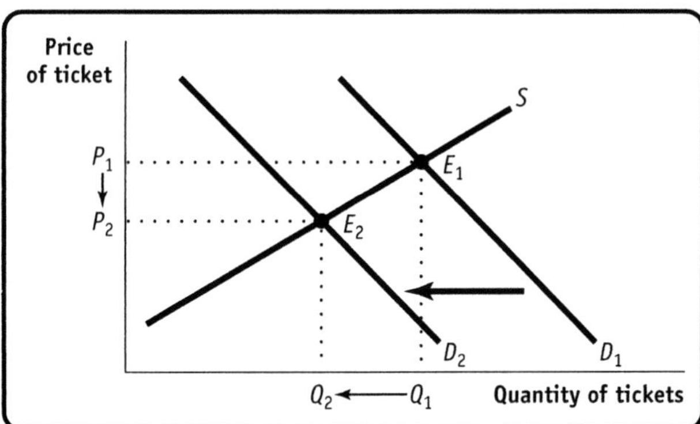

e. The announcement that this is the group's last tour causes the demand for tickets to increase. This is represented by a rightward shift of the demand curve from D_1 to D_2, resulting in an increase in both the equilibrium price and quantity as the equilibrium changes from E_1 to E_2.

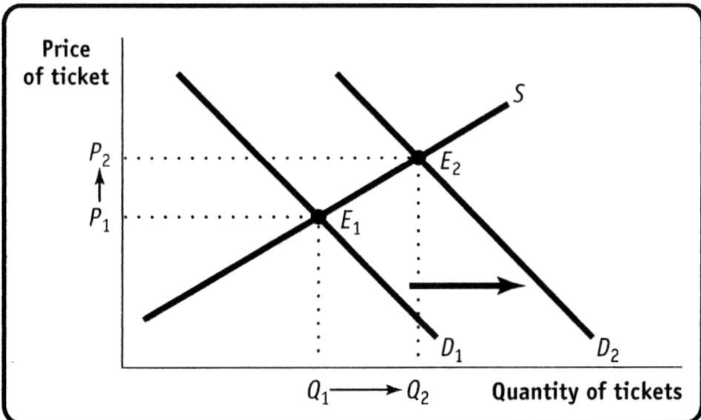

10. The accompanying table gives the annual U.S. demand and supply schedules for pickup trucks.

Price of truck	Quantity of trucks demanded (millions)	Quantity of trucks supplied (millions)
$20,000	20	14
25,000	18	15
30,000	16	16
35,000	14	17
40,000	12	18

a. Plot the demand and supply curves using these schedules. Indicate the equilibrium price and quantity on your diagram.

b. Suppose the tires used on pickup trucks are found to be defective. What would you expect to happen in the market for pickup trucks? Show this on your diagram.

c. Suppose that the U.S. Department of Transportation imposes costly regulations on manufacturers that cause them to reduce supply by one-third at any given price. Calculate and plot the new supply schedule and indicate the new equilibrium price and quantity on your diagram.

10. **a.** The supply curve is S_1 and the demand curve is D_1. The equilibrium in the market for pickup trucks is indicated by point E_1 in the diagram, with an equilibrium price of $30,000 and an equilibrium quantity of 16 million trucks bought and sold.

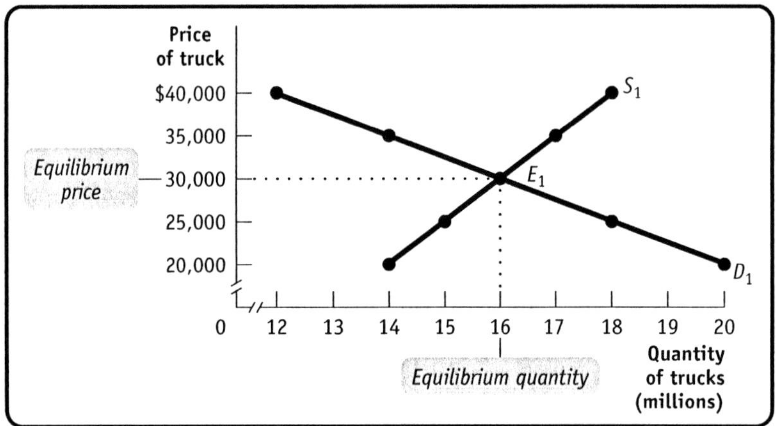

b. The announcement of a defect is likely to decrease the demand for pickup trucks. This is represented by a leftward shift of the demand curve, as shown by the shift from D_1 to D_2, and causes the equilibrium price and quantity to fall as the equilibrium changes from E_1 to E_2.

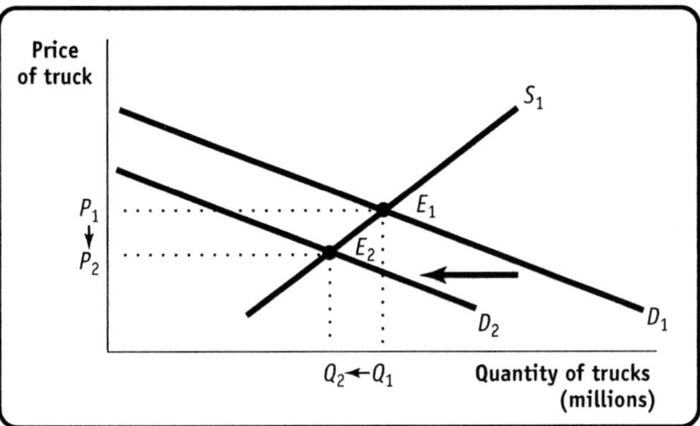

c. The new supply schedule is as follows.

Price of truck	Quantity of trucks supplied (millions)
$20,000	9.3
25,000	10.0
30,000	10.7
35,000	11.3
40,000	12.0

This one-third decrease in the quantity supplied at any given price is shown as a leftward shift of the supply curve from S_1 to S_2. It results in a new, higher equilibrium price, $40,000 per truck, and a lower equilibrium quantity, 12 million trucks, as shown by the change of the equilibrium from E_1 to E_3.

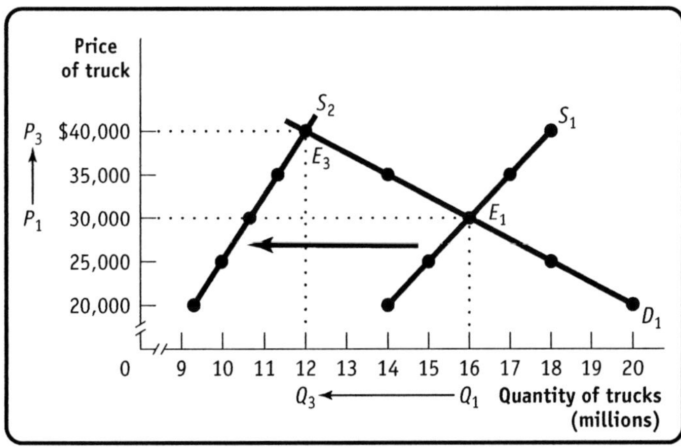

11. After several years of decline, the market for handmade acoustic guitars is making a comeback. These guitars are usually made in small workshops employing relatively few highly skilled luthiers. Assess the impact on the equilibrium price and quantity of handmade acoustic guitars as a result of each of the following events. In your answers indicate which curve(s) shift(s) and in which direction.

    a. Environmentalists succeed in having the use of Brazilian rosewood banned in the United States, forcing luthiers to seek out alternative, more costly woods.

    b. A foreign producer reengineers the guitar-making process and floods the market with identical guitars.

    c. Music featuring handmade acoustic guitars makes a comeback as audiences tire of heavy metal and grunge music.

    d. The country goes into a deep recession and the income of the average American falls sharply.

11.   **a.** The cost of producing handmade acoustic guitars rises as more costly woods are used to construct them. This reduces supply, as luthiers offer fewer guitars at any given price. This is represented by a leftward shift of the supply curve and results in a rise in the equilibrium price and a fall in the equilibrium quantity.

    b. This represents a rightward shift of the supply curve and results in a fall in the equilibrium price and a rise in the equilibrium quantity.

    c. As more people demand music played on acoustic guitars, the demand for these guitars by musicians increases as well. (Acoustic guitars are an "input" into the production of this music.) This represents a rightward shift of the demand curve, leading to a higher equilibrium price and quantity.

    d. If average American income falls sharply, then the demand for handmade acoustic guitars will decrease sharply as well because they are a normal good. This is represented by a leftward shift of the demand curve and results in a lower equilibrium price and quantity.

12. *Demand twisters*: Sketch and explain the demand relationship in each of the following statements.

    a. I would never buy a Britney Spears CD! You couldn't even give me one for nothing.

    b. I generally buy a bit more coffee as the price falls. But once the price falls to $2 per pound, I'll buy out the entire stock of the supermarket.

    c. I spend more on orange juice even as the price rises. (Does this mean that I must be violating the law of demand?)

    d. Due to a tuition rise, most students at a college find themselves with lower disposable income. Almost all of them eat more frequently at the school cafeteria and less often at restaurants, even though prices at the cafeteria have risen too. (This one requires that you draw both the demand and the supply curves for dormitory cafeteria meals.)

12. **a.** In this case the quantity demanded is 0 regardless of the price. So this person's demand curve for Britney Spears CDs is a vertical line at the quantity of 0—that is, a
vertical line that lies on top of the vertical axis.

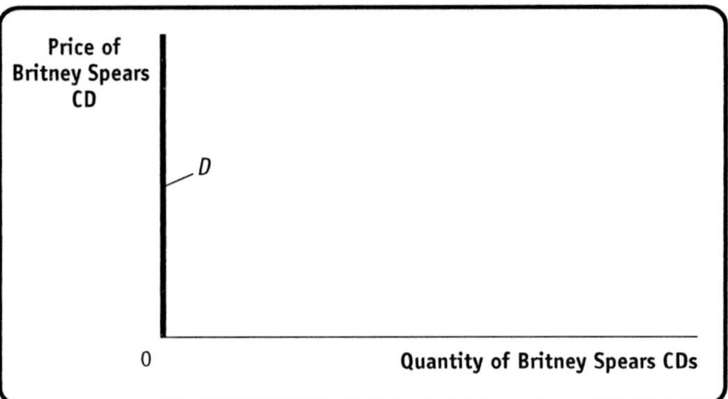

b. The person here has the typical downward-sloping demand curve for coffee until it
reaches the price of $2 per pound, at which point it becomes horizontal, showing
that he or she would buy a very large quantity at that price.

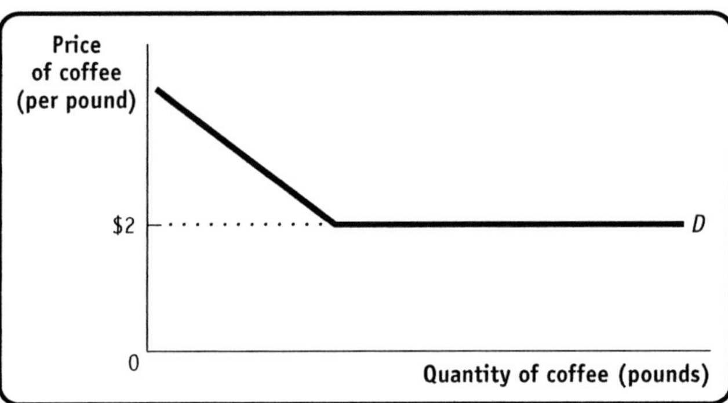

c. This person does not necessarily violate the law of demand: the quantity of orange juice demanded may in fact fall as price goes up. The likely explanation is the following: Spending is price times the quantity demanded. Although price goes up, the total amount of money this person spends on orange juice rises because he or she does not reduce the quantity demanded enough to offset the increased cost per unit. This person will have a steep demand curve as shown in the diagram: quantity demanded falls as price rises, but the fall in quantity demanded is proportionately less than the rise in price.

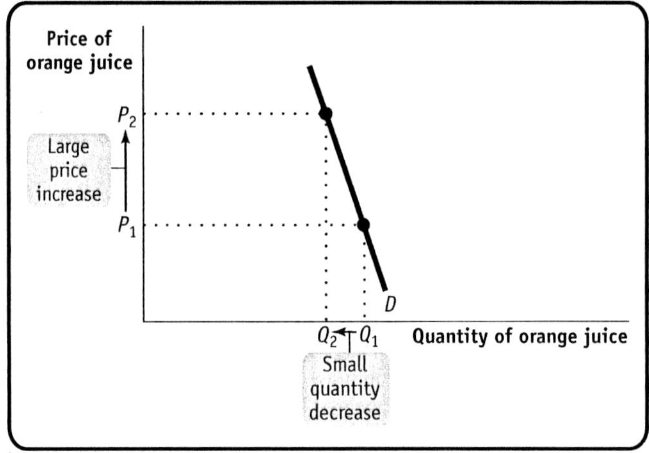

d. Since students' income has fallen, but the demand for cafeteria meals has increased, cafeteria meals must be an inferior good. The rightward shift of the demand curve, from D_1 to D_2, results in an increase in the equilibrium price and the equilibrium quantity of cafeteria meals, as the equilibrium changes from E_1 to E_2.

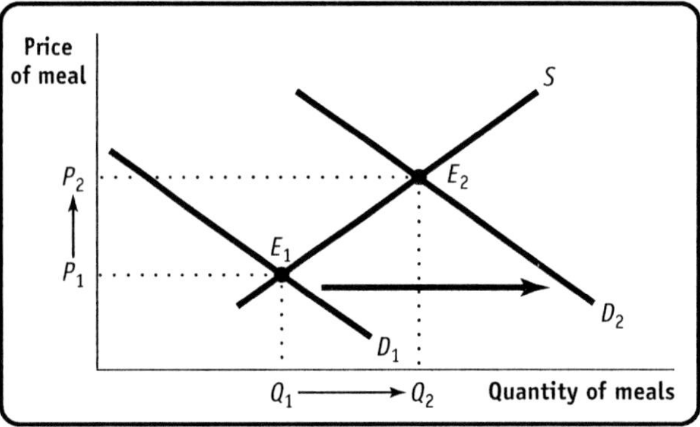

13. Will Shakespeare is a struggling playwright in sixteenth-century London. As the price he receives for writing a play increases, he is willing to write more plays. For the following situations, use a diagram to illustrate how each event affects the equilibrium price and quantity in the market for Shakespeare's plays.

a. The playwright Christopher Marlowe, Shakespeare's chief rival, is killed in a bar brawl.

b. The bubonic plague, a deadly infectious disease, breaks out in London.

c. To celebrate the defeat of the Spanish Armada, Queen Elizabeth declares several weeks of festivities, which involves commissioning new plays.

13. **a.** The death of Marlowe means that the supply of a substitute good (Marlowe's plays) has decreased, and therefore the price of Marlowe's plays will rise. As a result, the demand for Shakespeare's plays will increase, inducing a rightward shift of the demand curve in the market for Shakespeare's plays from D_1 to D_2. As a result, equilibrium price and quantity will rise as the equilibrium changes from E_1 to E_2.

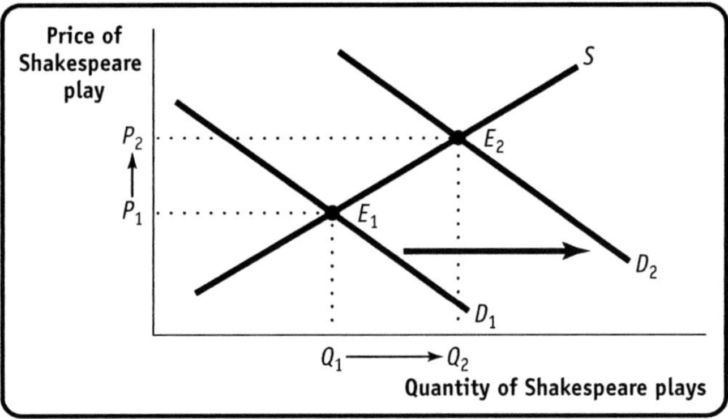

b. After the outbreak of the plague, fewer Londoners will wish to see Shakespeare's plays to avoid contracting the illness, inducing a leftward shift of the demand curve from D_1 to D_2. Equilibrium price and quantity will fall as the equilibrium changes from E_1 to E_2.

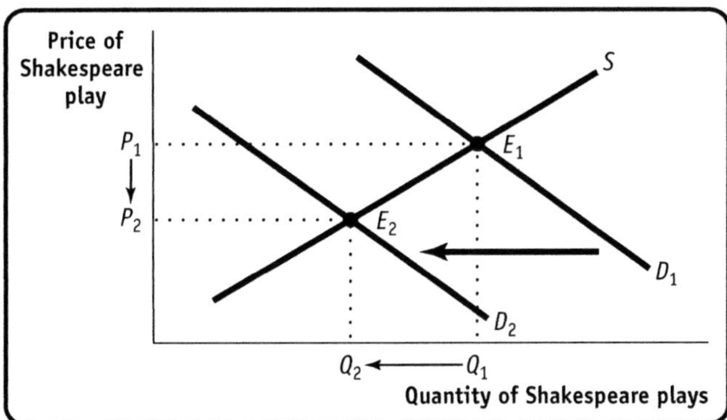

c. Queen Elizabeth's commissions result in a greater quantity of Shakespeare's plays demanded at any given price. This represents a rightward shift of the demand curve from D_1 to D_2, resulting in a higher equilibrium price and quantity as the equilibrium changes from E_1 to E_2.

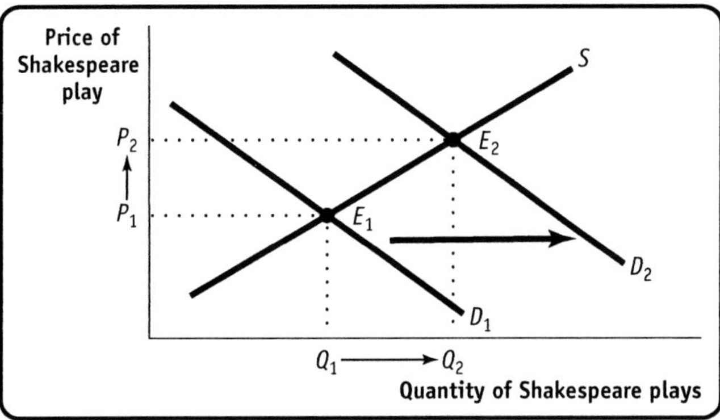

14. The small town of Middling experiences a sudden doubling of the birth rate. After three years, the birth rate returns to normal. Use a diagram to illustrate the effect of these events on the following.

   a. The market for an hour of babysitting services in Middling today

   b. The market for an hour of babysitting services 14 years into the future, after the birth rate has returned to normal, by which time children born today are old enough to work as babysitters

   c. The market for an hour of babysitting services 30 years into the future, when children born today are likely to be having children of their own

14. **a.** There are more babies today, so the demand for an hour of babysitting services has increased. This produces a rightward shift of the demand curve for babysitting services from D_1 to D_2, resulting in a rise in the equilibrium price and quantity as the equilibrium changes from E_1 to E_2.

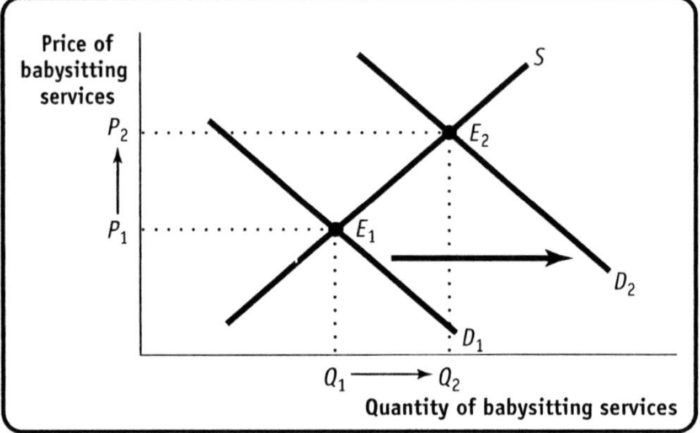

   b. The children born today will cause an increase in the supply of babysitters available 14 years from now, when there will be a rightward shift of the supply curve for babysitting services from S_1 to S_2. It will result in a lower equilibrium price and a higher equilibrium quantity as the equilibrium changes from E_1 to E_2.

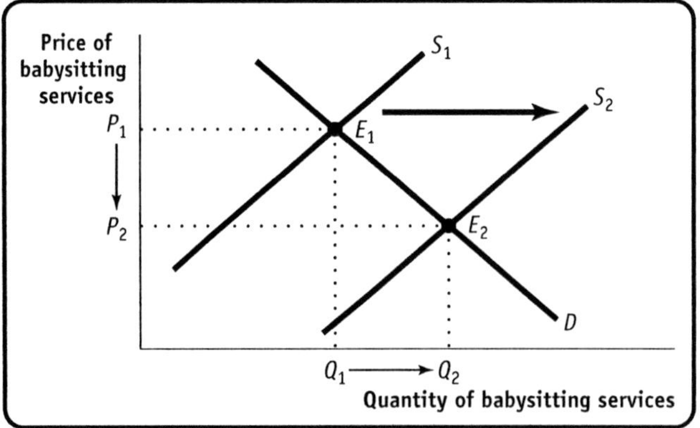

c. It is likely that there will be an increase in the birthrate 30 years from now. There-fore, there will be an increase in the demand for babysitting services, shifting the demand curve rightward from D_1 to D_2. It will result in a higher equilibrium quantity and price as the equilibrium changes from E_1 to E_2.

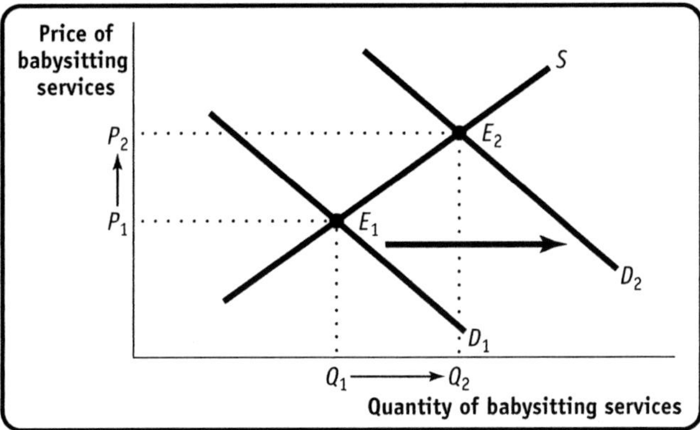

15. Use a diagram to illustrate how each of the following events affects the equilibrium price and quantity of pizza.

a. The price of mozzarella cheese rises.

b. The health hazards of hamburgers are widely publicized.

c. The price of tomato sauce falls.

d. The incomes of consumers rise and pizza is an inferior good.

e. Consumers expect the price of pizza to fall next week.

15. **a.** Mozzarella is an input in the production of pizza. Since the cost of an input has risen, pizza producers will reduce the quantity supplied at any given price, a left-ward shift of the supply curve from S_1 to S_2. As a result, the equilibrium price of pizza will rise and the equilibrium quantity will fall as the equilibrium changes from E_1 to E_2.

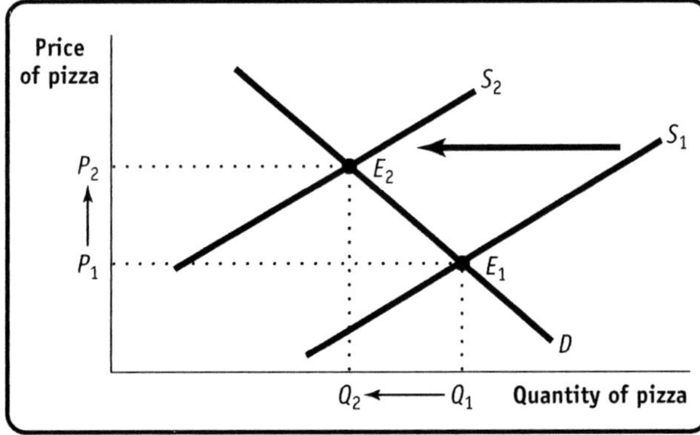

b. Consumers will substitute pizza for hamburgers, resulting in an increased demand for pizza at any given price. This generates a rightward shift of the demand curve from D_1 to D_2 and results in a rise in the equilibrium price and quantity as the equilibrium changes from E_1 to E_2.

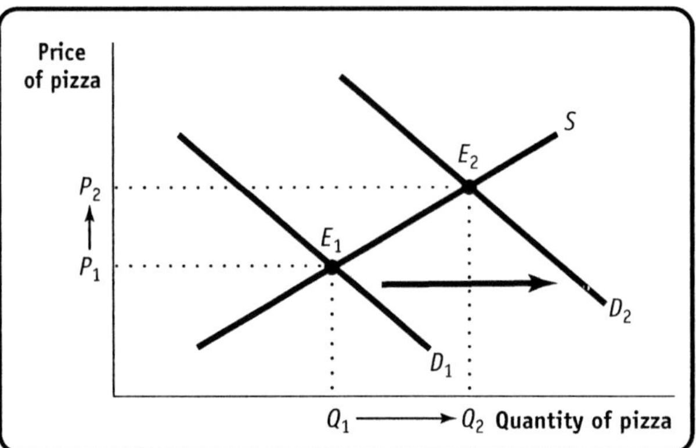

c. Tomato sauce is an input in the production of pizza. Since the cost of an input has fallen, pizza producers will increase the quantity supplied at any given price, a rightward shift of the supply curve from S_1 to S_2. As a result, the equilibrium price of pizza will fall and the equilibrium quantity will rise as the equilibrium changes from E_1 to E_2.

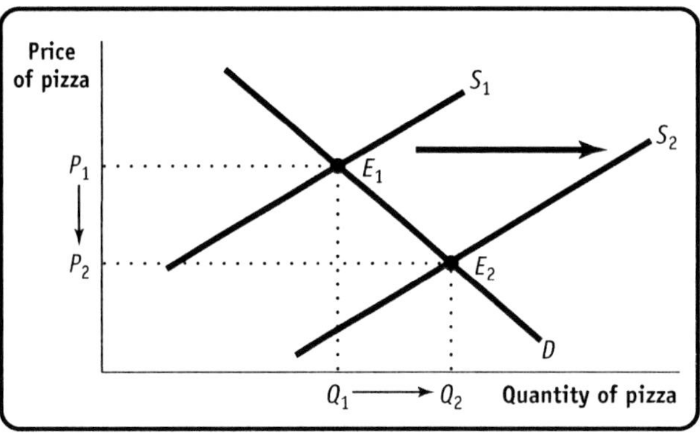

d. The demand for an inferior good decreases when the incomes of consumers rise. So a rise in consumer incomes produces a leftward shift of the demand curve from D_1 to D_2 and results in a lower equilibrium price and quantity as the equilibrium changes from E_1 to E_2.

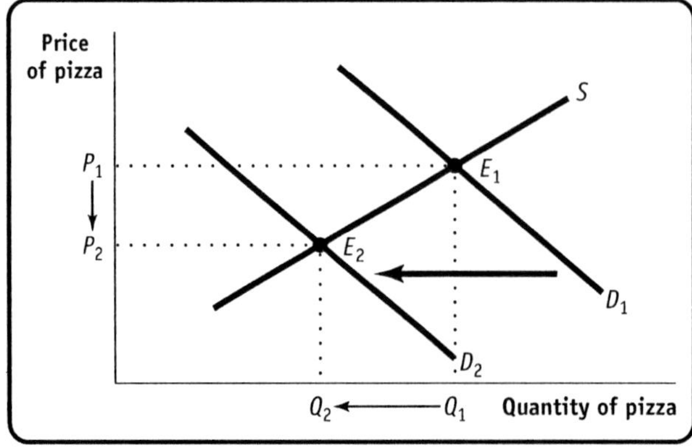

e. Consumers will delay their purchases of pizza today in anticipation of consuming more pizza next week. As a result, the demand curve shifts leftward from D_1 to D_2 and results in a lower equilibrium price and quantity as the equilibrium changes from E_1 to E_2.

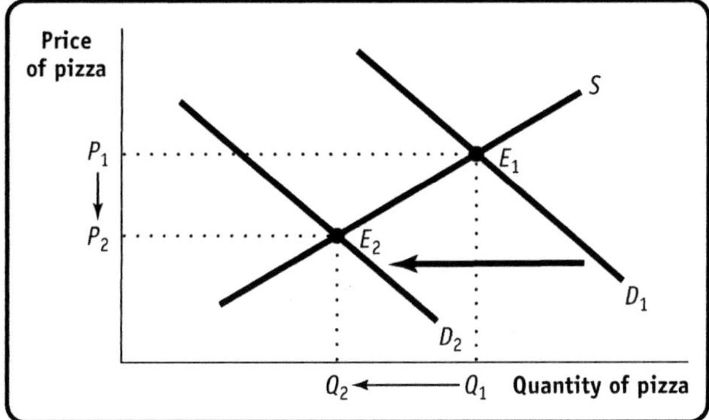

16. Although he was a prolific artist, Pablo Picasso painted only 1,000 canvases during his "Blue Period." Picasso is now dead, and all of his Blue Period works are currently on display in museums and private galleries throughout Europe and the United States.

a. Draw a supply curve for Picasso Blue Period works. Why is this supply curve different from ones you have seen?

b. Given the supply curve from part a, the price of a Picasso Blue Period work will be entirely dependent on what factor(s)? Draw a diagram showing how the equilibrium price of such a work is determined.

c. Suppose that rich art collectors decide that it is essential to acquire Picasso Blue Period art for their collections. Show the impact of this on the market for these paintings.

16. a. There are no more Picasso Blue Period works available. Hence the supply curve is a vertical line at the quantity 1,000.

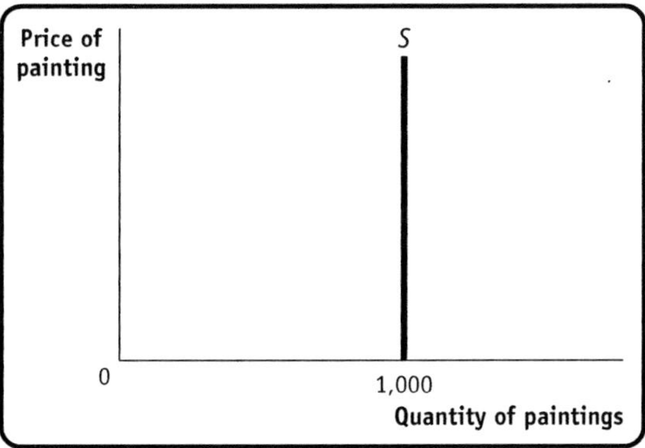

b. Since supply is fixed, the price of a Picasso Blue Period work is entirely determined by demand. Any change in demand is fully reflected in a change in price.

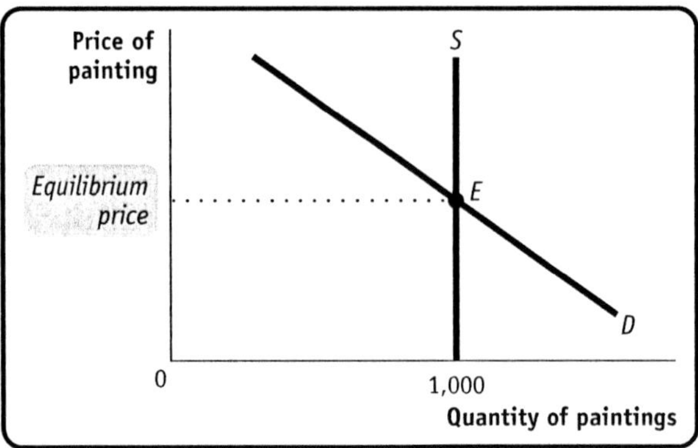

c. This results in a rightward shift of the demand curve for these works from D_1 to D_2, and the equilibrium changes from E_1 to E_2. But since no more works are available, this increase in demand simply results in an increase in the equilibrium price.

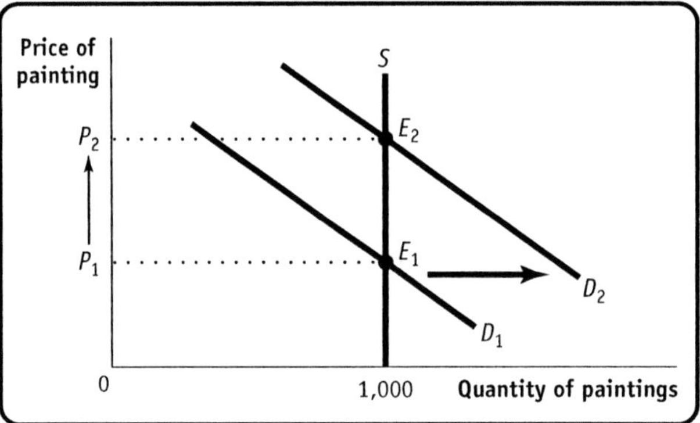

17. Draw the appropriate curve in each of the following cases. Is it like or unlike the curves you have seen so far? Explain.

    a. The demand for cardiac bypass surgery, given that the government pays the full cost for any patient

    b. The demand for elective cosmetic plastic surgery, given that the patient pays the full cost

    c. The supply of Rembrandt paintings

    d. The supply of reproductions of Rembrandt paintings

17. **a.** Since the government pays the full cost of cardiac bypass surgery, the price paid by the patient is always zero. Consequently, the demand for surgery is constant, regardless of the price actually paid by the government. The quantity demanded is constant at the quantity that would be demanded by patients if the government, not the patient, pays for surgery. That is, it is a vertical line at the quantity that patients would demand if the price of surgery to them were zero.

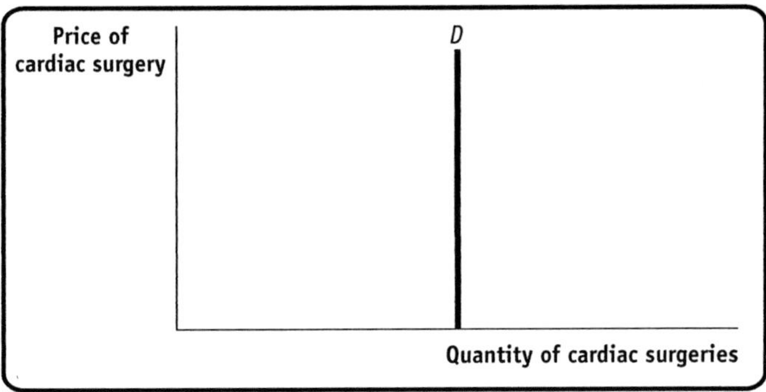

b. In this case the patient must pay the cost of the surgery; therefore, the quantity demanded is affected by price, and the demand curve has its usual downward-sloping shape.

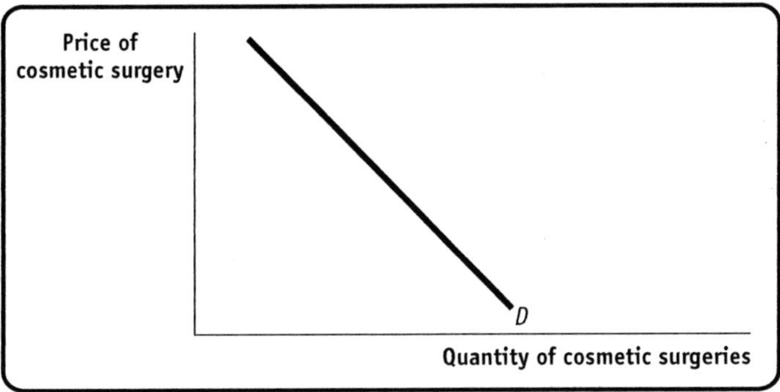

c. The supply of Rembrandt paintings is fixed because Rembrandt is dead. Therefore, unlike the typical upward-sloping supply curve, the supply curve is a vertical line, where the quantity supplied is equal to the number of Rembrandt paintings in existence.

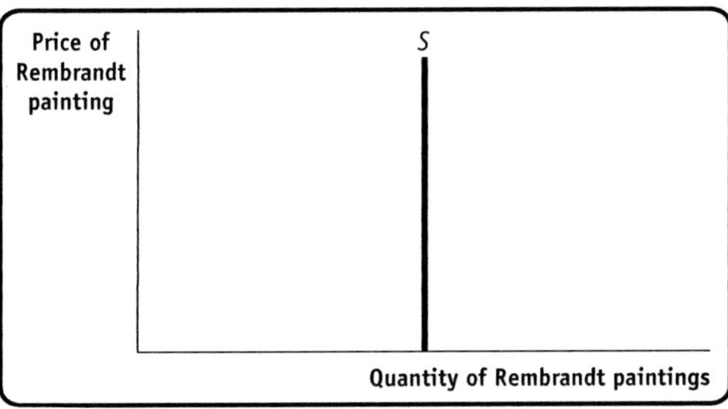

d. The supply of Rembrandt reproductions is not fixed because they can be created by existing artists. Therefore, the supply curve of these reproductions has the familiar upward-sloping shape.

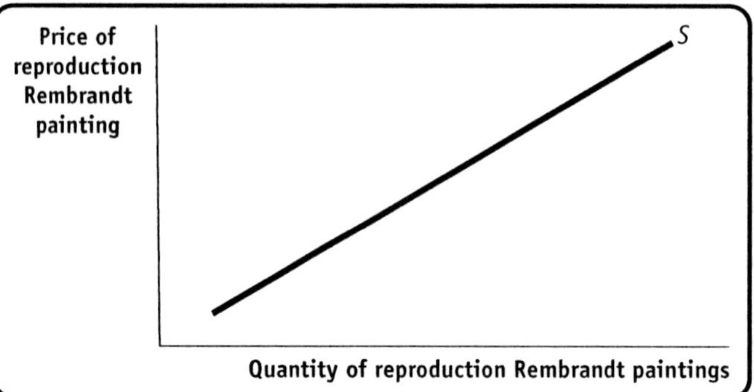

The Market Strikes Back

1. Suppose it is decided that rent control in New York City will be abolished and that market rents will now prevail. Assume that all rental units are identical and are therefore offered at the same rent. To address the plight of residents who may be unable to pay the market rent, an income supplement will be paid to all low-income households equal to the difference between the old controlled rent and the new market rent.

a. Use a diagram to show the effect on the rental market of the elimination of rent control. What will happen to the quality and quantity of rental housing supplied?

b. Now use a second diagram to show the additional effect of the income-supplement policy on the market. What effect does it have on the market rent and quantity of rental housing supplied in comparison to your answers to part a?

c. Are tenants better or worse off as a result of these policies? Are landlords better or worse off?

d. From a political standpoint, why do you think cities have been more likely to resort to rent control rather than a policy of income supplements to help low-income people pay for housing?

1. **a.** With a price ceiling at $P_{CEILING}$, the quantity bought and sold is $Q_{CEILING}$, indicated by point A. The ceiling at $P_{CEILING}$ is eliminated and the rent returns to the market equilibrium E_1, with an equilibrium rent of P_1. The quantity supplied increases from $Q_{CEILING}$ to the equilibrium quantity Q_1. At the same time, you should expect the quality of rental housing to improve. As you learned in this chapter, one of the inefficiencies caused by price ceilings is inefficiently low quality. As the rent returns to the equilibrium rent, landlords again have the incentive to invest in the quality of their apartments in order to attract renters.

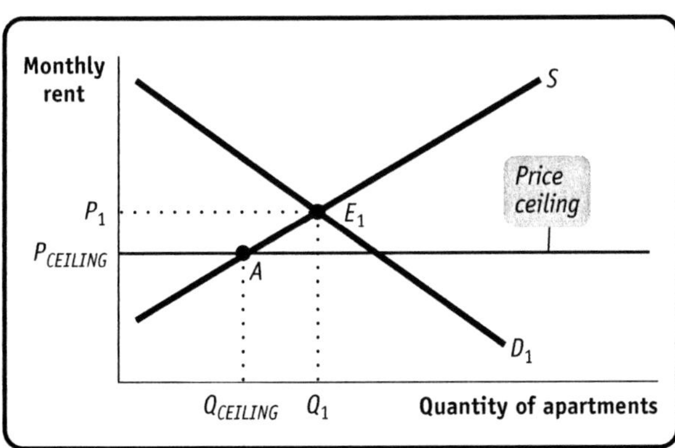

b. The income-supplement policy causes a rightward shift of the demand curve from D_1 to D_2. This results in an increase in the equilibrium rent, from P_1 to P_2, and an increase in the equilibrium quantity, from Q_1 to Q_2, as the equilibrium changes from E_1 to E_2.

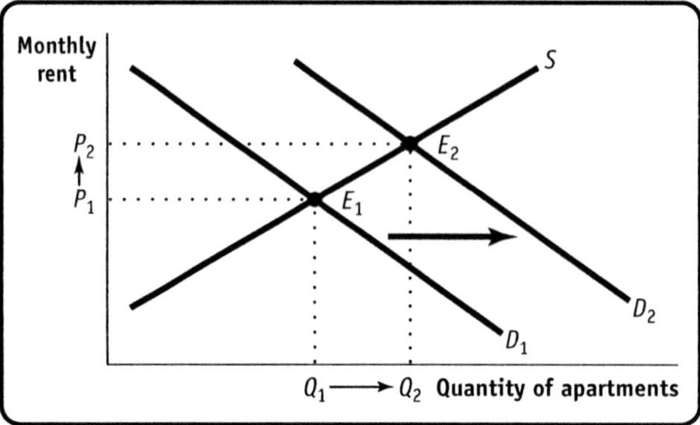

c. Landlords are clearly better off as a result of these two policies: more landlords rent out apartments, and at a higher monthly rent. It is not clear whether tenants are better or worse off. Some tenants who previously could not get apartments can now do so, but at a higher rent. In particular, those tenants who do not receive the income supplement and who used to rent cheap apartments under the price ceiling are now worse off.

d. It is likely that tenants who currently live in rent-controlled housing are better organized than tenants who cannot currently find rental housing. And more organized groups can generally exert greater influence over city policy.

2. In order to ingratiate himself with voters, the mayor of Gotham City decides to lower the price of taxi rides. Assume, for simplicity, that all taxi rides are the same distance and therefore cost the same. The accompanying table shows the demand and supply schedules for taxi rides.

Fare (per ride)	Quantity of rides (millions per year)	
	Quantity demanded	Quantity supplied
$7.00	10	12
6.50	11	11
6.00	12	10
5.50	13	9
5.00	14	8
4.50	15	7

a. Assume that there are no restrictions on the number of taxi rides that can be supplied in the city (i.e., there is no medallion system). Find the equilibrium price and quantity.

b. Suppose that the mayor sets a price ceiling at $5.50. How large is the shortage of rides? Illustrate with a diagram. Who loses and who benefits from this policy?

c. Suppose that the stock market crashes and, as a result, people in Gotham City are poorer. This reduces the quantity of taxi rides demanded by 6 million rides per year at any given price. What effect will the mayor's new policy have now? Illustrate with a diagram.

d. Suppose that the stock market rises and the demand for taxi rides returns to normal (that is, returns to the demand schedule given in the table). The mayor now decides to ingratiate himself with taxi drivers. He announces a policy in which operating licenses are given to existing taxi drivers; the number of licenses is restricted such that only 10 million rides per year can be given. Illustrate the effect of this policy on the market, and indicate the resulting price and quantity transacted. What is the quota rent per ride?

2. **a.** The equilibrium in the market for taxi rides is shown by E_1 in the accompanying diagram. The equilibrium price is $6.50; at that price, the quantity demanded equals the quantity supplied—11 million taxi rides per year. The demand and supply curves $(D_1$ and $S)$ illustrate this initial situation.

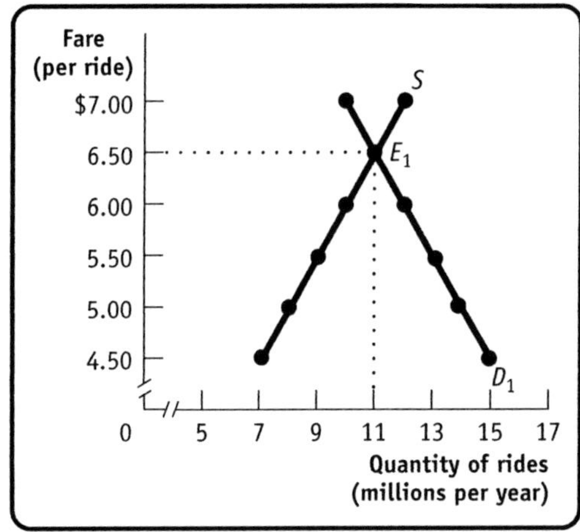

b. With a price ceiling of $5.50, the quantity supplied is 9 million taxi rides and the quantity demanded is 13 million. The shortage therefore is 13 million − 9 million = 4 million. Taxi drivers clearly lose out: there are fewer taxi rides supplied than before, and at a lower price. The impact on consumers is unclear: fewer people now manage to get rides, but those who do, get them at a lower price.

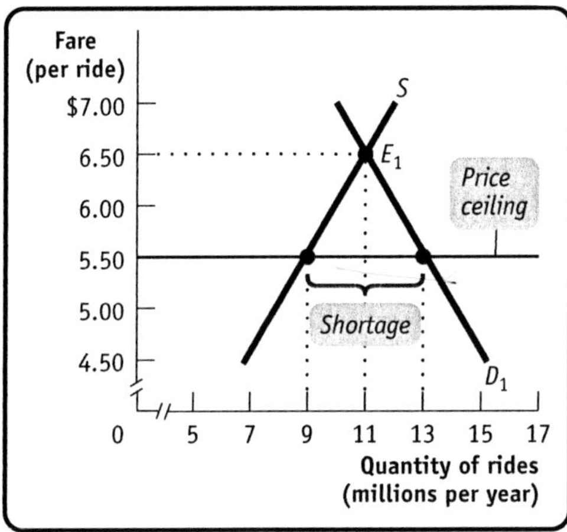

c. The new demand curve is D_2. Now the price ceiling has no effect: the equilibrium is point E_2 and the market price settles at $5, which is below the mandated price ceiling of $5.50. There will be 8 million taxi rides demanded and supplied, at a price of $5 each.

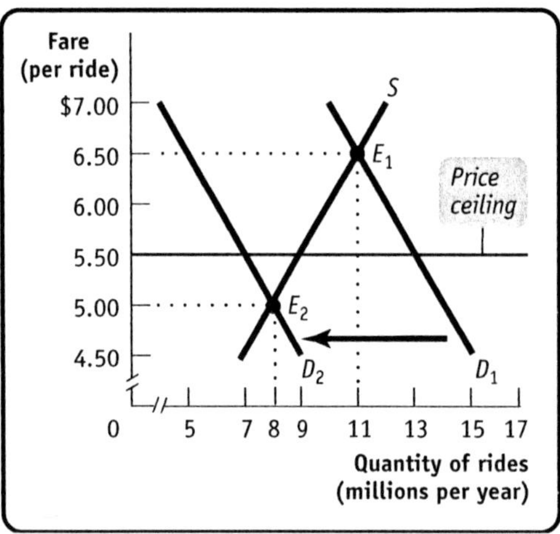

d. The accompanying diagram illustrates the effect of the quota of 10 million taxi rides. The quantity of taxi rides is now 10 million, at a price of $7. The quota rent per ride is $1.

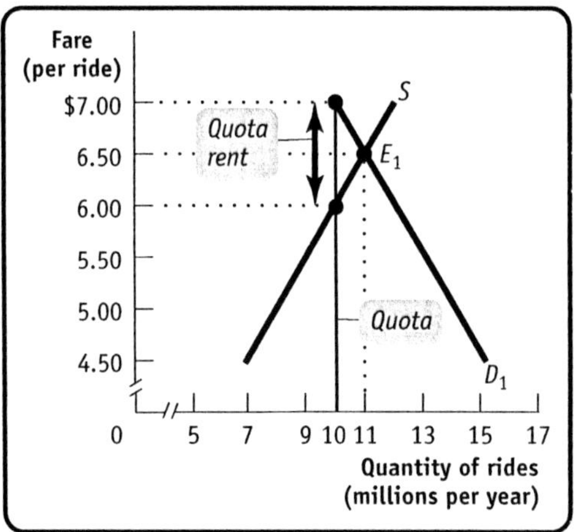

3. In the late eighteenth century, the price of bread in New York City was controlled, set at a predetermined price above the market price.

a. Draw a diagram showing the effect of the policy. Did the policy act as a price ceiling or a price floor?

b. What kinds of inefficiencies were likely to have arisen when the controlled price of bread was above the market price? Explain in detail.

One year during this period, a poor wheat harvest caused a leftward shift in the supply of bread and therefore an increase in its market price. New York bakers found that the controlled price of bread in New York was below the market price.

c. Draw a diagram showing the effect of the price control on the market for bread during this one-year period. Did the policy act as a price ceiling or a price floor?

d. What kinds of inefficiencies do you think occurred during this period? Explain in detail.

3. **a.** Panel (a) of the accompanying diagram illustrates the effect of this policy. Since the price is set *above* the market equilibrium price, this policy acts as a price floor: it raises the price artificially above the equilibrium. As a result, too much bread is produced: there is a surplus.

b. As with all price floors above the equilibrium price, there are several associated inefficiencies. Since bakers cannot compete on price, they will compete on quality: you should expect excessively high quality (bread that is more fancy than customers really want). You should also, of course, expect to see surplus production of bread that does not get bought but is thrown away instead. Furthermore, some bakers are less efficient than others (they operate at a higher cost); if the market were allowed to reach equilibrium, they would find it too costly to operate so there is an inefficient allocation among producers. Finally, there is always an opportunity for black market activity—illegal trade in bread that is priced below the set price.

c. Panel (b) illustrates the effect of the fixed price if the market equilibrium is above that price. The set price now acts like a price ceiling, preventing the price from rising to the equilibrium. There is a shortage, as occurs with every price ceiling below the equilibrium price.

d. One inefficiency is that, since there is an incentive for bakers to locate outside the city, where they can get higher prices, some consumers who cannot buy bread in the city (where there is a shortage) will travel outside the city to buy bread. And the opportunity cost of travel time is, of course, wasteful. Also, some people who manage to buy bread in the city are not those who value it most highly: there might be others who are in greater need but cannot buy bread so there is an inefficient allocation to consumers. Since the price of bread is kept artificially low, some bakers will skimp on quality. Finally, there is an opportunity for black market trade in bread that is resold at much higher prices.

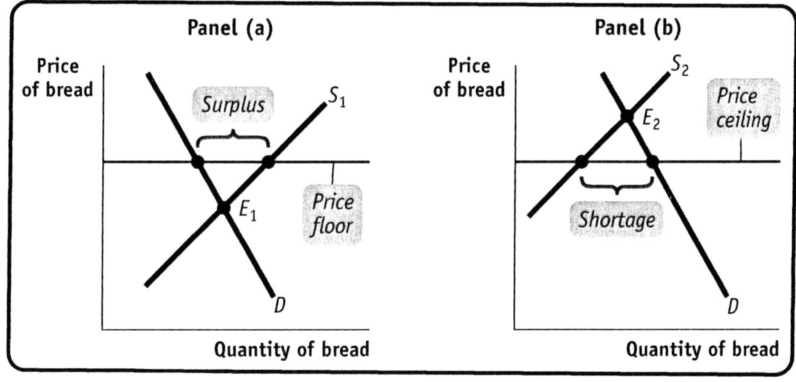

4. The accompanying table shows the demand and supply schedules for milk per year. The U.S. government decides that the incomes of dairy farmers should be maintained at a level that allows the traditional family dairy farm to survive. It therefore implements a price floor of $1 per pint by buying surplus milk until the market price is $1 per pint.

Price of milk (per pint)	Quantity of milk (millions of pints per year)	
	Quantity demanded	Quantity supplied
$1.20	550	850
1.10	600	800
1.00	650	750
0.90	700	700
0.80	750	650

a. How much surplus milk will be produced as a result of this policy?

b. What will be the cost to the government of this policy?

c. Since milk is an important source of protein and calcium, the government decides to provide the surplus milk it purchases to elementary schools at a price of only $0.60 per pint. Assume that schools will buy any amount of milk available at this low price. But parents now reduce their purchases of milk at any price by 50 million pints per year because they know their children are getting milk at school. How much will the dairy program now cost the government?

d. Give two examples of inefficiencies arising from wasted resources that are likely to result from this policy. What is the missed opportunity in each case?

4. **a.** With demand of D_1, and supply of S, the equilibrium would be at point E_1 in the accompanying diagram. However, with a price floor at $1, the quantity supplied is 750 million pints and the quantity demanded is 650 million pints. The policy therefore causes a surplus of milk of 100 million pints per year.

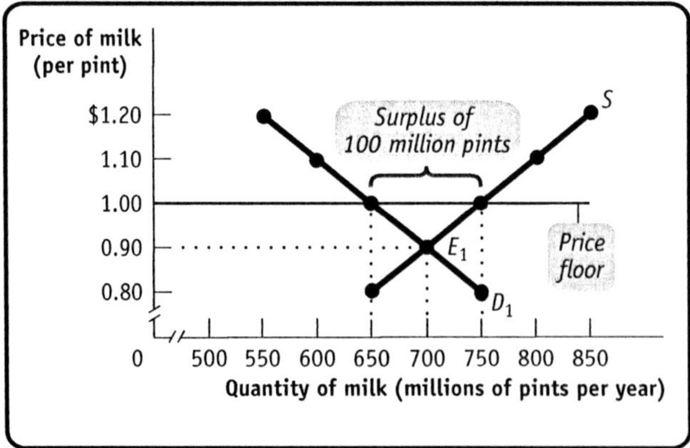

b. In order to sustain this price floor (to prevent black market sales of surplus milk below the price floor), the government would have to buy up the surplus of milk. Buying 100 million pints of milk at a price of $1 each costs the government $100 million.

c. As a result of sales of cheap milk to schools, the quantity demanded falls by 50 million pints per year at any price: the demand curve shifts leftward to the new demand curve D_2. Without the price floor, the equilibrium would now be at point E_2. However, with the price floor at \$1, there is now a surplus of 150 million pints. In order to sustain the price floor of \$1, the government needs to buy up 150 million pints at \$1 each; that is, it needs to spend \$150 million. It does, however, sell those 150 million pints to schools at \$0.60 each (and from those sales makes \$0.60 × 150 million = \$90 million), so that the policy costs the government \$150 million − \$90 million = \$60 million.

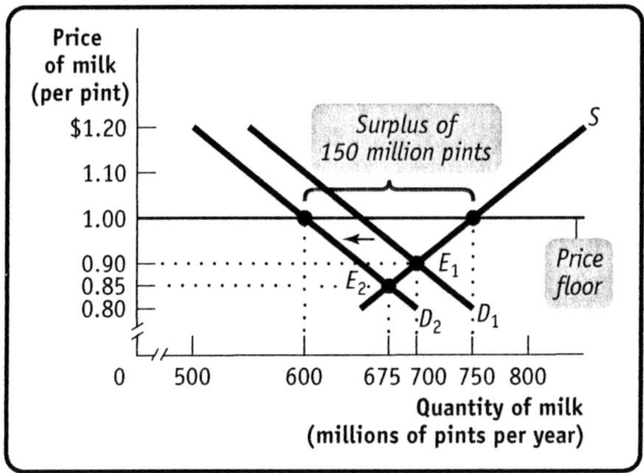

d. Some milk producers are inefficient: if the price were allowed to reach equilibrium, they would find it too costly to produce. In their absence, milk would be produced only by the most efficient producers. This is a missed opportunity. Furthermore, resources are being wasted: although no milk is poured away outright, the government spends significant amounts of money on purchases of milk. This is money that might be used more effectively for purposes other than providing cheap milk to schoolchildren, such as improving the quality of public schools. This, too, is a missed opportunity.

5. As noted in the text, European governments tend to make greater use of price controls than does the American government. For example, the French government sets minimum starting yearly wages for new hires who have completed *le bac*, certification roughly equivalent to a high school diploma. The demand schedule for new hires with *le bac* and the supply schedule for similarly credentialed new job seekers are given in the accompanying table. The price here—given in euros, the currency used in France— is the same as the yearly wage.

Wage (per year)	Quantity demanded (new job offers per year)	Quantity supplied (new job seekers per year)
€45,000	200,000	325,000
40,000	220,000	320,000
35,000	250,000	310,000
30,000	290,000	290,000
25,000	370,000	200,000

a. In the absence of government interference, what is the equilibrium wage and number of graduates hired per year? Illustrate with a diagram. Will there be anyone seeking a job at the equilibrium wage who is unable to find one—that is, will there be anyone who is involuntarily unemployed?

b. Suppose the French government sets a minimum yearly wage of €35,000. Is there any involuntary unemployment at this wage? If so, how much? Illustrate with a diagram. What if the minimum wage is set at €40,000? Also illustrate with a diagram.

c. Given your answer to part b and the information in the table, what do you think is the relationship between the level of involuntary unemployment and the level of the minimum wage? Who benefits from such a policy? Who loses? What is the missed opportunity here?

5. **a.** The equilibrium wage is €30,000, and 290,000 workers are hired. There is full employment: nobody is involuntarily unemployed. The equilibrium is at point *E*.

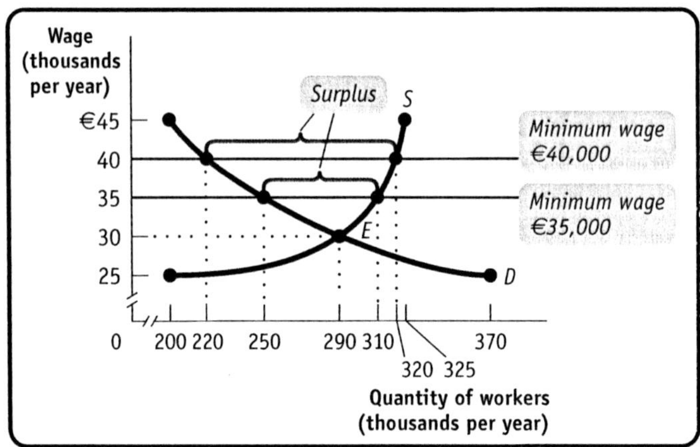

b. With a minimum wage of €35,000, there is a surplus of workers of 60,000 (the quantity supplied is 310,000 and the quantity demanded is 250,000). That is, there are 60,000 workers that are involuntarily unemployed. At a minimum wage of €40,000, there is a surplus of workers of 100,000: this is the number of involuntarily unemployed workers.

c. The higher the minimum wage, the larger the amount of involuntary unemployment. The people who benefit from this policy are those workers who succeed in getting hired: they now enjoy a higher wage. Those workers who do not get hired, however, lose: if the market were allowed to reach equilibrium, more workers would be employed. Employers also lose: fewer employers can now afford to hire workers, and they need to pay higher wages. The missed opportunity is that there are workers who want to work at a wage lower than the minimum wage and firms that would willingly hire them at a lower wage; but because the wage is not allowed to fall below the minimum wage, these hires are not made.

6. Until recently, the standard number of hours worked per week for a full-time job in France was 39 hours, just as in the United States. But in response to social unrest over high levels of involuntary unemployment, the French government instituted a 35-hour workweek—a worker could not work more than 35 hours per week even if both the worker and employer wanted it. The motivation behind this policy was that if current employees worked fewer hours, employers would be forced to hire more new workers. Assume that it is costly for employers to train new workers. French employers were greatly opposed to this policy and threatened to move their operations to neighboring countries that did not have such employment restrictions. Can you explain their attitude? Give an example of both an inefficiency and an illegal activity that are likely to arise from this policy.

6. The introduction of a quota limit, limiting the workweek to 35 hours, below the current equilibrium quantity, implies that there is quota rent earned by the suppliers of labor. So it should not come as a surprise that workers who expected to keep their jobs under the new policy were in favor of the policy. The demand price (the price paid by the demanders of labor, that is, firms), compared to what the wage had been before the introduction of the policy, had risen. Furthermore, since it is costly to train new workers, firms could not completely make up through new hiring for the shortfall in the hours that their current employees were working. As a result, firms had to produce less output and earn lower revenue than before the policy. Like every quota that is below the equilibrium quantity, this quota introduced inefficiency: even if workers wanted to work more (and firms were willing to employ them for longer), such trades were no longer legally possible. You might expect a certain amount of black market activity to occur: workers working longer hours off the books.

7. For the last 70 years the U.S. government has used price supports to provide income assistance to American farmers. At times the government has used price floors, which it maintains by buying up the surplus farm products. At other times, it has used target prices, a policy by which the government gives the farmer an amount equal to the difference between the market price and the target price for each unit sold. Consider the market for corn depicted in the accompanying figure.

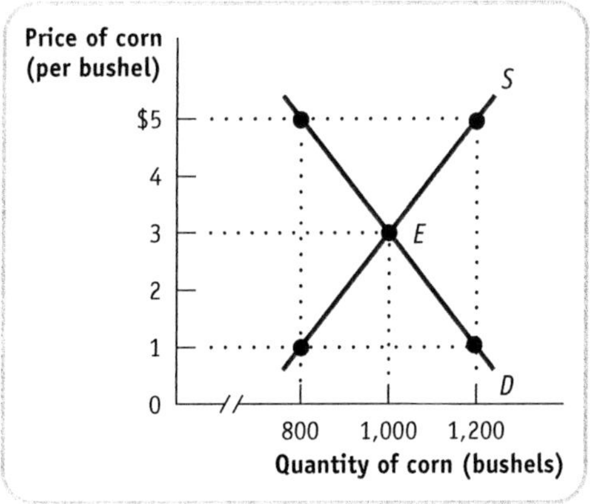

a. If the government sets a price floor of $5 per bushel, how many bushels of corn are produced? How many are purchased by consumers? By the government? How much does the program cost the government? How much revenue do corn farmers receive?

b. Suppose the government sets a target price of $5 per bushel for any quantity supplied up to 1,000 bushels. How many bushels of corn are purchased by consumers and at what price? By the government? How much does the program cost the government? How much revenue do corn farmers receive?

c. Which of these programs (in parts a and b) costs corn consumers more? Which program costs the government more? Explain.

d. What are the inefficiencies that arise in each of these cases (parts a and b)?

7. **a.** With a price floor of $5, the quantity of corn supplied is 1,200 bushels. The quantity demanded is only 800 bushels: there is a surplus of 400 bushels. The government therefore has to buy up the surplus of 400 bushels, at a price of $5 each: the program costs the government $400 \times \$5 = \$2,000$. Corn farmers sell 1,200 bushels (800 to consumers and 400 to the government) and therefore make $1,200 \times \$5 = \$6,000$ in revenue.

b. If the government sets a target price of $5, the market reaches equilibrium at a price of $3 and a quantity of 1,000 bushels. There is no surplus (or shortage). The government does not buy any corn under this policy. On each bushel sold the government pays farmers $2 (to make up the difference between the market price of $3 and the target price of $5), so the government pays a total of $1,000 \times \$2 = \$2,000$. Corn farmers sell 1,000 bushels and make $5 for each bushel ($3 come from consumers and $2 from the government), for a total of $5,000 of revenue.

c. The price-floor policy is more expensive for consumers: they pay $5 per bushel (compared to the $3 under the target price policy). Both policies are equally expensive for the government.

d. When there is a price floor for corn, the most striking inefficiency is the waste of resources (the corn bought by the government is presumably thrown away). This does not occur under the target price policy: under that policy all corn that is produced is also bought by consumers.

8. The waters off the North Atlantic coast were once teeming with fish. Now, due to overfishing by the commercial fishing industry, the stocks of fish are seriously depleted. In 1991, the National Marine Fishery Service of the U.S. government implemented a quota to allow fish stocks to recover. The quota limited the amount of swordfish caught per year by all U.S.-licensed fishing boats to 7 million pounds. As soon as the U.S. fishing fleet had met the quota limit, the swordfish catch was closed down for the rest of the year. The accompanying table gives the hypothetical demand and supply schedules for swordfish caught in the United States per year.

	Quantity of swordfish (millions of pounds per year)	
Price of swordfish (per pound)	Quantity demanded	Quantity supplied
$20	6	15
18	7	13
16	8	11
14	9	9
12	10	7

a. Use a diagram to show the effect of the quota on the market for swordfish in 1991.

b. How do you think fishermen will change how they fish in response to this policy?

c. Use your diagram from part a to show an excise tax that achieves the same reduction in the amount of pounds of swordfish caught as the quota. What is the amount of the tax per pound?

d. What kinds of activities do you think an excise tax will tempt people to engage in?

e. The excise tax is collected from the fishermen, who protest that they alone are bearing the burden of this policy. Why might this protest be misguided?

8. **a.** The quantity sold is 7 million pounds, at a price of $18 per pound. On each pound of fish caught, each fisherman earns quota rent of $6, as shown in the accompanying diagram.

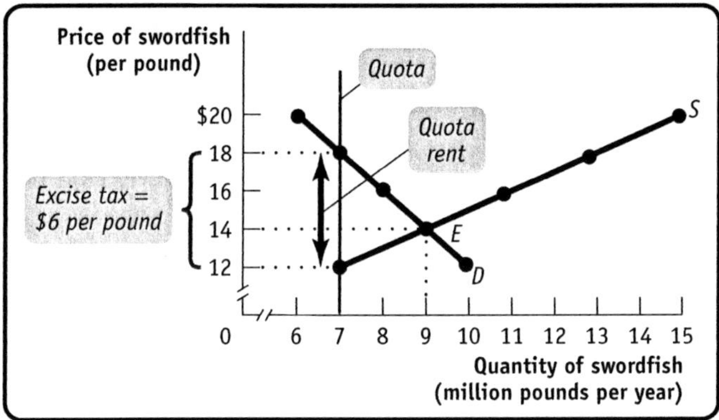

b. Because each pound of swordfish gives a fisherman $6 quota rent, each fisherman will attempt to fish as much as possible as soon as the swordfish catch opens. You should therefore see fishermen scramble to fish right at the beginning of the season, and you should see the catch being closed down very soon thereafter. (Which is exactly what happens.)

c. If an excise tax of $6 per pound were introduced, this would similarly reduce the quantity bought and sold to 7 million pounds, as shown in the accompanying diagram.

d. Any tax always creates the incentive for tax evasion—in this case, selling fish privately, or in the black market, while circumventing the imposition of the tax on those sales.

e. The fishermen are confusing who is responsible for paying the excise tax with the economic *incidence* of the tax: the burden of the tax is normally shared between consumers and producers. In this case, consumers pay $4 more per pound than they would in an equilibrium without tax (point E in the diagram); and fishermen receive $2 less per pound than they would in an equilibrium without tax. Both sides suffer from the missed opportunity to trade further amounts of fish.

9. The U.S. government would like to help the American auto industry compete against foreign automakers that sell trucks in the United States. It can do this either by imposing a quota on the number of foreign trucks imported or by imposing an excise tax on each foreign truck sold in the United States. The hypothetical demand and supply schedules for imported trucks are given in the accompanying table.

Price of imported truck	Quantity of imported trucks (thousands)	
	Quantity demanded	Quantity supplied
$32,000	100	400
31,000	200	350
30,000	300	300
29,000	400	250
28,000	500	200
27,000	600	150

a. In the absence of government interference, what is the price of an imported truck? How many are sold in the United States? Illustrate with a diagram.

b. Suppose the government adopts a quota, allowing no more than 200,000 foreign trucks to be imported. What is the effect on the market for these trucks? Illustrate using your diagram from part a and explain.

c. Now suppose that, instead of a quota, the government imposes an excise tax of $3,000 per truck. Illustrate the effect of this excise tax in your diagram from part a. How many trucks will now be purchased and at what price? What will the foreign automaker receive per truck?

d. Calculate the government revenue raised by the excise tax in part c. Then illustrate it on your diagram from that part. Do you think the government, from a revenue standpoint, prefers an excise tax or a quota?

e. Explain how the government policy, whether it be a quota or an excise tax, benefits American automakers. Whom does it hurt? What is the missed opportunity here and how does it reflect inefficiency?

9. **a.** The equilibrium price without government interference is $30,000, and 300,000 trucks are bought and sold, as shown by point E in the accompanying diagram.

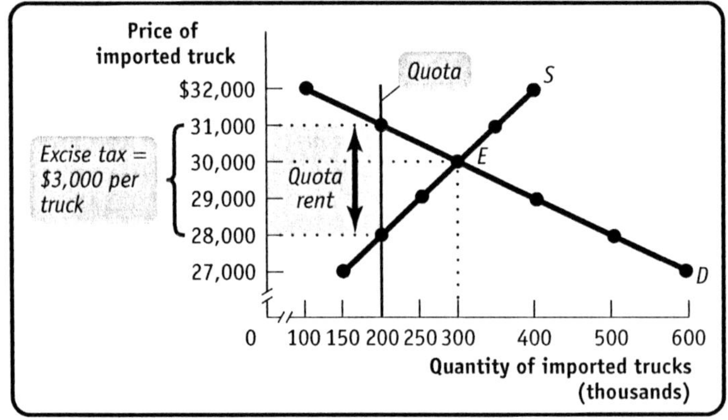

b. The effect of the quota is illustrated in the diagram: 200,000 trucks are sold at a price of $31,000, and producers receive a quota rent of $3,000 per truck.

c. The excise tax is also illustrated in the diagram: a tax of $3,000 per truck puts a wedge between the price paid by consumers, or the demand price ($31,000), and the price received by producers, or the supply price ($28,000). The quantity sold is 200,000 trucks. The foreign automaker receives $28,000 per truck (after tax).

d. Since 200,000 trucks are sold, and the government earns a tax of $3,000 on each truck, the total tax revenue is 200,000 × $3,000 = $600 million. This is the shaded square in the diagram. The government, of course, prefers the tax to a quota. Under the quota policy, the foreign automakers benefit (in the form of quota rent); under the tax policy, the government benefits (in the form of tax revenue).

e. Since American trucks are substitutes for imported trucks, a rise in the price of imported trucks (such as would occur both with the quota and the excise tax) increases the domestic demand for American trucks. As a result, buyers of both American and foreign trucks will pay higher prices. Some of the opportunities for mutually beneficial exchanges between buyers and sellers of foreign trucks will be missed due to the quotas or prohibitively high prices, constituting a loss of efficiency.

10. In Maine, you must have a license to harvest lobster commercially; these licenses are issued yearly. The state of Maine is concerned about the dwindling supplies of lobsters found off its coast. The state fishery department has decided to place a yearly quota of 80,000 pounds of lobsters harvested in all Maine waters. It has also decided to give licenses this year only to those fishermen who had licenses last year. The accompanying figure shows the demand and supply curves for Maine lobsters.

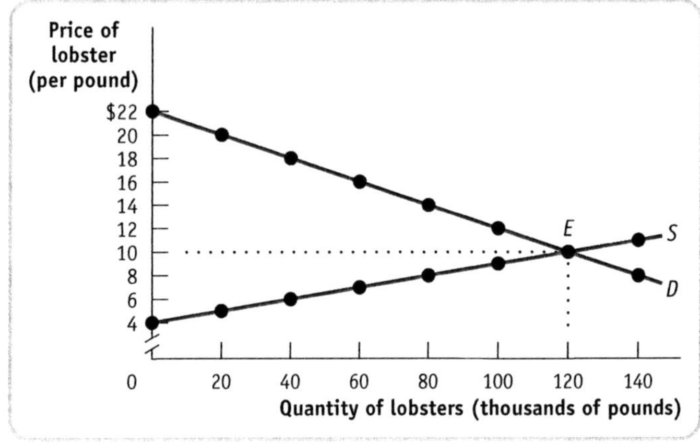

a. In the absence of government restrictions, what are the equilibrium price and quantity?

b. What is the *demand price* at which consumers wish to purchase 80,000 pounds of lobsters?

c. What is the *supply price* at which suppliers are willing to supply 80,000 pounds of lobsters?

d. What is the *quota rent* per pound of lobster when 80,000 pounds are sold?

e. Find an excise tax that achieves the same reduction in the harvest of lobsters. Show it on the figure. What is the government revenue collected from this tax?

f. Explain a transaction that benefits both buyer and seller but is prevented by the quota restriction. Explain a transaction that benefits both buyer and seller but is prevented by the excise tax.

10. **a.** Without government intervention, the equilibrium in the market for lobsters is at point E. The equilibrium price for lobsters is $10 per pound. At that price, the quantity demanded and the quantity supplied is 120,000 pounds of lobsters.

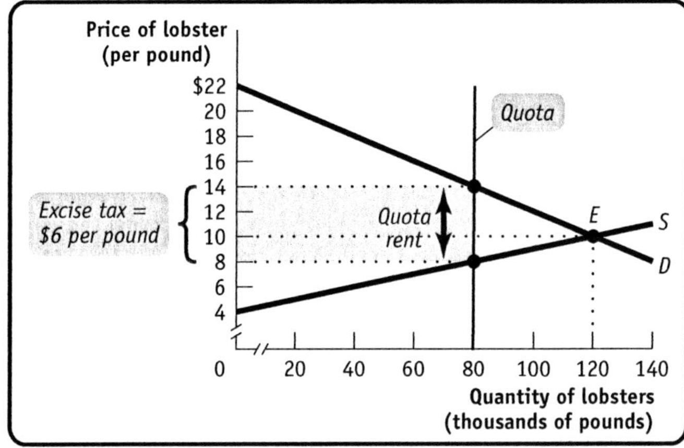

b. The demand price of 80,000 pounds of lobsters is $14.

c. The supply price of 80,000 pounds of lobsters is $8.

d. The quota rent per pound of lobster is $14 − $8 = $6.

e. An excise tax of $6 per pound would have the same effect, as the diagram illustrates. The tax reduces the quantity sold to 80,000 pounds; since the government earns a tax of $6 per pound, the government tax revenue is 80,000 × $6 = $480,000, the area of the shaded rectangle in the diagram.

f. Under the quota policy, if the 80,001st producer could sell a lobster to the 80,001st consumer, they could both be better off: the producer would be willing to sell for just a little more than $8, and the consumer would be willing to buy for just a little less than $14. The quota, however, prevents this trade. Under the tax policy, the 80,001st producer would be willing to sell to the 80,001st consumer if the tax on that 80,001st pound of lobster was reduced to a little less than $6. But since the tax is $6, selling the 80,001st pound of lobster does not cover the producer's cost, and therefore that trade is not made.

11. In each of the following cases involving taxes, explain: (i) whether the incidence of the tax falls more heavily on consumers or producers, (ii) why government revenue raised from the tax is not a good indicator of the true cost of the tax, and (iii) what missed opportunity, or inefficiency, arises.

a. The government imposes an excise tax on the sale of all college textbooks. Before the tax was imposed, 1 million textbooks were sold every year at a price of $50. After the tax is imposed, 600,000 books are sold yearly; students pay $55 per book, $30 of which publishers receive.

b. The government imposes an excise tax on the sale of all airplane tickets. Before the tax was imposed, 3 million airline tickets were sold every year at a price of $500. After the tax is imposed, 1.5 million tickets are sold yearly; travelers pay $550 per ticket, $450 of which the airlines receive.

c. The government imposes an excise tax on the sale of all toothbrushes. Before the tax, 2 million toothbrushes were sold every year at a price of $1.50. After the tax is imposed, 800,000 toothbrushes are sold every year; consumers pay $2 per toothbrush, $1.25 of which producers receive.

11. **a.** After the imposition of the tax, consumers pay $5 more per book than before; publishers receive $20 less per book than before. Producers (publishers) bear more of the tax. The tax is $55 − $30 = $25 per book, and 600,000 books are sold. Government revenue is therefore $15 million. This, however, is a poor estimate of the cost of the tax, since it does not take into account the fact that, in addition to the higher price, there are now 400,000 potential consumers who would have bought the books without the tax but no longer will buy them. The missed opportunity is that, were it not for the tax, there are 400,000 potential consumers that would buy the books and to whom publishers would sell them; but with the tax these trades are not made.

b. After the imposition of the tax, travelers pay $50 more per ticket than before; airlines receive $50 less than before. The tax is split evenly between consumers and producers. The tax is $550 − $450 = $100 per ticket, and 1.5 million tickets are sold. Government revenue is therefore $150 million. This, however, is a poor estimate of the cost of the tax, since it does not take into account the fact that, in addition to 1.5 million travelers paying higher prices, there are now 1.5 million potential consumers who would have bought tickets without the tax but no longer buy tickets. The missed opportunity is that, were it not for the tax, there are 1.5 million potential consumers who would want to travel and to whom airlines would want to sell tickets; but with the tax these trades are not made.

c. After the imposition of the tax, consumers pay $0.50 more per toothbrush than before; producers receive $0.25 less than before. The incidence of the tax falls mainly on consumers. The tax is $2.00 − $1.25 = $0.75 per toothbrush, and 800,000 toothbrushes are sold. Government revenue therefore is $600,000. This, however, is a poor estimate of the cost of the tax, since it does not take into account the fact that, in addition to 800,000 toothbrushes now being more expensive, there are 1.2 million toothbrushes that would have been sold without the tax but are no longer sold. The missed opportunity is that, were it not for the tax, there are 1.2 million toothbrushes that could be produced at a lower cost than consumers are willing to pay for them: this would be an improvement for both consumers and producers.

Consumer and Producer Surplus

1. Determine the amount of consumer surplus generated in each of the following situations.

   a. Paul goes to the clothing store to buy a new T-shirt, for which he is willing to pay up to $10. He picks out one he likes with a price tag of exactly $10. At the cash register, he is told that his T-shirt is on sale for half the posted price.

   b. Robin goes to the CD store hoping to find a used copy of the *Eagles Greatest Hits* for up to $10. The store has one copy selling for $10.

   c. After soccer practice, Phil is willing to pay $2 for a bottle of mineral water. The 7-Eleven sells mineral water for $2.25 per bottle.

1. a. Paul's consumer surplus is $5. This is the difference between how much he is willing to pay ($10) and how much he does pay ($5).

   b. Since Robin's willingness to pay is $10 and the price of the CD is $10, she gets no consumer surplus if she buys the CD.

   c. No trade will take place since Phil's willingness to pay is less than the price. So no consumer surplus is created.

2. Determine the amount of producer surplus generated in each of the following situations.

   a. Bob lists his old Lionel electric trains on eBay. He sets a minimum acceptable price, known as his *reserve price*, of $75. After five days of bidding, the final high bid is exactly $75.

   b. Jenny advertises her car for sale in the used-car section of the student newspaper for $2,000, but she is willing to sell the car for any price higher than $1,500. The best offer she gets is $1,200.

   c. Sanjay likes his job so much that he would be willing to do it for free. However, his annual salary is $80,000.

2. a. Bob will receive no producer surplus since the price paid for the trains is equal to his cost.

   b. No trade will take place since Jenny's cost is $1,500, which is higher than the price of $1,200 she is offered. So no producer surplus is created.

   c. Sanjay's cost is zero. The price he is paid for his time is $80,000, so his producer surplus is $80,000.

3. Hollywood writers negotiate a new agreement with movie producers that they will receive 10 percent of the revenue from every video rental of a movie they worked on. They have no such agreement for movies shown on pay-per-view television.

   a. When the new writers' agreement comes into effect, what will happen in the market for video rentals—that is, will supply or demand shift, and how? As a result, how will consumer surplus in the market for video rentals change? Illustrate with a diagram. Do you think the writers' agreement will be popular with consumers who rent videos?

b. Consumers consider video rentals and pay-per-view movies substitutable to some extent. When the new writers' agreement comes into effect, what will happen in the market for pay-per-view movies—that is, will supply or demand shift, and how? As a result, how will producer surplus in the market for pay-per-view movies change? Illustrate with a diagram. Do you think the writers' agreement will be popular with cable television companies that show pay-per-view movies?

3. a. The payment to writers will increase the cost of providing video rentals. In the accompanying diagram, the supply curve shifts leftward from S_1 to S_2, the equilibrium price of video rentals rises from P_1 to P_2 and the quantity of video rentals bought and sold falls from Q_1 to Q_2. As a result, consumer surplus will decrease by the shaded amount. The writers' agreement will not be popular with consumers.

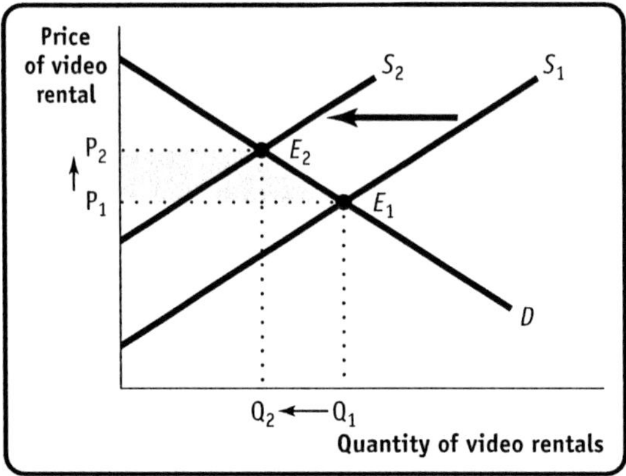

b. The higher price of video rentals will make pay-per-view movies more popular. They are substitute goods, and the demand for them will increase when the price of video rentals rises. In the accompanying diagram, demand shifts rightward from D_1 to D_2. The price rises from P_1 to P_2, and the equilibrium quantity rises from Q_1 to Q_2. Producer surplus will increase by the shaded amount. This change will be popular with the cable television companies that show pay-per-view movies.

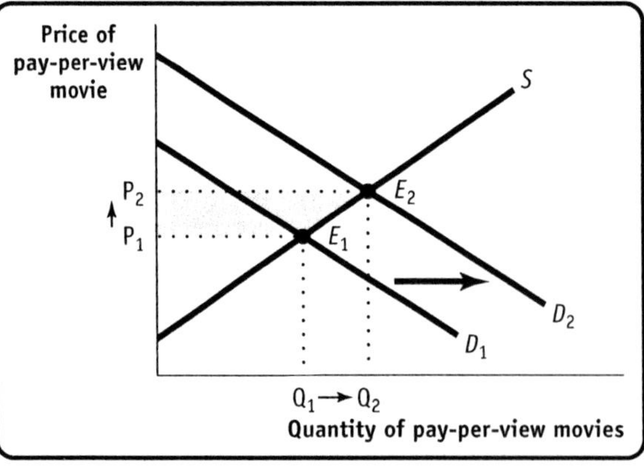

4. There are six potential consumers of computer games, each willing to buy only one game. Consumer 1 is willing to pay $40 for a computer game, consumer 2 is willing to pay $35, consumer 3 is willing to pay $30, consumer 4 is willing pay $25, consumer 5 is willing to pay $20, and consumer 6 is willing to pay $15.

a. Suppose the market price is $29. What is the total consumer surplus?

b. Now the market price decreases to $19. What is the total consumer surplus now?

c. When the price fell from $29 to $19, how much did each consumer's individual consumer surplus change?

4. **a.** Consumer 1 buys a game since her willingness to pay is greater than the price. She gains $40 − $29 = $11.

Consumer 2 buys a game since his willingness to pay is greater than the price. He gains $35 − $29 = $6.

Consumer 3 buys a game since her willingness to pay is greater than the price. She gains $30 − $29 = $1.

The total consumer surplus is $11 + $6 + $1 = $18.

b. Consumer 1 buys a game since her willingness to pay is greater than the price. She gains $40 − $19 = $21.

Consumer 2 buys a game since his willingness to pay is greater than the price. He gains $35 − $19 = $16.

Consumer 3 buys a game since her willingness to pay is greater than the price. She gains $30 − $19 = $11.

Consumer 4 buys a game since his willingness to pay is greater than the price. He gains $25 − $19 = $6.

Consumer 5 buys a game since her willingness to pay is greater than the price. She gains $20 − $19 = $1.

The total consumer surplus is $21 + $16 + $11 + $6 + $1 = $55.

c. Total consumer surplus has increased by $55 − $18 = $37 as a result of the price decrease. For consumers 1, 2, and 3 (the consumers who would also have bought games at the higher price), individual consumer surplus increases by $10 each, the amount of the price reduction. This accounts for $30 of the increase in consumer surplus. But consumers 4 and 5 now also get consumer surplus, since the lower price leads them to buy computer games also. Consumer 4 gets $6 of consumer surplus, and consumer 5 gets $1.

5. In an effort to provide more affordable rental housing for low-income families, the city council of Collegetown decides to impose a rent ceiling well below the current market equilibrium rent.

a. Illustrate the effect of this policy in a diagram. Indicate consumer and producer surplus before and after the introduction of the rent ceiling.

b. Will this policy be popular with renters? With landlords?

c. An economist explains to the city council that this policy is creating a deadweight loss. Illustrate the deadweight loss in your diagram.

5. a. Before the introduction of the rent ceiling, the market is in equilibrium at a price of P_E and a quantity of Q_E. Consumer surplus is the area P_EEA. Producer surplus is the area P_EBE. The rent ceiling at $P_{CEILING}$ leads to a reduction in the quantity from Q_E to $Q_{CEILING}$. Consumer surplus is the area $P_{CEILING}FCA$. Producer surplus is the area $P_{CEILING}BF$.

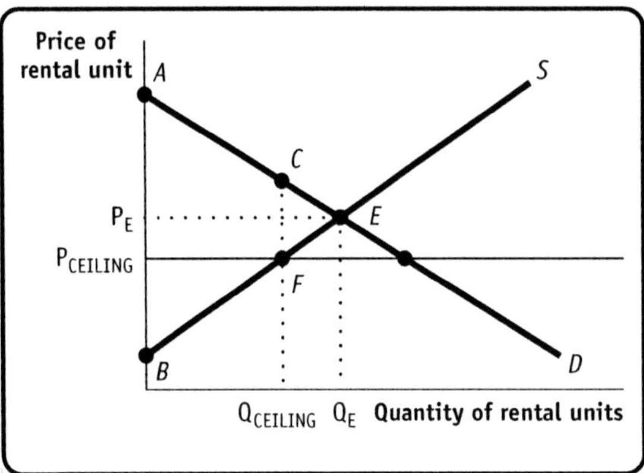

b. It is not clear whether consumers are better off with the rent ceiling: The consumers who rent housing both before and after the introduction of the price ceiling gain consumer surplus. However, some consumers who used to rent housing can no longer do so after the introduction of the price ceiling, and they lose all consumer surplus. It is clear that the policy will be unpopular with landlords: producer surplus decreases unambiguously.

c. The deadweight loss from this policy is the area *CFE*: it is a measure of how much consumer surplus and producer surplus is lost because of the introduction of the rent ceiling.

6. On Thursday nights, a local restaurant has a pasta special. Ari likes the restaurant's pasta, and his willingness to pay for each serving is shown in the accompanying table.

Quantity of pasta (servings)	Willingness to pay for pasta (per serving)
1	$10
2	8
3	6
4	4
5	2
6	0

a. If the price of a serving of pasta is $4, how many servings will Ari buy? How much consumer surplus does he receive?

b. The following week, Ari is back at the restaurant again, but now the price of a serving of pasta is $6. By how much does his consumer surplus decrease compared to the previous week?

c. One week later, he goes to the restaurant again. He discovers that the restaurant is offering an "all you can eat" special for $25. How much pasta will Ari eat, and how much consumer surplus does he receive now?

d. Suppose you own the restaurant and Ari is a "typical" customer. What is the highest price you can charge for the "all you can eat" special and still attract customers?

6. **a.** Ari will buy four servings of pasta. His consumer surplus is equal to $12, that is:
($10 – $4) + ($8 – $4) + ($6 – $4) + ($4 – $4) = $12.

   b. Ari will buy three servings of pasta. His consumer surplus is ($10 – $6) +
   ($8 – $6) + ($6 – $6) = $6, so his consumer surplus falls by $6, from $12 to $6.

   c. If there is an "all you can eat" special, the price Ari pays per serving is zero. Therefore, he will eat six servings of pasta. The total amount he is willing to pay for those
   six servings is $30: the sum of the amount he is willing to pay for each individual
   serving. Since he actually pays $25, his consumer surplus is $5.

   d. When there is an "all you can eat" special, Ari will consume six servings. His consumer surplus from consuming six servings is $30. Therefore, the most he is will-
   ing to pay for an "all you can eat" special is $30. This is the highest price you can
   charge for the special.

7. The accompanying diagram shows the market for cigarettes. The current equilibrium
price per pack is $4, and every day 40 million packs of cigarettes are sold. In order to
recover some of the health care costs associated with smoking, the government imposes a tax of $2 per pack. This will raise the equilibrium price to $5 per pack and reduce the equilibrium quantity to 30 million packs.

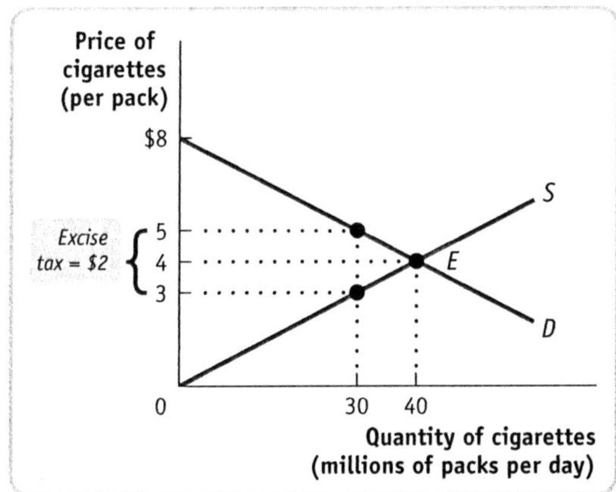

   The economist working for the tobacco lobby claims that this tax will reduce consumer surplus for smokers by $40 million per day, since 40 million packs now cost $1
more per pack. The economist working for the lobby for sufferers of second-hand
smoke argues that this is an enormous overestimate and that the reduction in consumer surplus will be only $30 million per day, since after the imposition of the tax
only 30 million packs of cigarettes will be bought and each of these packs will now
cost $1 more. They are both wrong. Why?

7. The economist working for the tobacco lobby is overestimating the change in consumer surplus. She is assuming that there will be no change in the quantity demanded and that consumers will continue to smoke 40 million packs of cigarettes
   per day even when the price has risen by $1 per pack. The economist working for
   the second-hand smoke lobby is underestimating the loss of consumer surplus. He
   expects that the quantity demanded will be reduced to 30 million packs per day. He
   is then looking at the loss of consumer surplus experienced by the consumers of
   those 30 million packs per day. The loss is $1 per pack, the increase in the price per
   pack. He is not counting the loss of consumer surplus experienced by those who
   are no longer smoking 10 million packs per day because consumption dropped
   from 40 million to 30 million packs per day.

The reduction in consumer surplus resulting from the new tax is the $30 million reduction experienced by the smokers of the 30 million packs plus the $5 million reduction in consumer surplus experienced by those smokers who are smoking 10 million fewer packs. The total reduction in consumer surplus is $35 million.

One way of calculating this answer is to look at the total consumer surplus before and after the new tax. Before the tax the consumer surplus was $\frac{1}{2} \times (\$8 - \$4) \times 40$ million = $80 million. After the tax, the consumer surplus is $\frac{1}{2} \times (\$8 - \$5) \times 30$ million = $45 million. The reduction in consumer surplus is $80 million − $45 million = $35 million. (Recall that the area of a triangle is $\frac{1}{2} \times$ the base of the triangle $\times$ the height of the triangle.)

8. Consider the original market for pizza in Collegetown, illustrated in the accompanying table. Collegetown officials decide to impose an excise tax on pizza of $4 per pizza.

Price of pizza	Quantity of pizza demanded	Quantity of pizza supplied
$10	0	6
9	1	5
8	2	4
7	3	3
6	4	2
5	5	1
4	6	0
3	7	0
2	8	0
1	9	0

a. What is the quantity of pizza bought and sold after the imposition of the tax? What is the price paid by consumers? What is the price received by producers?

b. Calculate the consumer surplus and the producer surplus after the imposition of the tax. By how much has the imposition of the tax reduced consumer surplus? By how much has it reduced producer surplus?

c. How much tax revenue does Collegetown earn from this tax?

d. Calculate the deadweight loss from this tax.

8. a. The tax drives a wedge between the price paid by consumers and the price received by producers. Consumers now pay $9, and producers receive $5. After the imposition of the tax, the quantity bought and sold will therefore be one pizza.

b. Consumer surplus is now zero (the one consumer who still buys a pizza at $9 has a willingness to pay of just $9, so that the consumer surplus is $9 − $9 = $0). Compared to the situation before the imposition of the tax where the equilibrium price was $7, consumer surplus has been reduced by $3. Similarly, the producer of the one pizza has a cost of $5, and this is the price he receives, so producer surplus is also zero: compared to the situation before, it has decreased by $3.

c. Collegetown earns a tax of $4 per pizza sold, that is, a total tax revenue of $4.

d. Total surplus has been decreased by $6. Of those $6, the town earns $4 in revenue, but $2 of surplus is lost. That is the deadweight loss from this tax.

9. Consider once more the original market for pizza in Collegetown, illustrated in the table in Problem 8. Now Collegetown officials impose a price floor on pizza of $8.

   a. What is the quantity of pizza bought and sold after the imposition of the price floor?

   b. Calculate the consumer surplus and the producer surplus after the imposition of the price floor.

9. **a.** After the imposition of the price floor, the price of pizza is $8. The demand schedule tells you that the quantity bought and sold is now two pizzas.

   b. At a price of $8, consumer surplus is now ($9 − $8) + ($8 − $8) = $1. Producer surplus is ($8 − $5) + ($8 − $6) = $5.

10. You are the manager of Fun World, a small amusement park. The accompanying diagram shows the demand curve of a typical customer at Fun World.

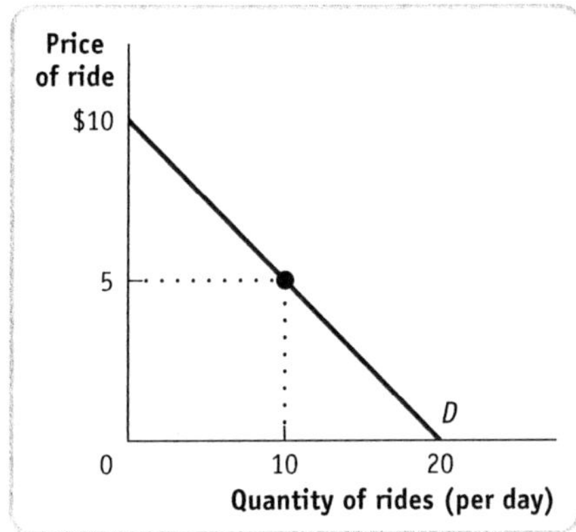

   a. Suppose that the price of each ride is $5. At that price, how much consumer surplus does an individual consumer get? (Recall that the area of a triangle is ½ × the base of the triangle × the height of the triangle.)

   b. Suppose that Fun World considers charging an admission fee, even though it maintains the price of each ride at $5. What is the maximum admission fee it could charge? (Assume that all potential customers have enough money to pay the fee.)

   c. Suppose that Fun World lowered the price of each ride to zero. How much consumer surplus does an individual consumer get? What is the maximum admission fee Fun World could therefore charge?

10. **a.** From the demand curve, you can see that with a price per ride of $5, the customer takes 10 rides. At this point her consumer surplus is ½ × ($10 − $5) × 10 = $25.

   b. Since a consumer obtains consumer surplus of $25 from going to Fun World when each ride costs $5, that is the most that she would be willing to pay to go to Fun World. And it is therefore the maximum admission fee that Fun World could charge. (Charging consumers both an entrance fee and a price for each unit of a good bought is called a *two-part tariff*.)

   c. If Fun World charged nothing for each ride, a typical consumer would consume 20 rides, and this would give her a consumer surplus of ½ × $10 × 20 = $100. This is therefore the maximum admission fee that Fun World can charge with a price per ride of zero.

11. The accompanying diagram illustrates a taxi driver's individual supply curve (assume that each taxi ride is the same distance).

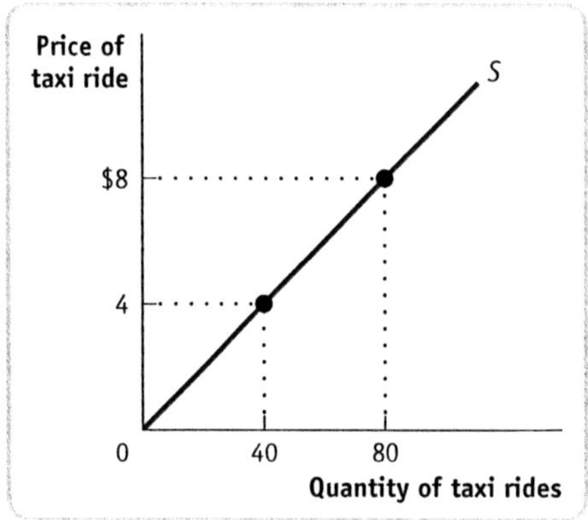

a. Suppose the city sets the price of taxi rides at $4 per ride. What is this taxi driver's producer surplus? (Recall that the area of a triangle is ½ × the base of the triangle × the height of the triangle.)

b. Suppose now that the city keeps the price of a taxi ride set at $4, but it decides to charge taxi drivers a "licensing fee." What is the maximum licensing fee the city could extract from this taxi driver?

c. Suppose that the city allowed the price of taxi rides to increase to $8 per ride. How much producer surplus does an individual taxi driver now get? What is the maximum licensing fee the city could charge this taxi driver?

11. **a.** At a price of $4, the taxi driver supplies 40 rides. His producer surplus is therefore ½ × $4 × 40 = $80.

b. Since the taxi driver's producer surplus is $80, this is the most he is willing to pay to supply 40 rides at $4. And it is therefore the most the city can charge him as a licensing fee.

c. At a price of $8, the taxi driver supplies 80 rides. His producer surplus is therefore ½ × $8 × 80 = $320. Therefore, $320 is the most the city can charge as a licensing fee when the price per ride is $8.

12. The state needs to raise money, and the governor has a choice of imposing an excise tax of the same amount on one of two previously untaxed goods: the state can tax either sales of restaurant meals or sales of gasoline. Both the demand for and the supply of restaurant meals are more elastic than the demand for and the supply of gasoline. If the governor wants to minimize the deadweight loss caused by the tax, which good should be taxed? For each good, draw a diagram that illustrates the deadweight loss from taxation.

12. The tax should be imposed on sales of gasoline. Since both demand for and supply of gasoline are less elastic, changes in the price of gasoline will result in smaller reductions in the quantity demanded and quantity supplied. As a result, fewer transactions are discouraged by the tax—in other words, less total surplus (consumer and producer surplus) is lost. Panel (a) of the accompanying diagram illustrates a tax imposed on sales of gasoline, for which both demand and supply are less elastic; panel (b) illustrates a tax imposed on sales of restaurant meals, for which both demand and supply are more elastic. As you can see, deadweight loss, the shaded triangle, is larger in panel (b) than in panel (a).

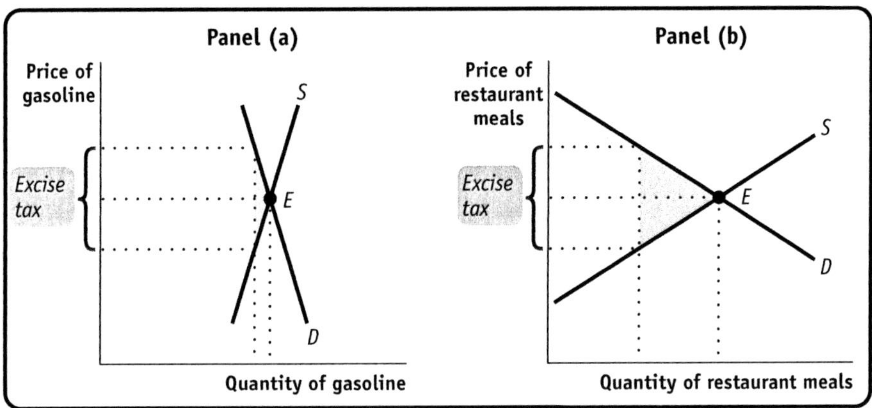

Macroeconomics: The Big Picture

1. Which of the following questions are relevant for the study of macroeconomics and which for microeconomics?

   a. How will Ms. Martin's tips change when a large manufacturing plant near the restaurant where she works closes?

   b. What will happen to spending by consumers when the economy enters a downturn?

   c. How will the price of oranges change when a late frost damages Florida's orange groves?

   d. How will wages at a manufacturing plant change when its workforce is unionized?

   e. What will happen to U.S. exports as the dollar becomes less expensive in terms of other currencies?

   f. What is the relationship between a nation's unemployment rate and its inflation rate?

1. a. This is a microeconomic question because it addresses the effects of a single firm's actions (the closure of a manufacturing plant) on a single individual (the waitress).

   b. This is a macroeconomic question because it considers how overall spending by consumers is affected by the state of the macroeconomy.

   c. This is a microeconomic question because it looks at how a single market (oranges) will be affected by a late frost.

   d. This is a microeconomic question because it addresses how wages in a particular plant will change when the firm's workforce is unionized.

   e. This is a macroeconomic question because it considers the change in the overall level of exports as the exchange rate changes.

   f. This is a macroeconomic question because it addresses the relationship between two aggregate measures of economic activity, inflation and unemployment.

2. When one person saves, that person's wealth is increased, meaning that he or she can consume more in the future. But when everyone saves, everyone's income falls, meaning that everyone must consume less today. Explain this seeming contradiction.

2. This question concerns the Paradox of Thrift; what is true for an individual—that saving makes you better off—is not always true for the economy as a whole. When an individual saves, she adds to her wealth, providing for higher consumption in the future. However, if everyone saves, firms will not sell as much and will lay off workers. Individuals find that their incomes fall as a result. Hence they must consume less today.

3. What was the Great Depression? How did it affect the role of government in the economy and the macroeconomic toolkit?

3. Great Depression refers to the high rates of unemployment that the United States and other nations experienced during the 1930s. In the United States, unemployment rates reached a high of almost 25%. Economists focused on understanding how such a prolonged period of unemployment could have happened and how it could be alleviated. John Maynard Keynes's *The General Theory of Employment, Interest, and Money,* as well as interpretations and critiques of his work, are seen as the beginning of macroeconomics as we know it today. It is from this that the modern macroeconomic toolkit of fiscal policy (control of government spending and taxation) and monetary policy (control of interest rates and money supply in circulation) was developed.

4. Why do we consider a business-cycle expansion different from long-run economic growth? Why do we care about the size of the long-run growth rate of real GDP versus the size of the growth rate of the population?

4. Long-run economic growth is the sustained upward trend in aggregate output over long periods of time. Long-run growth per capita is the key to rising wages and sustained increases in the standard of living. From 1000 to 1800, aggregate output grew less than 0.2% per year and, with population rising at about the same rate, the standard of living remained about constant. However, since that time, long-run economic growth has increased significantly. In the last 50 or so years, long-run economic growth in the United States has averaged about 3.5% per year. A business-cycle expansion results in a short-run (many months or a few years) increase in real GDP, but long-run growth results in a long-run (many decades) increase in real GDP per capita. We care about the relative size of the long-run growth rate of real GDP and the population growth rate because living standards will fall unless the long-run growth rate of real GDP is at least as high as the rate of growth of the population.

5. There are 100,000 inhabitants in Macronesia. Among those 100,000 inhabitants, 25,000 are too old to work and 15,000 inhabitants are too young to work. Among the remaining 60,000 inhabitants, 10,000 are not working and have given up looking for work, 45,000 are currently employed, and the remaining 5,000 are looking for work but do not currently have a job.

    a. What is the number of people in the labor force in Macronesia?

    b. What is the unemployment rate in Macronesia?

    c. How many people in Macronesia are discouraged workers?

5.   **a.** The labor force is the sum of employed and unemployed people. There are 45,000 employed people and 5,000 unemployed people. The size of the labor force therefore is 45,000 + 5,000 = 50,000 people.

    b. The unemployment rate is the ratio of people unemployed to the total number of people in the labor force. Here it is (5,000/50,000) × 100 = 10%.

    c. There are 10,000 people in Macronesia who are discouraged workers, since they are capable of working but not actively looking for a job.

6. In 1798, Thomas Malthus's "Essay on the Principle of Population" was published. In it, he wrote: "Population, when unchecked, increases in a geometrical ratio. Subsistence increases only in an arithmetical ratio . . . . This implies a strong and constantly operating check on population from the difficulty of subsistence." Malthus was saying that the growth of the population is limited by the amount of food available to eat; people will live at the subsistence level forever. Why didn't Malthus's description apply to the world after 1800?

6. Malthus expected that life would continue as it had for the previous 800 or so years. He did not know that advances in technology would bring large changes in productivity and that the long-run growth of aggregate output would exceed population growth. As we learned in the chapter, aggregate output per capita in the United States grew sevenfold from 1900 to 2004. Most of the United States population has a standard of living that far exceeds subsistence.

7. At the start of 2005 in Macroland, aggregate output was $10 billion ($10,000 million) and the population was 1 million. During 2005, aggregate output increased by 3.5%, the population increased by 2.5%, and the aggregate price level remained constant.

    a. What was aggregate output per capita in Macroland at the start of 2005?

    b. What was aggregate output in Macroland at the end of 2005?

    c. What was the population of Macroland at the end of 2005?

    d. What was aggregate output per capita in Macroland at the end of 2005?

    e. What was the annual growth rate of aggregate output per capita in Macroland during 2005? *Hint:* the 2005 growth rate is equal to:

$$\frac{\text{Change in aggregate output during 2005}}{\text{Aggregate output at start of 2005}} \times 100$$

7.   **a.** We can calculate aggregate output per capita in Macroland at the start of 2005 by dividing aggregate output at that time by the population.

$$\text{Aggregate output per capita at start of 2005} =$$
$$\$10,000 \text{ million}/1 \text{ million} = \$10,000$$

    b. We can calculate the increase in aggregate output in Macroland at the end of 2005 by multiplying aggregate output at the start of 2005 by the growth rate.

    Increase in aggregate output = $10,000 million × .035 = $350 million

    So aggregate output at the end of 2005 equaled $10,350 million (= $10,000 million + $350 million).

    c. We can calculate the increase in population in Macroland by multiplying the population at the start of 2005 by the population growth rate.

    Increase in population = 1,000,000 × .025 = 25,000

    The population at the end of 2005 equaled 1,025,000 (= 1,000,000 + 25,000).

    d. Using the answers to part b (aggregate output at the end of 2005) and part c (population at the end of 2005), aggregate output per capita at the end of 2005 was $10,087.56.

$$\text{Aggregate output per capita at end of 2005} =$$
$$\$10,350 \text{ million}/1,025,000 = \$10,097.56$$

    e. The growth rate of aggregate output per capita in 2005 equals the increase in aggregate output per capita during 2005 as a percentage of aggregate output per capita at the start of 2005.

$$\text{Growth Rate in aggregate output per capita in 2005} =$$
$$(\$10,097.56 - \$10,000)/\$10,000 = 0.9756\%$$

8. College tuition has risen significantly in the last few decades. From the 1971–1972 academic year to the 2001–2002 academic year, total tuition, room, and board paid by full-time undergraduate students went from $1,357 to $8,022 at public institutions and from $2,917 to $21,413 at private institutions. This is an average annual tuition increase of 6.1% at public institutions and 6.9% at private institutions. Over the same time, average personal income after taxes rose from $3,860 to $26,156 per year, which is an average annual rate of growth of personal income of 6.6%. Have these tuition increases made it more difficult for the average student to afford college tuition?

8. To determine whether it is more or less difficult for a typical person to afford college, we would need to know how much tuition had increased relative to average income in the United States. Average personal income after taxes rose from $3,860 to $26,156 from 1971 to 2001, or an average annual increase of 6.6%. So it was easier for the average person to afford a public institution, where tuition increased 6.1% annually, but more difficult to afford a private institution, where tuition rose 6.9% annually.

9. In May of each year, *The Economist* publishes data on the price of the Big Mac in different countries and exchange rates. The accompanying table shows some data used for the index from 2001 and 2003. Use this information to answer the questions below.

	2001		2003	
Country	Price of Big Mac (in local currency)	Exchange rate (foreign currency per U.S. dollar)	Price of Big Mac (in local currency)	Exchange rate (foreign currency per U.S. dollar)
Argentina	peso2.50	1.00 pesos per US$1	peso4.10	2.88 pesos per US$1
Canada	C$3.33	C$1.56 per US$1	C$3.20	C$1.45 per US$1
Euro area	€2.57	€1.14 per US$1	€2.71	€0.91 per US$1
Japan	¥294	¥124 per US$1	¥262	¥120 per US$1
United States	US$2.54		US$2.71	

a. Where was it cheapest to buy a Big Mac in U.S. dollars in 2001?

b. Where was it cheapest to buy a Big Mac in U.S. dollars in 2003?

c. If the increase in the local currency price of the Big Mac in each country represented the average inflation rate in that country over the two-year period from 2001 to 2003, which nation experienced the most inflation? Did any of the nations experience deflation?

d. For each currency, explain whether the dollar became more or less valuable in terms of that currency from 2001 to 2003.

9. The accompanying table shows the implied dollar price of the Big Mac in the countries below. To calculate the dollar price, you need to find the U.S. dollar price of the local currency

> US$ price of local currency = 1/(local currency price of the US$)

and multiply the U.S. dollar price of the foreign currency times the foreign price of the Big Mac.

a. In U.S. dollars, a Big Mac was cheapest in Canada in 2001.

	2001			2003		
Country	Price of Big Mac (in local currency)	Exchange rate (foreign currency per U.S. dollar)	Price of Big Mac (in U.S. dollars)	Price of Big Mac (in local currency)	Exchange rate (foreign currency per U.S. dollar)	Price of Big Mac (in U.S. dollars)
Argentina	peso2.50	peso1.00	$2.50	peso4.10	peso2.88	$1.42
Canada	C$3.33	C$1.56	$2.13	C$3.20	C$1.45	$2.21
Euro area	€2.57	€1.14	$2.25	€2.71	€0.91	$2.98
Japan	¥294	¥124	$2.37	¥262	¥120	$2.18
United States	US$2.54		$2.54	US$2.71		$2.71

b. In U.S. dollars, a Big Mac was cheapest in Argentina in 2003.

c. To calculate the rate of inflation over the two-year period from 2001 to 2003, we need to calculate the rate of change in the local currency price of the Big Mac in each country.

Inflation Rate in Argentina = (peso4.10 − peso2.50)/peso2.50 = 64.0%

Inflation Rate in Canada = (C$3.20 − C$3.33)/C$3.33 = −3.9%

Inflation Rate in Euro area = (€ 2.71 − € 2.57)/€ 2.57 = 5.4%

Inflation Rate in Japan = (¥262 − ¥294)/¥294 = −10.9%

Inflation Rate in the U.S. = (US$2.71 − US$2.54)/US$2.54 = 6.7%

Argentina experienced the highest rate of inflation over the two-year period; Canada and Japan experienced deflation.

d. From 2001 to 2003, the amount of the local currency received for each dollar rose in Argentina; the U.S. dollar became more valuable against the Argentine peso. However, the amount of local currency received for each dollar fell in Canada, the Euro area, and Japan; the U.S. dollar became less valuable against the currencies of these nations.

Tracking the Macroeconomy

1. Below is a simplified circular-flow diagram for the economy of Micronia.

   a. What is the value of GDP in Micronia?

   b. What is the value of net exports?

   c. What is the value of disposable income?

   d. Does the total flow of money out of households—the sum of taxes paid, consumer spending, and private savings—equal the total flow of money into households?

   e. How does the government of Micronia finance its purchases of goods and services?

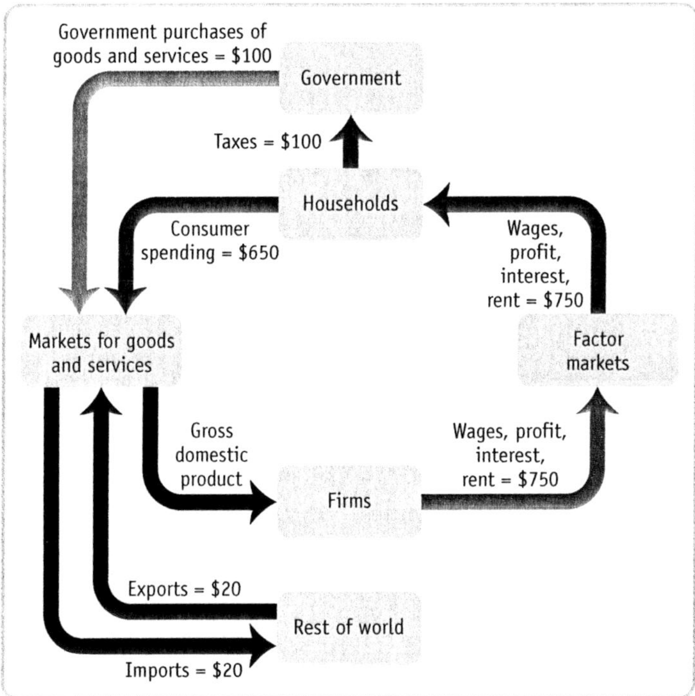

1. **a.** We can measure GDP in Micronia as the sum of all spending on domestically produced final goods and services. Spending consists of consumer spending, government purchases of goods and services, and exports less imports, or $750 ($650 + $100 + $20 − $20).

   b. Net exports are exports less imports. In Micronia, net exports equal zero ($20 − $20).

   c. Disposable income is income received by households less taxes plus government transfers. In Micronia, disposable income equals $650 ($750 − $100).

   d. Yes, consumer spending plus taxes equals $750—the same as the wages, profit, interest, and rent received by households.

   e. The government finances its purchases of goods and services with tax revenue.

2. A more complex circular-flow diagram for the economy of Macronia is shown below.

   a. What is the value of GDP in Macronia?

   b. What is the value of net exports?

   c. What is the value of disposable income?

   d. Does the total flow of money out of households—the sum of taxes paid, consumer spending, and private savings—equal the total flow of money into households?

   e. How does the government finance its spending?

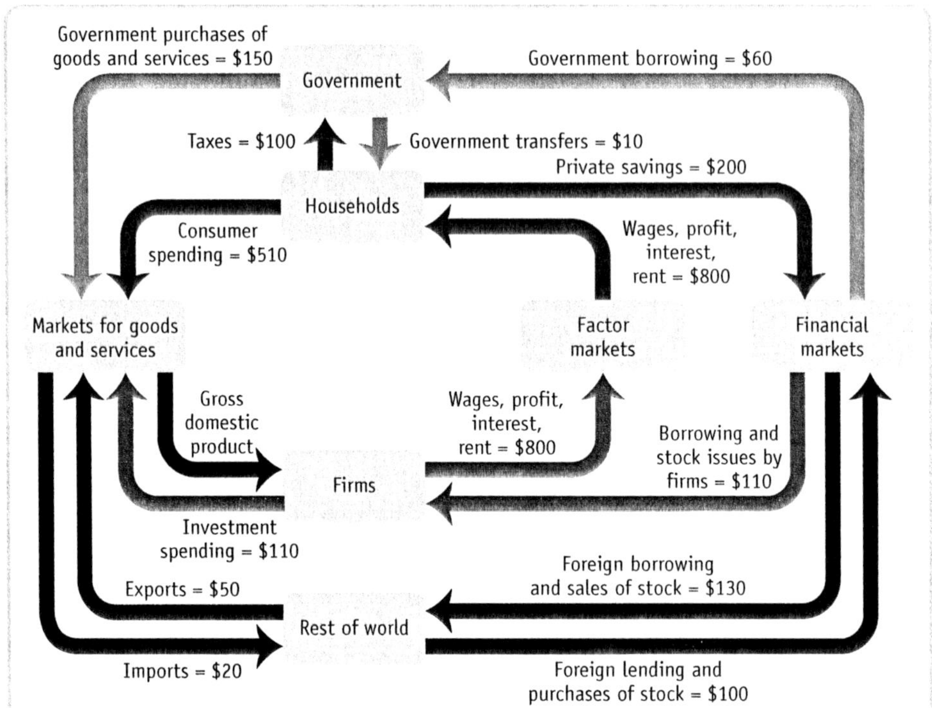

2. a. We can measure GDP in Macronia as the sum of all spending on domestically produced final goods and services. Spending consists of consumer spending, investment spending, government purchases of goods and services, and exports less imports, or $800 ($510 + $110 + $150 + $50 − $20).

   b. Net exports are exports less imports. In Macronia, net exports equal $30 ($50 − $20).

   c. Disposable income is income received by households less taxes plus government transfers. In Macronia, disposable income equals $710 ($800 − $100 + $10).

   d. Yes, consumer spending plus taxes plus private savings equals $810—the same as the wages, profit, interest, rent, and government transfers received by households.

   e. In Macronia, the government needs to finance $160 in spending ($150 on purchases of goods and services and $10 in government transfers). The government finances $100 of its spending with tax revenue and the other $60 through borrowing in financial markets.

3. The small economy of Pizzania produces three goods (bread, cheese, and pizza), each produced by a separate company. The bread and cheese companies produce all the inputs they need to make bread and cheese, respectively; the pizza company uses the bread and cheese from the other companies to make its pizzas. All three companies employ labor to help produce their goods, and the difference between the value of goods sold and the sum of labor and input costs is the firm's profit. This table summarizes the activities of the three companies when all the bread and cheese produced are sold to the pizza company as inputs in the production of pizzas.

	Bread company	Cheese company	Pizza company
Cost of inputs	$0	$0	$50 Bread
			35 Cheese
Wages	15	20	75
Value of output	50	35	200

a. Calculate GDP as the value added in production.

b. Calculate GDP as spending on final goods and services.

c. Calculate GDP as factor income.

3. a. To calculate GDP as the value added in production, we need to sum all value added (value of output less input costs) for each company. Value added in the bread company is $50; in the cheese company, $35; and in the pizza company, $115 ($200 − $50 − $35). The total value added in production is $200.

b. To calculate GDP as spending on final goods and services, we only need to estimate the value of pizzas because all bread and cheese produced are intermediate goods used in the production of pizzas. Spending on final goods and services is $200.

c. To calculate GDP as factor income, we need to sum factor income (wages and profits) for each firm. For the bread company, factor income is $50: labor earns $15 and profit is $35. For the cheese company, factor income is $35: labor earns $20 and profit is $15. For the pizza company, factor income is $115; labor earns $75 and profit is $40 ($200 − $75 − $50 − $35). Factor income is $200 ($50 + $35 + $115).

4. In the economy of Pizzania (from Problem 3), bread and cheese produced are sold both to the pizza company for inputs in the production of pizzas and to consumers as final goods. The accompanying table summarizes the activities of the three companies.

	Bread company	Cheese company	Pizza company
Cost of inputs	$0	$0	$50 Bread
			35 Cheese
Wages	25	30	75
Value of output	100	60	200

a. Calculate GDP as the value added in production.

b. Calculate GDP as spending on final goods and services.

c. Calculate GDP as factor income.

4. a. To calculate GDP as the value added in production, we need to sum all value added (value of output less input costs) for each company. Value added in the bread company is $100; in the cheese company, $60; and in the pizza company, $115 ($200 − $50 − $35). The total value added in production is $275.

b. To calculate GDP as spending on final goods and services, we need to sum the value of bread, cheese, and pizzas sold as final goods. GDP equals $275 because the bread company sells $50 worth as final goods, the cheese company sells $25 worth as final goods, and all $200 worth of pizzas are final goods.

c. To calculate GDP as factor income, we need to sum factor income (labor and profits) for each firm. For the bread company, factor income is $100: labor earns $25 and profit is $75. For the cheese company, factor income is $60: labor earns $30 and profit is $30. For the pizza company, factor income is $115: labor earns $75 and profit is $40 ($200 − $75 − $50 − $35). As factor income, GDP equals $275 ($100 + $60 + $115).

5. Which of the following transactions will be included in GDP for the United States?

a. Coca-Cola builds a new bottling plant in the United States.

b. Delta sells one of its existing airplanes to Korean Air.

c. Ms. Moneybags buys an existing share of Disney stock.

d. A California winery produces a bottle of Chardonnay and sells it to a customer in Montreal, Canada.

e. An American buys a bottle of French perfume.

f. A book publisher produces too many copies of a new book; the books don't sell this year, so the publisher adds the surplus books to inventories.

5. a. When Coca-Cola builds a new bottling plant, it is investment spending and included in GDP.

b. If Delta sells one of its airplanes to Korean Air, this transaction is not included in GDP because it does not represent production during the current time period. The airplane would have been included in GDP when it was produced; now it is just a sale of a used item.

c. When an individual buys an existing share of stock, the transaction is not included in GDP because there is no production.

d. If a California winery sells a bottle of Chardonnay to a customer in Montreal, it is a U.S. export and is entered as such in U.S. GDP.

e. When an American buys a bottle of French perfume, it is a consumption expenditure as measured by GDP. But since it does not represent production in the United States, it is also deducted from GDP as an import. The net effect of the transaction does not change GDP in the United States.

f. If a book publisher produces too many copies of a new book and the books don't sell in the year they are produced, the publisher adds the surplus books to inventories. These books are considered investment spending and added to GDP. It is as if the publisher bought the books itself.

6. The economy of Britannica produces three goods: computers, DVDs, and pizza. The accompanying table shows the prices and output of the three goods for the years 2002, 2003, and 2004.

	Computers		DVDs		Pizza	
Year	Price	Quantity	Price	Quantity	Price	Quantity
2002	$900	10	$10	100	$15	2
2003	1,000	10.5	12	105	16	2
2004	1,050	12	14	110	17	3

a. What is the percent change in production of each of the goods from 2002 to 2003 and from 2003 to 2004?

b. What is the percent change in prices of each of the goods from 2002 to 2003 and from 2003 to 2004?

c. Calculate nominal GDP in Britannica for each of the three years. What is the percent change in nominal GDP from 2002 to 2003 and from 2003 to 2004?

d. Calculate real GDP in Britannica using 2002 prices for each of the three years. What is the percent change in real GDP from 2002 to 2003 and from 2003 to 2004?

6. a. From 2002 to 2003, the percent change in the production of computers is 5.0% (equal to (10.5 − 10)/10 × 100); of DVDs, 5.0% (equal to (105 − 100)/100 × 100); and of pizza, 0% (equal to (2 − 2)/2 × 100). From 2003 to 2004, the percent change in the production of computers is 14.3% (equal to (12 − 10.5)/10.5 × 100); of DVDs, 4.8% (equal to (110 − 105)/105 × 100); and of pizza, 50.0% (equal to (3 − 2)/2 × 100).

b. From 2002 to 2003, the percent change in the price of computers is 11.1% (equal to ($1,000 − $900)/$900 × 100); of DVDs, 20.0% (equal to ($12 − $10)/$10 × 100); and of pizza, 6.7% (equal to ($16 − $15)/$15 × 100). From 2003 to 2004, the percent change in the price of computers is 5.0% (equal to ($1,050 − $1,000)/$1,000 × 100); of DVDs, 16.7% (equal to ($14 − $12)/$12 × 100); and of pizza, 6.25% (equal to ($17 − $16)/$16 × 100).

c. Nominal GDP for each year is calculated by summing up the value of the three goods produced in that year:

Year	Nominal GDP	Nominal GDP rate of change
2002	$10,030	
2003	11,792	17.6%
2004	14,191	20.3%

d. Real GDP in 2002 prices is calculated by summing up the value of the three goods produced each year using 2002 prices:

Year	Real GDP (2002 dollars)	Real GDP rate of change
2002	$10,030	
2003	10,530	5.0%
2004	11,945	13.4%

7. The accompanying table shows data on nominal GDP (in billions of dollars), real GDP (in billions of dollars) using 2000 as the base year, and population (in thousands) of the U.S. in 1960, 1970, 1980, 1990, 2000, and 2004, years in which the U.S. price level consistently rose.

Year	Nominal GDP (billions of dollars)	Real GDP (billions of 2000 dollars)	Population (thousands)
1960	$526.4	$2,501.8	180,671
1970	1,038.5	3,771.9	205,052
1980	2,789.5	5,161.7	227,726
1990	5,803.1	7,112.5	250,132
2000	9,817.0	9,817.0	282,388
2004	11,734.0	10,841.9	293,907

a. Why is real GDP greater than nominal GDP for all years before 2000 and lower for 2004? Does nominal GDP have to equal real GDP in 2000?

b. Calculate the percent change in real GDP from 1960 to 1970, 1970 to 1980, 1980 to 1990, and 1990 to 2000. Which period had the highest growth rate?

c. Calculate real GDP per capita for each of the years in the table.

d. Calculate the percent change in real GDP per capita from 1960 to 1970, 1970 to 1980, 1980 to 1990, and 1990 to 2000. Which period had the highest growth rate?

e. How do the percent change in real GDP and the percent change in real GDP per capita compare? Which is larger? Do we expect them to have this relationship?

7. **a.** Real GDP is greater than nominal GDP for all years before 2000 because from 1960 to 2000 prices rose. So to calculate real GDP for the years 1960, 1970, 1980, and 1990, we would multiply output in those years by the higher prices that existed in 2000. To calculate nominal GDP, we would multiply output by the lower prices that existed in those particular years. Since prices rose from 2000 to 2004, valuing the output in 2004 using 2000 prices (real GDP) will result in a lower number than valuing the output in 2004 using 2004 prices. Real GDP equals nominal GDP in 2000 because the year 2000 is the base year and we use the same set of prices to value both real and nominal GDP in that year.

b. The accompanying table shows the percent change in real GDP from 1960 to 1970, 1970 to 1980, 1980 to 1990, and 1990 to 2000. The percent change in real GDP was the highest during the 1960s.

Year	Real GDP (billions of 2000 dollars)	Real GDP rate of change
1960	$2,501.8	
1970	3,771.9	50.8%
1980	5,161.7	36.8%
1990	7,112.5	37.8%
2000	9,817.0	38.0%

c. We can calculate real GDP per capita by dividing real GDP by population. The accompanying table shows real GDP per capita for each of the years in the table. Remember that real GDP is measured in billions and population is measured in thousands. Real GDP per capita in 1960 was $13,847.27 ($2,501,800,000,000/180,671,000).

Year	Real GDP (billions of 2000 dollars)	Population (thousands)	Real GDP per capita
1960	$2,501.8	180,671	$13,847.27
1970	3,771.9	205,052	18,394.85
1980	5,161.7	227,726	22,666.27
1990	7,112.5	250,132	28,434.99
2000	9,817.0	282,388	34,764.23
2004	10,841.9	293,907	36,888.88

d. The accompanying table shows the percent change in real GDP per capita from 1960 to 1970, 1970 to 1980, 1980 to 1990, and 1990 to 2000. The percent change in real GDP per capita was the highest during the 1960s.

Year	Real GDP (billions of 2000 dollars)	Population (thousands)	Real GDP per capita	Real GDP per capita rate of change
1960	$2,501.8	180,671	$13,847.27	
1970	3,771.9	205,052	18,394.85	32.8%
1980	5,161.7	227,726	22,666.27	23.2%
1990	7,112.5	250,132	28,434.99	25.5%
2000	9,817.0	282,388	34,764.23	22.3%

e. The percent change in real GDP is always larger than the percent change in GDP per capita; as long as the population is growing, the two will always have this relationship.

8. This table shows the Human Development Index (HDI) and real GDP per capita in U.S. dollars for six nations in 2002.

	HDI	Real GDP per capita
Brazil	0.775	$7,770
Canada	0.943	29,480
Japan	0.938	26,940
Mexico	0.802	8,970
Saudi Arabia	0.768	12,650
United States	0.939	35,750

Rank the nations according to HDI and according to real GDP per capita. Why do the two vary?

8. The accompanying table shows the Human Development Index (HDI) and real GDP per capita in dollars for six nations in 2002, along with their HDI and real GDP per capita rank. The two differ in that a nation's rank in real GDP per capita relates how much production is available per person in that country compared with other nations and the rank in HDI relates how a nation stands relative to various determinants of human welfare (such as infant mortality, life expectancy, and literacy).

	HDI	Real GDP per capita	Rank HDI	Rank real GDP per capita
Brazil	0.775	$7,770	5	6
Canada	0.943	29,480	1	2
Japan	0.938	26,940	3	3
Mexico	0.802	8,970	4	5
Saudi Arabia	0.768	12,650	6	4
United States	0.939	35,750	2	1

9. In general, how do changes in the unemployment rate vary with changes in real GDP? After several quarters of a severe recession, explain why we might observe a decrease in the official unemployment rate. Could we see an increase in the official unemployment rate after several quarters of a strong expansion?

9. In general, the change in the unemployment rate varies inversely with the rate of growth in real GDP: when the economy is growing, we expect the unemployment rate to be falling rapidly. However, after several quarters of a severe recession, unemployed workers may become discouraged and stop looking for work. Since the definition of unemployed persons requires that they be looking for work, unemployment falls as workers become discouraged and stop looking. We could see an increase in the official unemployment rate after several quarters of a strong expansion as existing workers, encouraged by an increase in wages to attract new workers, leave existing jobs to search for new ones and discouraged workers begin to search for a job again.

10. Each month, usually on the first Friday of the month, the Bureau of Labor Statistics releases the Employment Situation Summary for the previous month. Go to www.bls.gov and find the latest report. (On the Bureau of Labor Statistics home page, click on "National unemployment rate" and then choose "Employment Situation Summary.") How does the unemployment rate compare to the rate one year earlier? What percentage of unemployed workers are long-term unemployed workers?

10. Answers will vary with the latest data. For September 2005, the unemployment rate was 5.1%, unchanged from September 2004 when it was also 5.1%. The number of long-term unemployed workers represented 19.4% of the unemployed in September 2005.

11. Eastland College is concerned about the rising price of textbooks that students must purchase. To better identify the increase in the price of textbooks, the dean asks you, the Economics Department's star student, to create an index of textbook prices. The average student purchases three English, two math, and four economics textbooks. The prices of these books are given in the accompanying table.

	2002	2003	2004
English textbook	$50	$55	$57
Math textbook	70	72	74
Economics textbook	80	90	100

a. Create the price index for these books for all years with a base year of 2002.

b. What is the percent change in the price of an English textbook from 2002 to 2004?

c. What is the percent change in the price of a math textbook from 2002 to 2004?

d. What is the percent change in the price of an economics textbook from 2002 to 2004?

e. What is the percent change in the market index from 2002 to 2004?

11. a. To create an index of textbook prices, you must first calculate the cost of the market basket (three English, two math, and four economics textbooks) in each of the three years; then normalize it by dividing the cost of the market basket in a given year by the cost of the market basket in the base period; and then multiply by 100 to get an index value (base period of 2002 = 100).

$$\text{Cost of textbooks in 2002} = 3 \times \$50 + 2 \times \$70 + 4 \times \$80 = \$610$$

$$\text{Cost of textbooks in 2003} = 3 \times \$55 + 2 \times \$72 + 4 \times \$90 = \$669$$

$$\text{Cost of textbooks in 2004} = 3 \times \$57 + 2 \times \$74 + 4 \times \$100 = \$719$$

$$\text{Index value for 2002} = \$610/\$610 \times 100 = 100$$

$$\text{Index value for 2003} = \$669/\$610 \times 100 = 109.7$$

$$\text{Index value for 2004} = \$719/\$610 \times 100 = 117.9$$

b. The percent change in the price of an English textbook from 2002 to 2004 is 14.0% (equal to ($57 − $50)/$50 × 100).

c. The percent change in the price of a math textbook from 2002 to 2004 is 5.7% (equal to ($74 − $70)/$70 × 100).

d. The percent change in the price of an economics textbook from 2002 to 2004 is 25% (equal to ($100 − $80)/$80 × 100).

e. The percent change in the market index for textbooks from 2002 to 2004 is 17.9% (equal to (117.9 − 100)/100 × 100).

12. The consumer price index, or CPI, measures the cost of living for the average consumer by multiplying the price for each category of expenditure (housing, food, and so on) times a measure of the importance of that expenditure in the average consumer's market basket and summing over all categories. However, using data from the consumer price index, we can see that changes in the cost of living for different types of consumers can vary a great deal. Let's compare the cost of living for a hypothetical retired person and a hypothetical college student. Let's assume that the market basket of a retired person is allocated in the following way: 10% on housing, 15% on food,

5% on transportation, 60% on medical care, 0% on education, and 10% on recreation. The college student's market basket is allocated as follows: 5% on housing, 15% on food, 20% on transportation, 0% on medical care, 40% on education, and 20% on recreation. The accompanying table shows the December 2004 CPI for each of the relevant categories.

	CPI, December 2004
Housing	190.7
Food	188.9
Transportation	164.8
Medical care	314.9
Education	112.6
Recreation	108.5

Calculate the overall CPI for the retired person and for the college student by multiplying the CPI for each of the categories by the relative importance of that category to the individual and then summing each of the categories. The CPI for all items in December 2004 was 190.3. How do your calculations for a CPI for the retired person and the college student compare to the overall CPI?

12. To calculate the CPI for the retired person and for the college student, we need to weight the CPI for each component with the importance of that component in his or her market basket. The CPI for the retired person is 255.45 and for the college student is 138.58. Since the CPI for the average consumer was 190.3, the CPI overstates the increase in the cost of living for the college student and understates it for the retired person.

For the retired person:

	Weight	CPI—December 2004	CPI for retired person
Housing	0.10	190.7	19.07
Food	0.15	188.9	28.34
Transportation	0.05	164.8	8.24
Medical Care	0.60	314.9	188.94
Education	0.00	112.6	0.00
Recreation	0.10	108.5	10.85
			255.44

For the college student:

	Weight	CPI—December 2004	CPI for college student
Housing	0.05	190.7	9.54
Food	0.15	188.9	28.34
Transportation	0.20	164.8	32.96
Medical Care	0.00	314.9	0.00
Education	0.40	112.6	45.04
Recreation	0.20	108.5	21.70
			137.58

13. Each month the Bureau of Labor Statistics releases the Consumer Price Index Summary for the previous month. Go to www.bls.gov and find the latest report. (On the Bureau of Labor Statistics home page, click on "CPI" under "Latest Numbers" and then choose "Consumer Price Index Summary.") What was the CPI for the previous month? How did it change from the previous month? How does the CPI compare to the same month one year ago?

13. Answers will vary with the latest data. For September 2005, the CPI was 198.8; it rose 1.2% from August 2005. The CPI was 4.7% higher than in September 2004.

14. The accompanying table contains two price indexes for the years 2002, 2003, and 2004: the GDP deflator and the CPI. For each price index, calculate the inflation rate from 2002 to 2003 and from 2003 to 2004.

Year	GDP deflator	CPI
2002	104.1	179.9
2003	106.0	184.0
2004	108.3	188.9

14. The accompanying table calculates the inflation rates based on the GDP deflator and on the CPI.

Year	GDP deflator	Inflation rate (based on GDP deflator)	CPI	Inflation rate (based on CPI)
2002	104.1		179.9	
2003	106.0	1.8%	184.0	2.3%
2004	108.3	2.2%	188.9	2.7%

Long-Run Economic Growth

1. The accompanying table shows data from the Penn World Table, Version 6.1, for real GDP per capita in 1996 U.S. dollars for Argentina, Ghana, South Korea, and the United States for 1960, 1970, 1980, 1990, and 2000.

	Argentina			Ghana		
Year	Real GDP per capita (1996 dollars)	Percentage of 1960 real GDP per capita	Percentage of 2000 real GDP per capita	Real GDP per capita (1996 dollars)	Percentage of 1960 real GDP per capita	Percentage of 2000 real GDP per capita
1960	$7,395	?	?	$832	?	?
1970	9,227	?	?	1,275	?	?
1980	10,556	?	?	1,204	?	?
1990	7,237	?	?	1,183	?	?
2000	10,995	?	?	1,349	?	?

	South Korea			United States		
Year	Real GDP per capita (1996 dollars)	Percentage of 1960 real GDP per capita	Percentage of 2000 real GDP per capita	Real GDP per capita (1996 dollars)	Percentage of 1960 real GDP per capita	Percentage of 2000 real GDP per capita
1960	$1,571	?	?	$12,414	?	?
1970	2,777	?	?	16,488	?	?
1980	4,830	?	?	21,337	?	?
1990	9,959	?	?	26,470	?	?
2000	15,881	?	?	33,308	?	?

a. Complete the table by expressing each year's real GDP per capita as a percentage of its 1960 and 2000 levels.

b. How does the growth in living standards from 1960 to 2000 compare across these four nations? What might account for these differences?

1. a. The accompanying table shows each nation's real GDP per capita in terms of its 1960 and 2000 levels.

	Argentina			Ghana		
Year	Real GDP per capita (1996 dollars)	Percentage of 1960 real GDP per capita	Percentage of 2000 real GDP per capita	Real GDP per capita (1996 dollars)	Percentage of 1960 real GDP per capita	Percentage of 2000 real GDP per capita
1960	$7,395	100%	67%	$832	100%	62%
1970	9,227	125	84	1,275	153	95
1980	10,556	143	96	1,204	145	89
1990	7,237	98	66	1,183	142	88
2000	10,995	149	100	1,349	162	100

	South Korea			United States		
Year	Real GDP per capita (1996 dollars)	Percentage of 1960 real GDP per capita	Percentage of 2000 real GDP per capita	Real GDP per capita (1996 dollars)	Percentage of 1960 real GDP per capita	Percentage of 2000 real GDP per capita
1960	$ 1,571	100%	10%	$12,414	100%	37%
1970	2,777	177	17	16,488	133	50
1980	4,830	307	30	2 1,337	172	64
1990	9,959	634	63	26,470	213	79
2000	15,881	1,011	100	33,308	268	100

b. South Korea experienced the greatest increase in living standards from 1960 to 2000; in 2001 it produced 1,011% ($15,881/$1,571 × 100) of what it produced in 1960. Argentina and Ghana experienced only a modest growth in living standards over the same period. Argentina's path was less consistent than that of Ghana, where living standards remained low throughout the period. Compared with real GDP per capita in 1960, the United States in 2000 produced 268% ($33,308/$12,414 × 100) of what it produced in 1960. The growth in living standards in Argentina, Ghana, and South Korea reflects the pattern for their different regions of the world. South Korea, like many other East Asian countries, had high productivity growth because of high savings and investment rates, a good education system, and substantial technological progress. Living standards grew more modestly in Argentina, as in other Latin American countries, because of low savings and investment spending rates, underinvestment in education, political instability, and irresponsible government policies. Although the growth in living standards was similar in Ghana and Argentina, Ghana had started from a much lower level. Real GDP per capita in Ghana was only 11% of that in Argentina in 1960 and 12% in 2000. Living standards in Africa suffered from major political instabilities, poor education and infrastructure, and disease.

2. The accompanying table shows the average annual growth rate in real GDP per capita for Argentina, Ghana, and South Korea using data from the Penn World Table, Version 6.1, for the past few decades.

	Average annual growth rate of real GDP per capita		
Years	Argentina	Ghana	South Korea
1960–1970	2.24%	4.36%	5.86%
1970–1980	1.35	−0.57	5.69
1980–1990	−3.70	−0.18	7.51
1990–2000	4.27	1.33	4.78

a. For each decade and for each country, use the Rule of 70 where possible to calculate how long it would take for that country's real GDP per capita to double.

b. Suppose that the average annual growth rate that each country achieved over the period 1990–2000 continues indefinitely into the future. Starting from 2000, use the Rule of 70 to calculate, where possible, the year in which a country will have doubled its real GDP per capita.

2. a. The accompanying table shows the number of years it would take for real GDP per capita to double according to the Rule of 70 using the average annual growth rate in real GDP per capita per decade in each country. Values corresponding to years with negative growth rates are left uncalculated because we cannot apply the Rule of 70 to a negative growth rate.

Years for real GDP per capita to double according to the Rule of 70

Years	Argentina	Ghana	South Korea
1960–1970	31.3	16.1	11.9
1970–1980	51.9	—	12.3
1980–1990	—	—	9.3
1990–2000	16.4	52.6	14.7

b. If each nation continues to grow as it did from 1990 to 2000, real GDP per capita will have doubled in Argentina by 2016, in Ghana by 2052, and in South Korea by 2014.

3. You are hired as an economic consultant to the countries of Albernia and Brittania. Each country's current relationship between physical capital per worker (K/L) and output per worker (Y/L) is given by the curve labeled Productivity$_1$ in the accompanying diagram. Albernia is at point A and Brittania is at point B.

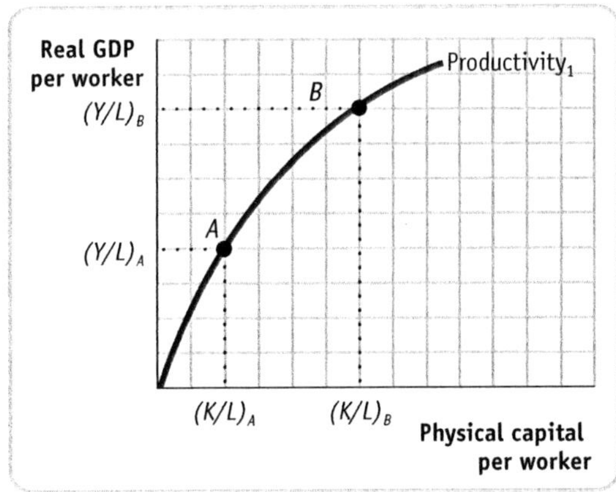

a. In the relationship depicted by the curve Productivity$_1$, what factors are held fixed? Do these countries experience diminishing returns to physical capital per worker?

b. Assuming that the amount of human capital per worker and the technology are held fixed in each country, can you recommend a policy to generate a doubling of real GDP per capita in each country?

c. How would your policy recommendation change if the amount of human capital per worker and the technology were not fixed? Draw a curve on the diagram that represents this policy for Albernia.

3. a. The curve reflecting the relationship between physical capital per worker (K/L) and output per worker (Y/L) is drawn holding human capital per worker and technology fixed. Both Albernia and Brittania experience diminishing returns to physical capital since in both countries equal successive increases in physical capital per worker—holding human capital per worker and technology constant—will result in smaller and smaller increases in real GDP per worker.

b. Albernia should increase its physical capital per worker to $(K/L)_B$. Brittania will have to add a huge amount of physical capital per worker.

c. If it were possible to increase the amount of human capital per worker or improve the technology, or both, then Productivity$_1$ could shift to Productivity$_2$ and Albernia could double real GDP per worker without a change in the physical capital per worker. On the accompanying diagram, Albernia would move from point *A* to point *C*.

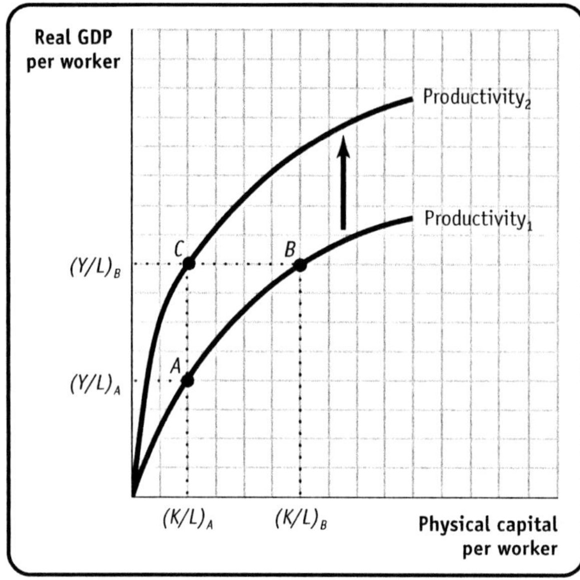

4. Why would you expect real GDP per capita in California and Pennsylvania to exhibit convergence but not in California and Baja California, a state of Mexico that borders the United States? What changes would allow California and Baja California to converge?

4. According to the conditional convergence hypothesis, *other things equal*, countries with relatively low real GDP per capita tend to have higher rates of growth than countries with relatively high real GDP per capita. We can apply this hypothesis to regions as well. It is more likely that the factors that affect growth will be equal in California and Pennsylvania: both states have similar educational systems, infrastructure, rule of law, and so on. But that is not true of California and Baja California: in comparing them, the factors that affect growth are not likely to be equal. California and Baja California have very different educational systems, different infrastructures, and there are differences in how the rule of law is applied. So it is less likely that they will converge. For California and Baja California to converge in real GDP per capita, they would have to become more similar in the factors that affect growth.

5. The economy of Profunctia has estimated its aggregate production function, when holding human capital per worker and technology constant, as

$$\frac{Y}{L} = 100 \times \sqrt{\frac{K}{L}}$$

Y is real GDP, L is the number of workers, and K is the quantity of physical capital. Given that Profunctia has 1,000 workers, calculate real GDP per worker and the quantity of physical capital per worker for the differing amounts of physical capital shown in the accompanying table.

K	L	K/L	Y/L
$0	1,000	?	?
10	1,000	?	?
20	1,000	?	?
30	1,000	?	?
40	1,000	?	?
50	1,000	?	?
60	1,000	?	?
70	1,000	?	?
80	1,000	?	?
90	1,000	?	?
100	1,000	?	?

a. Plot the aggregate production function for Profunctia.

b. Does the aggregate production function exhibit diminishing returns to physical capital? Explain your answer.

5. a. The accompanying table and diagram show the aggregate production function for Profunctia.

K	L	K/L	Y/L
$0	1,000	$0.00	$0.00
10	1,000	0.01	10.00
20	1,000	0.02	14.14
30	1,000	0.03	17.32
40	1,000	0.04	20.00
50	1,000	0.05	22.36
60	1,000	0.06	24.49
70	1,000	0.07	26.46
80	1,000	0.08	28.28
90	1,000	0.09	30.00
100	1,000	0.10	31.62

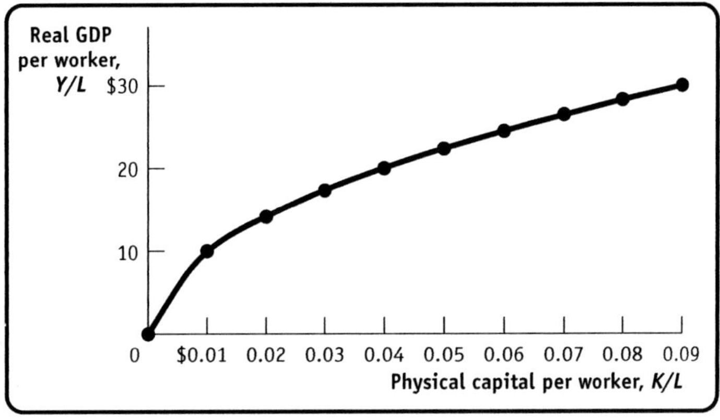

b. The aggregate production function does exhibit diminishing returns to physical capital. For example, the table shows that as K increases from \$30 to \$40, Y/L increases by \$2.68, but as K increases from \$70 to \$80, Y/L increases only by \$1.82.

6. The Bureau of Labor Statistics regularly releases the "Productivity and Costs" report for the previous month. Go to www.bls.gov and find the latest report. (On the Bureau of Labor Statistics home page, click on "Productivity" under Latest Numbers and then choose the latest "Productivity and Costs" report.) What were the percent changes in business and nonfarm business productivity for the previous quarter? How does the percent change in that quarter's productivity compare to previous data?

6. Answers will vary with the latest data. For the third quarter of 2005, business and nonfarm business productivity grew by 4.8% and 4.1%, respectively. These were higher than the productivity growth figures for the second quarter of 2005, which were 0.81% and 2.1%, respectively.

7. What roles do physical capital, human capital, technology, and natural resources play in influencing long-run economic growth of aggregate output per capita?

7. Physical capital, human capital, technology, and natural resources play important roles in influencing long-run growth in real GDP per capita. Increases in both physical capital and human capital help a given labor force to produce more over time. Although economic studies have suggested that increases in human capital may explain increases in productivity better than increases in physical capital per worker, technological progress is probably the most important driver of productivity growth. While natural resources played a prominent role historically in determining productivity, they play a less important role in increasing productivity than do increases in human or physical capital in most countries today.

8. Through its policies and institutions, how has the United States influenced U.S. long-run economic growth? Why might persistently large borrowing by the U.S. government ultimately limit long-run economic growth in the future?

8. Institutions and policies in the United States have greatly aided U.S. economic growth. The country has been politically stable, and its laws and institutions protect private property. The economy has attracted significant savings, both domestic and foreign, that have allowed investment spending to spur the growth of the capital stock and fund research and development. The government has directly supported economic growth through its support of public education as well as research and development. However, the government's persistently large borrowing may reduce private investment spending (a phenomenon known as "crowding out"), consequently slowing economic growth.

9. Over the next 100 years, real GDP per capita in Groland is expected to grow at an average annual rate of 2.0%. In Sloland, however, growth is expected to be somewhat slower, at an average annual growth rate of 1.5%. If both countries have a real GDP per capita today of \$20,000, how will their real GDP per capita differ in 100 years? (*Hint:* A country that has a real GDP today of \$x and grows at y% per year will achieve a real GDP of $\$x \times (1 + 0.0y)^z$ in z years.)

9. If real GDP per capita in Groland grows at an average annual rate of 2.0%, real GDP per capita in 100 years will be $144,893 [$20,000 $\times$ (1 + 0.02)^{100}]. At an average annual rate of growth of 1.5%, real GDP per capita in Sloland in 100 years will be $88,641 [$20,000 $\times$ (1 + 0.015)^{100}]. Although both nations start with the same real GDP per capita today, the differential growth rates will result in living standards in Sloland that are 61.2% ($88,641/$144,893 $\times$ 100) of those in Groland.

10. The accompanying table shows data from the Penn World Table, Version 6.1, for real GDP per capita (1996 U.S. dollars) in France, Japan, the United Kingdom, and the United States in 1950 and 2000. Complete the table. Have these countries converged economically?

	1950		2000	
	Real GDP per capita (1996 dollars)	Percentage of U.S. real GDP per capita	Real GDP per capita (1996 dollars)	Percentage of U.S. real GDP per capita
France	$5,561	?	$22,254	?
Japan	2,445	?	24,495	?
United Kingdom	7,498	?	22,849	?
United States	10,601	?	33,308	?

10. The accompanying table shows real GDP per capita (1996 U.S. dollars) in France, Japan, and the United Kingdom as a percentage of real GDP per capita in the United States.

	1950		2000	
	Real GDP per capita (1996 dollars)	Percentage of U.S. real GDP per capita	Real GDP per capita (1996 dollars)	Percentage of U.S. real GDP per capita
France	$5,561	52.5%	$22,254	66.8%
Japan	2,445	23.1	24,495	73.5
United Kingdom	7,498	70.7	22,849	68.6
United States	10,601	100.0	33,308	100.0

Real GDP per capita in France and Japan, the two nations with the lowest real GDP per capita in 1950, closed some of the gap in living standards with the United States. Japan's real GDP per capita grew from only 23.1% of that in the United States to 73.5%, and France's rose from 52.5% to 66.8%. But living standards in the United Kingdom relative to those in the United States actually declined; real GDP per capita fell from 70.7% of that in the United States to 68.6%. France and Japan have converged, but the United Kingdom has not.

11. The accompanying table shows data from the Penn World Table, Version 6.1, for real GDP per capita (1996 U.S. dollars) for Argentina, Ghana, South Korea, and the United States in 1960 and 2000. Complete the table. Have these countries converged economically?

	1960		2000	
	Real GDP per capita (1996 dollars)	Percentage of U.S. real GDP per capita	Real GDP per capita (1996 dollars)	Percentage of U.S. real GDP per capita
Argentina	$7,395	?	$10,995	?
Ghana	832	?	1,349	?
South Korea	1,571	?	15,881	?
United States	12,414	?	33,308	?

11. The accompanying table shows real GDP per capita (1996 U.S. dollars) in Argentina, Ghana, and South Korea as a percentage of real GDP per capita in the United States.

	1960		2000	
	Real GDP per capita (1996 dollars)	Percentage of U.S. real GDP per capita	Real GDP per capita (1996 dollars)	Percentage of U.S. real GDP per capita
Argentina	$7,395	59.6%	$10,995	33.0%
Ghana	832	6.7	1,349	4.0
South Korea	1,571	12.7	15,881	47.7
United States	12,414	100.0	33,308	100.0

There is little evidence of convergence for either Argentina or Ghana. Living standards in both nations declined relative to those in the United States. In Argentina real GDP per capita fell from 59.6% of that of the United States to 33.0%; Ghana's fell from 6.7% to 4.0%. But South Korea's real GDP per capita showed signs of convergence with those in the United States; real GDP per capita rose from 12.7% of that in the United States to 47.7%.

Savings, Investment Spending, and the Financial System

1. Given the following information about the closed economy of Brittania, what is the level of investment spending and private savings, and what is the budget balance? What is the relationship among the three? Is national savings equal to investment spending? There are no government transfers.

GDP = $1,000 million   T = $50 million
C = $850 million   G = $100 million

1. In a closed economy, investment spending is equal to GDP minus consumer spending minus government purchases of goods and services. In Brittania, investment spending is $50 million:

$$I = GDP - C - G$$

$$I = \$1,000 \text{ million} - \$850 \text{ million} - \$100 \text{ million} = \$50 \text{ million}$$

Private savings is equal to disposable income (income net of taxes—and recall that there are no government transfers) minus consumer spending. In Brittania, private savings is $100 million:

$$S_{Private} = GDP - T - C = \$1,000 \text{ million} - \$50 \text{ million} - \$850 \text{ million} = \$100 \text{ million}$$

The budget balance is equal to tax revenue minus government purchases of goods and services. In Brittania, the government is running a budget deficit of $50 million:

$$S_{Government} = T - G = \$50 \text{ million} - \$100 \text{ million} = -\$50 \text{ million}$$

National savings is the sum of private savings and the budget balance; that is, it is $100 million − $50 million = $50 million. So investment spending does equal national savings.

2. Given the following information about the open economy of Regalia, what is the level of investment spending and private savings, and what are the budget balance and capital inflow? What is the relationship among the four? There are no government transfers.

GDP = $1,000 million   G = $100 million
C = $850 million   X = $100 million
T = $50 million   IM = $125 million

2. In an open economy, investment spending is equal to GDP minus consumer spending minus government purchases of goods and services plus capital inflow, the value of imports minus the value of exports. In Regalia, investment spending is $75 million:

$$I = (GDP - C - G) + (IM - X)$$

$$I = (\$1,000 \text{ million} - \$850 \text{ million} - \$100 \text{ million}) + (\$125 \text{ million} - \$100 \text{ million})$$

$$I = \$50 \text{ million} + \$25 \text{ million} = \$75 \text{ million}$$

Private savings and the budget balance are measured in the same way in open and closed economies. (Again, recall that there are no government transfers.) In Regalia, private savings is $100 million and the budget balance is −$50 million (that is, the government is running a deficit of $50 million):

$$S_{Private} = GDP - T - C = \$1,000 \text{ million} - \$50 \text{ million} - \$850 \text{ million} = \$100 \text{ million}$$

$$S_{Government} = T - G = \$50 \text{ million} - \$100 \text{ million} = -\$50 \text{ million}$$

An economy will experience a positive capital inflow equal to the difference between imports and exports when imports exceed exports; it will experience a capital outflow (a negative capital inflow) equal to the difference between imports and exports when exports exceed imports. Regalia has a positive capital inflow equal to $25 million:

$$KI = IM - X = \$125 \text{ million} - \$100 \text{ million} = \$25 \text{ million}$$

Investment spending must equal the sum of private savings, the budget balance, and the capital inflow. In Regalia, we can see that this relationship holds among the four:

$$I = S_{Private} + S_{Government} + KI = \$75 \text{ million}$$

3. The accompanying table shows the percentage of GDP accounted for by private savings, investment spending, and capital inflow in the economies of Capsland and Marsalia. Capsland is currently experiencing a net capital inflow and Marsalia, a net capital outflow. What is the budget balance (as a percentage of GDP) in both countries? Are Capsland and Marsalia running a budget deficit or surplus?

	Capsland	Marsalia
Investment spending as a percentage of GDP	20%	20%
Private savings as a percentage of GDP	10	25
Capital inflow as a percentage of GDP	5	−2

3. In both countries, investment spending as a percentage of GDP must be equal to the sum of private savings, the budget balance, and capital inflow as a percentage of GDP. We can calculate the budget balance as investment spending minus the sum of private savings and capital inflow:

$$I = S_{Private} + S_{Government} + KI$$
$$S_{Government} = I - S_{Private} - KI$$

In Capsland, the budget balance is 5% of GDP; the government is running a budget surplus equal to 5% of GDP:

$$S_{Government} = 20\% - 10\% - 5\%$$
$$S_{Government} = 5\%$$

In Marsalia, the budget balance is −3% of GDP; the government is running a budget deficit equal to 3% of GDP:

$$S_{Government} = 20\% - 25\% - (-2\%) = 20\% - 25\% + 2\%$$
$$S_{Government} = -3\%$$

4. Assume the economy is open. Answer each of the following questions.

a. $X = \$125$ million
$IM = \$80$ million
$S_{Government} = -\$200$ million
$I = \$350$ million
Calculate $S_{Private}$.

b. $X = \$85$ million
$IM = \$135$ million
$S_{Government} = \$100$ million
$S_{Private} = \$250$ million
Calculate I.

c. $X = \$60$ million
$IM = \$95$ million
$S_{Private} = \$325$ million
$I = \$300$ million
Calculate $S_{Government}$.

d. $S_{Private} = \$325$ million
$I = \$400$ million
$S_{Government} = \$10$ million
Calculate $IM - X$.

4. According to the savings–investment spending identity in an open economy, the following must hold: $I = S_{Private} + S_{Government} + (IM - X)$. We use this to solve for the missing variable in each problem.

a. $350 million $= S_{Private} - $200 million $+ ($80 million $- $125 million$)$
Hence, $S_{Private} = $595 million

b. $I = $250 million $+ $100 million $+ ($135 million $- $85 million$)$
Hence, $I = $400 million

c. $300 million $= $325 million $+ S_{Government} + ($95 million $- $60 million$)$
Hence, $S_{Government} = -$60 million

d. $400 million $= $325 million $+ $10 million $+ (IM - X)$
Hence, $(IM - X) = $65 million

5. Use the market for loanable funds shown in the accompanying diagram to explain what happens to private savings, private investment spending, and the rate of interest if the following events occur. Assume the economy is closed.

a. The government reduces the size of its deficit to zero.

b. At any given interest rate, consumers decide to save more. Assume the budget balance is zero.

c. At any given interest rate, businesses become very optimistic about the future profitability of investment spending. Assume the budget balance is zero.

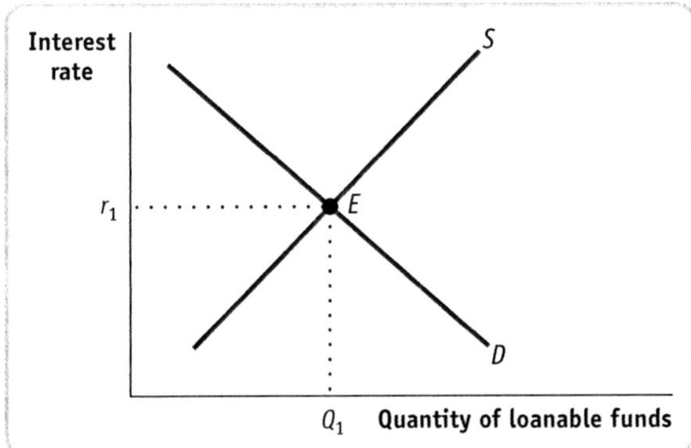

5. a. If the government reduces its deficit to zero, there will be a decrease in the demand for loanable funds equal to the reduction in the size of the deficit. In the accompanying figure, the amount $Q_1 - Q_3$ represents the amount by which the government decreases its deficit. In response to the decrease in demand, the interest rate falls from r_1 to r_2. This fall in interest rates will increase private investment spending from Q_3 to Q_2 and decrease private savings from Q_1 to Q_2.

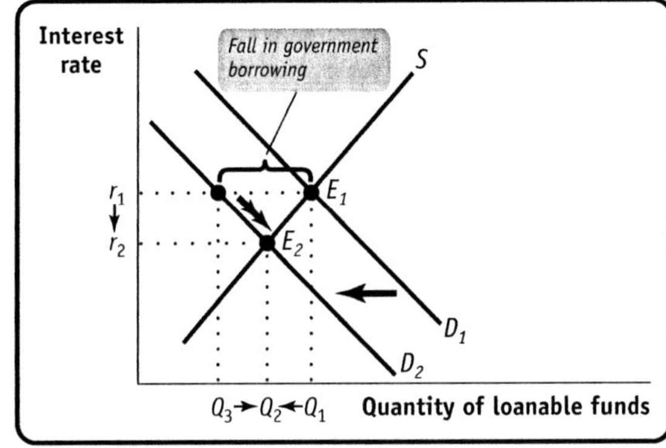

b. If consumers decide to save more, there will be an increase in the supply of loanable funds. In the accompanying figure, this is represented by the rightward shift of the supply curve from S_1 to S_2. The increase in the supply of loanable funds reduces the equilibrium interest rate from r_1 to r_2. In response to the lower interest rate, private investment spending will rise from Q_1 to Q_2.

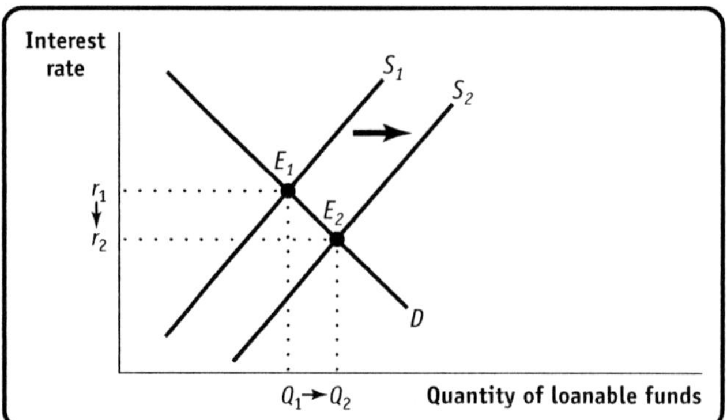

c. Higher investment spending at any given interest rate leads to an increase in the demand for loanable funds. In the accompanying figure, the increase in the demand for loanable funds raises the equilibrium interest rate from r_1 to r_2. In response to the higher interest rate, private savings will rise from Q_1 to Q_2.

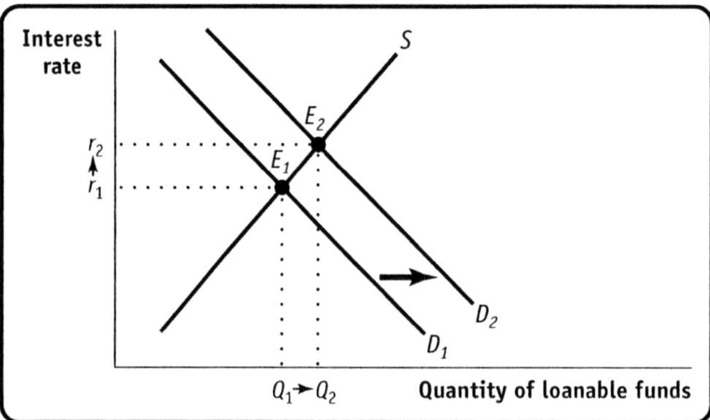

6. The government is running a budget balance of zero when it decides to increase education spending by \$200 billion and finance the spending by selling bonds. The accompanying diagram shows the market for loanable funds before the government sells the bonds. Assume the economy is closed. How will the equilibrium interest rate and the equilibrium quantity of loanable funds change? Is there any crowding out in the market?

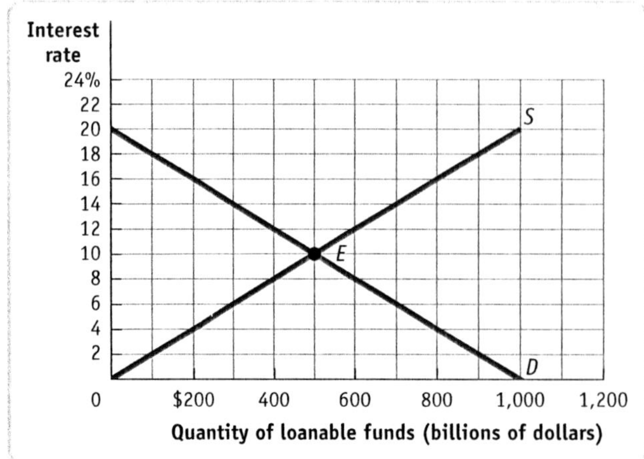

6. The $200 billion in government borrowing will increase the demand for loanable funds from D_1 to D_2 as shown in the accompanying diagram. The equilibrium interest rate rises from 10% to 12%, and the equilibrium quantity of loanable funds increases from $500 billion to $600 billion. The rise in the interest rates will lead to an increase in private savings of $100 billion, and private investment spending will fall by $100 billion. Through the rise in the interest rate, the increase in government borrowing crowded out $100 billion in private investment spending.

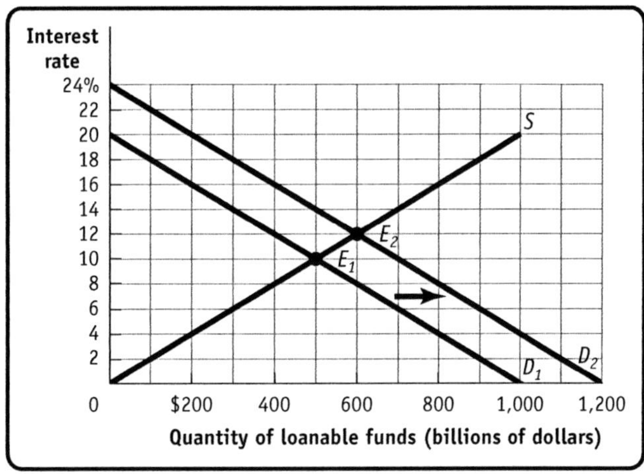

7. Explain why equilibrium in the loanable funds market maximizes efficiency.

7. Equilibrium in the loanable funds market maximizes efficiency because it ensures that investment spending projects with higher rates of return get funded before those with lower rates of return. At the same time, private savers with the lowest opportunity cost for their funds will have their offers of loans accepted before savers with higher opportunity costs of funds. So in equilibrium the projects with the highest rates of return will be funded by savers with the lowest costs of lending. No mutually beneficial trades between lenders or borrowers are left unexploited.

8. How would you respond to a friend who claims that the government should eliminate all purchases that are financed by borrowing because such borrowing crowds out private investment spending?

8. You might first acknowledge that when the government runs a budget deficit, there is an increase in the demand for loanable funds. The increase in demand raises interest rates and decreases private investment spending. This means that businesses will add less physical capital each year and productivity growth may be slower than it would be if the government had not borrowed to cover its deficit. However, you might then explain that some government purchases are necessary for economic growth. Government funds much of the infrastructure within which the economy operates (for example, the legal framework, the court system, and the communications network), and the government also invests in education, roads, and airports necessary for economic growth.

9. Which of the following are examples of investment spending, investing in financial assets, or investing in physical assets?

   a. Rupert Moneybucks buys 100 shares of existing Coca-Cola stock.

   b. Rhonda Moviestar spends $10 million to buy a mansion built in the 1970s.

   c. Ronald Basketballstar spends $10 million to build a new mansion with a view of the Pacific Ocean.

   d. Rawlings builds a new plant to make catcher's mitts.

   e. Russia buys $100 million in U.S. government bonds.

9. **a.** When Rubert Moneybucks buys 100 shares of existing Coca-Cola stock, he is investing in a financial asset. He has a paper claim that entitles him to future income from Coca-Cola. It is not an example of investment spending because it does not add to the stock of physical capital in the economy.

   b. When Rhonda Moviestar spends $10 million to buy a mansion built in the 1970s, she is investing in a physical asset; she has bought something that she has the right to use or to dispose of as she wishes. It is not an example of investment spending because it does not add to the stock of physical capital in the economy because the mansion was pre-existing.

   c. When Ronald Basketballstar spends $10 million to build a new mansion with a view of the Pacific Ocean, he has engaged in investment spending because he has added to the amount of housing in the economy.

   d. When Rawlings builds a new plant to make catcher's mitts, it has engaged in investment spending because it has added to the economy's stock of physical capital.

   e. When the government of Russia buys $100 million in U.S. government bonds, it has invested in a financial asset. The Russian government has a paper claim on the United States that entitles it to future income. It is not an example of investment spending because it does not add to the stock of physical capital in either economy.

10. Explain how a well-functioning financial system increases savings and investment spending, holding the budget balance and any capital flows fixed.

10. A well-functioning financial system increases both the supply of loanable funds and the demand for loanable funds in three ways: by reducing transaction costs of making financial deals incurred by either lenders or borrowers; by reducing the risk associated with making investments or engaging in investment spending; and by increasing liquidity of financial assets, therefore making saving and the purchasing of financial assets more attractive to potential lenders, and thereby increasing investment spending.

11. What are the important types of financial intermediaries in the U.S. economy? What are the primary assets of these intermediaries, and how do they facilitate investment spending and saving?

11. Mutual funds, pension funds, life insurance companies, and banks are the most important types of financial intermediaries in the U.S. economy. Mutual funds are companies that buy stocks of other companies (the mutual funds companies' primary assets) and resell shares of the portfolio composed of those stocks to individual investors. Pension funds are a type of mutual fund that hold financial assets of other companies (the pension funds' primary assets) and sell shares to individual savers for retirement income. A life insurance company also holds financial assets (the life insurance company's primary assets) and sells policies that guarantee a payment to a policyholder's beneficiary when the policyholder dies. A bank makes loans to individuals and corporations (the bank's primary assets) and accepts deposits from the public that are payable on demand.

12. Explain the effect on a company's stock price today of the following events, other things held constant.

a. The interest rate on bonds falls.

b. Several companies in the same sector announce surprisingly slow sales.

c. A change in the tax law passed last year reduces this year's profit.

d. The company unexpectedly announces that due to an accounting error, it must amend last year's accounting statement and reduce last year's reported profit by $5 million. It also announces that this change has no implications for future profits.

12. **a.** Because bonds are a substitute asset for stocks, this will lead to a rise in all stock prices, including this company's stock price.

b. This will lead to an immediate fall in the company's stock price because it is unexpected information that communicates to investors that the company's sector is doing poorly, and therefore it is likely that the company will also experience slow sales and a lower-than-expected profit.

c. This will have no effect on the company's stock price today because the effect of the change in the tax law on this year's profit would have been incorporated in the company's stock price when the tax law change was announced.

d. This will have no effect on the company's stock price today because the stock price is based on expectations about the future stock price, and this is unaffected by changes in previous year's profits.

Aggregate Supply and Aggregate Demand

1. Your study partner is confused by the upward-sloping short-run aggregate supply curve and the vertical long-run aggregate supply curve. How would you explain this?

1. The short-run aggregate supply curve slopes upward because nominal wages are sticky in the short run. Nominal wages are fixed by either formal contracts or informal agreements in the short run. So, as the aggregate price level falls and nominal wages remain the same, production costs will not fall by the same proportion as the aggregate price level. This will reduce profit per unit of output, leading producers to reduce output in the short run. Similarly, as the aggregate price level rises, production costs will not rise by the same proportion because nominal wages will remain fixed in the short run. Profit per unit of output will increase, leading producers to increase output in the short run. So there is a positive relationship between the aggregate price level and the quantity of aggregate output producers are willing to supply in the short run because nominal wages are fixed. However, in the long run, nominal wages can and will be renegotiated. Nominal wages will change along with the aggregate price level. As the aggregate price level rises, production costs will rise by the same proportion. When the aggregate price level and production costs rise by the same percentage, every unit of output that had been profitable to produce before the price rise is still profitable, and every unit of output that had been unprofitable to produce before the price rise is still unprofitable. So aggregate output does not change. In the long run, when nominal wages are perfectly flexible, an increase or decrease in the aggregate price level will not change the quantity of aggregate output produced. So the long-run aggregate supply curve is vertical.

2. Suppose that in Wageland all workers sign annual wage contracts each year on January 1. No matter what happens to prices of final goods and services during the year, all workers earn the wage specified in their annual contract. This year, prices of final goods and services fall unexpectedly after the contracts are signed. Answer the following questions using a diagram and assume that the economy starts at potential output.

a. In the short run, how will the quantity of aggregate output supplied respond to the fall in prices?

b. What will happen when firms and workers renegotiate their wages?

2. a. In the short run, the prices of final goods and services in Wageland fall unexpectedly but nominal wages don't change; they are fixed in the short run by the annual contract. So firms earn a lower profit per unit and reduce output. In the accompanying diagram, Wageland moves along $SRAS_1$ from point A on January 1 to
point B after the fall in prices.

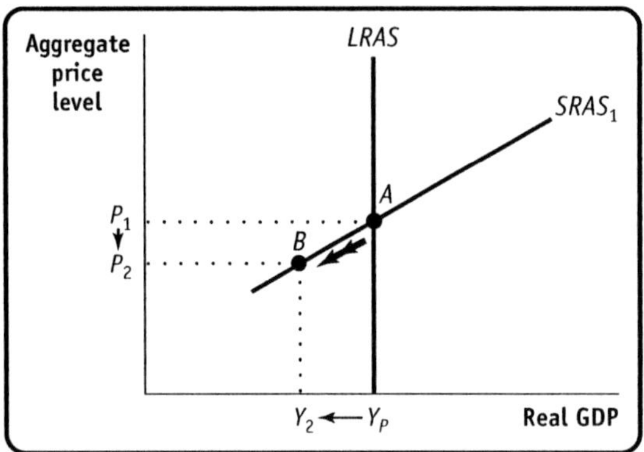

b. When firms and workers renegotiate their wages, nominal wages will decrease,
shifting the short-run aggregate supply curve rightward from $SRAS_1$ to a curve
such as $SRAS_2$.

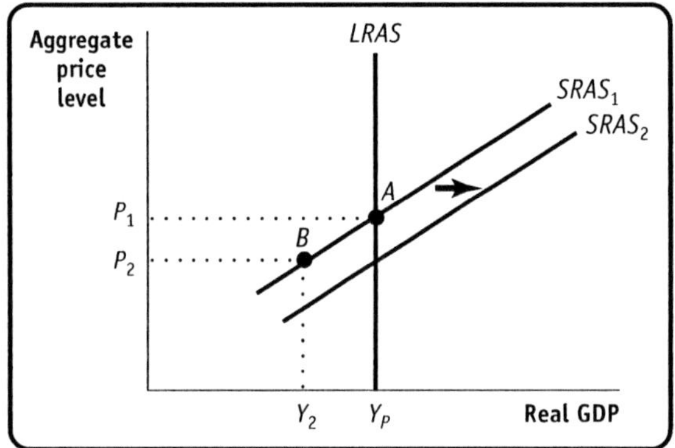

3. In each of the following cases, in the short run, determine whether the events cause
a shift of a curve or a movement along a curve. Determine which curve is involved
and the direction of the change.

a. As a result of an increase in the value of the dollar in relation to other currencies,
American producers now pay less in dollar terms for foreign steel, a major commodity used in production.

b. An increase in the quantity of money by the Federal Reserve increases the quantity
of money that people wish to lend, lowering interest rates.

c. Greater union activity leads to higher nominal wages.

d. A fall in the aggregate price level increases the purchasing power of households'
money holdings. As a result, they borrow less and lend more.

3. a. As the value of the dollar in terms of other currencies increases and American
producers pay less in dollar terms for foreign steel, producers' profit per unit
increases and they are willing to supply a greater quantity of aggregate output at
any given aggregate price level. The short-run aggregate supply curve will shift to
the right.

b. As the Federal Reserve increases the quantity of money, households and firms have more money, which they are willing to lend out, and interest rates fall. The lower interest rates will increase investment spending and consumer spending, leading to a greater quantity of aggregate output demanded at any given aggregate price level. The aggregate demand curve will shift to the right.

c. If unions are able to negotiate higher nominal wages for a large portion of the workforce, this will increase production costs and reduce profit per unit at any given aggregate price level. The short-run aggregate supply curve will shift to the left.

d. As the aggregate price level falls and the purchasing power of households' and firms' money holdings increases, the public tries to reduce its money holdings by borrowing less and lending more. So interest rates fall, leading to a rise in both investment spending and consumer spending. This is the interest rate effect of a change in the aggregate price level, represented as a movement down along the aggregate demand curve.

4. A fall in the value of the dollar against other currencies makes U.S. final goods and services cheaper to foreigners even though the U.S. aggregate price level stays the same. As a result, foreigners demand more American aggregate output. Your study partner says that this represents a movement down the aggregate demand curve because foreigners are demanding more in response to a lower price. You, however, insist that this represents a rightward shift of the aggregate demand curve. Who is right? Explain.

4. You are right. When a fall in the value of the dollar against other currencies makes U.S. final goods and services cheaper to foreigners, this represents a shift of the aggregate demand curve. Although foreigners may be demanding more U.S. goods because the price of those goods in their own currency is lower, there is no change in the U.S. aggregate price level. From the U.S. perspective, there is an increase in aggregate output demanded at any given aggregate price level.

5. Suppose that local, state and federal governments were obliged to cut government purchases whenever consumer spending falls. Then suppose that consumer spending falls due to a fall in the stock market. Draw a diagram and explain the full effect of the fall in the stock market on the aggregate demand curve and on the economy. How is this similar to the experience of stagflation in the 1970s?

5. If a fall in the stock market reduces consumer spending, the aggregate demand curve will shift to the left from AD_1 to AD_2 in the accompanying diagram. At any given aggregate price level, consumer spending is lower and the amount of aggregate output demanded falls. However, if governments must cut government purchases whenever consumer spending falls, this will lead to a further leftward shift of the aggregate demand curve from AD_2 to AD_3. At any given aggregate price level, government purchases are lower and the amount of aggregate output demanded falls again. This is similar to the "knock on" effect during the stagflation of the 1970s in that one adverse change led to another. The increase in the price of oil during the 1970s reduced short-run aggregate supply (the short-run aggregate supply curve shifted leftward) and raised aggregate prices. At this time many wage contracts included cost-of-living allowances that automatically raised the nominal wage when consumer prices increased. As nominal wages rose, there was a second leftward shift of the short-run aggregate supply curve.

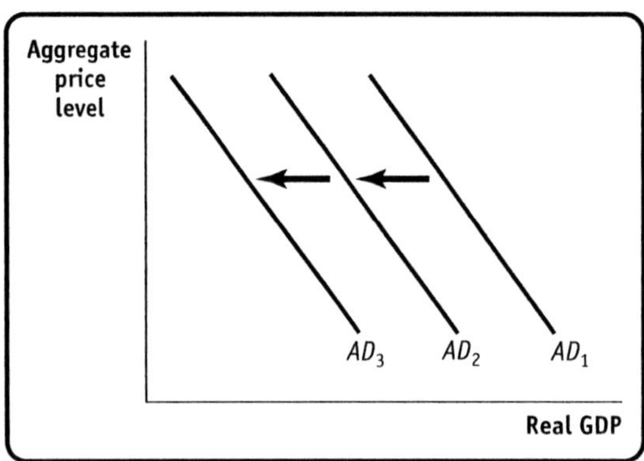

6. Due to an increase in consumer wealth, there is a $40 billion autonomous increase in consumer spending in the economies of Westlandia and Eastlandia. Assuming that the aggregate price level is constant, the interest rate is fixed in both countries, and there are no taxes and no foreign trade, complete the accompanying tables to show the various rounds of increased spending that will occur in both economies if the marginal propensity to consume is 0.5 in Westlandia and 0.75 in Eastlandia. What do your results indicate about the relationship between the size of the marginal propensity to consume and the multiplier?

Westlandia

Rounds	Incremental change in GDP		Total change in GDP
1		$\Delta C = \$40$ billion	?
2	$MPC \times \Delta C =$	?	?
3	$MPC \times MPC \times \Delta C =$	?	?
4	$MPC \times MPC \times MPC \times \Delta C =$	?	?
. . .		. . .	. . .
Total change in GDP		$(1/(1 - MPC)) \times \Delta C =$	?

Eastlandia

Rounds	Incremental change in GDP		Total change in GDP
1		$\Delta C = \$40$ billion	?
2	$MPC \times \Delta C =$	?	?
3	$MPC \times MPC \times \Delta C =$	?	?
4	$MPC \times MPC \times MPC \times \Delta C =$	?	?
. . .	. . .	. . .	
Total change in GDP		$(1/(1 - MPC)) \times \Delta C =$	?

6.

Westlandia

Rounds	Incremental change in GDP	Total change in GDP
1	$\Delta C = \$40$ billion	$40 billion
2	$MPC \times \Delta C = \$20$ billion	$60 billion
3	$MPC \times MPC \times \Delta C = \$10$ billion	$70 billion
4	$MPC \times MPC \times MPC \times \Delta C = \$5$ billion	$75 billion
. . .	. . .	. . .
Total change in GDP	$(1/(1 - MPC)) \times \Delta C - 1/(1 - 0.5) \times \$40$ billion	$80 billion

Eastlandia

Rounds	Incremental change in GDP	Total change in GDP
1	$\Delta C = \$40$ billion	$40 billion
2	$MPC \times \Delta C = \$30$ billion	$70 billion
3	$MPC \times MPC \times \Delta C = \$22.5$ billion	$92.5 billion
4	$MPC \times MPC \times MPC \times \Delta C = \$16.88$ billion	$109.38 billion
. . .	. . .	. . .
Total change in GDP	$(1/(1 - MPC)) \times \Delta C = 1/(1 - 0.75) \times \$40$ billion	$160 billion

The accompanying tables clearly show that the larger the marginal propensity to consume, the larger the size of the multiplier. In Westlandia, with the marginal propensity to consume of 0.5, the multiplier equals 2. In Eastlandia, with the marginal propensity to consume of 0.75, the multiplier equals 4.

7. Assuming that the aggregate price level is constant, the interest rate is fixed, and there are no taxes and no foreign trade, how much will the aggregate demand curve shift and in what direction if the following events occur?

a. An autonomous increase in consumer spending of $25 billion; the marginal propensity to consume is 2/3.

b. Firms reduce investment spending by $40 billion; the marginal propensity to consume is 0.8.

c. The government increases its purchases of military equipment by $60 billion; the marginal propensity to consume is 0.6.

7. a. An autonomous increase in consumer spending of $25 billion, with a marginal propensity to consume of 2/3, will shift the aggregate demand curve to the right by $75 billion.

Total change in real GDP $= (1/(1 - MPC)) \times \Delta C$

Total change in real GDP $= (1/(1 - 2/3)) \times \$25$ billion

Total change in real GDP $= 3 \times \$25$ billion

Total change in real GDP $= \$75$ billion

b. If firms reduce investment spending by $40 billion and the marginal propensity to consume is 0.8, the aggregate demand curve will shift to the left by $200 billion.

Total change in GDP = $(1/(1 - MPC)) \times \Delta I$

Total change in GDP = $(1/(1 - 0.8)) \times (-\$40$ billion$)$

Total change in GDP = $5 \times (-\$40$ billion$)$

Total change in GDP = $-\$200$ billion

c. If government purchases of goods and services rise by $60 billion and the marginal propensity to consume is 0.6, the aggregate demand curve will shift to the right by $150 billion.

Total change in GDP = $(1/(1 - MPC)) \times \Delta G$

Total change in GDP = $(1/(1 - 0.6)) \times \$60$ billion

Total change in GDP = $2.5 \times \$60$ billion

Total change in GDP = $\$150$ billion

8. The economy is at point A in the accompanying diagram. Suppose that the aggregate price level rises from P_1 to P_2. How will aggregate supply adjust in the short run and in the long run to the increase in the aggregate price level?

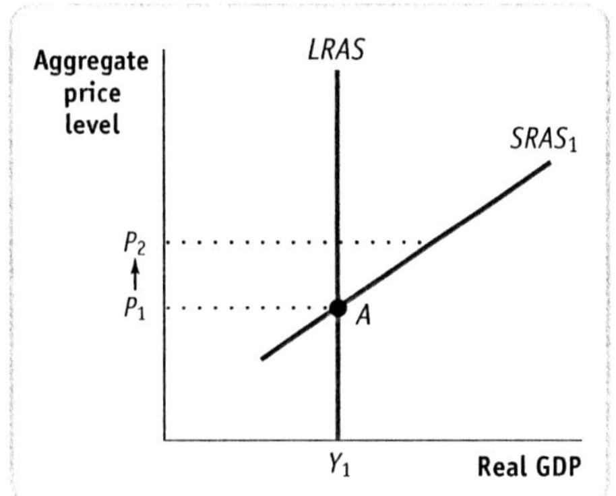

8. In the short run, as the aggregate price level rises from P_1 to P_2, nominal wages will not change. So profit per unit will rise, leading to an increase in production from Y_1 to Y_2. The economy will move from point A to point B in the accompanying diagram. In the long run, however, nominal wages will be renegotiated upward in reaction to low unemployment at Y_2. As nominal wages increase, the short-run aggregate supply curve will shift leftward from $SRAS_1$ to a position such as $SRAS_2$. The exact position of $SRAS_2$ depends on factors such as the aggregate demand curve.

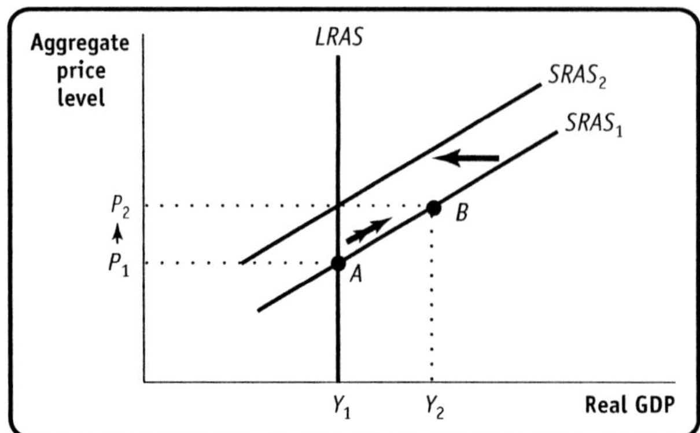

9. Suppose that all households hold all their wealth in assets that automatically rise in value when the aggregate price level rises (an example of this is what is called an "inflation-indexed bond"—a bond whose interest rate, among other things, changes one-for-one with the inflation rate). What happens to the wealth effect of a change in the aggregate price level as a result of this allocation of assets? What happens to the slope of the aggregate demand curve? Will it still slope downward? Explain.

9. If all households hold all their wealth in assets that automatically rise in value when the aggregate price level rises, this will eliminate the wealth effect of a change in the aggregate price level. The purchasing power of consumers' wealth will not vary with a change in the aggregate price level, so there will be no change in consumer spending due to the change in the aggregate price level. The aggregate demand curve will still slope downward because of the interest rate effect of a change in the aggregate price level. As the aggregate price level rises, the purchasing power of households' money holdings will decrease and they will be eager to borrow more and lend less, increasing interest rates. The increase in interest rates will discourage investment spending and consumer spending. The aggregate demand curve will be steeper because the wealth effect of a change in the aggregate price level has been eliminated. As prices rise, the amount of aggregate output demanded will fall by a smaller amount, an amount corresponding to the interest rate effect of a change in the aggregate price level.

10. Suppose that the economy is currently at potential output. Also suppose that you are an economic policy maker and that a college economics student asks you to rank, if possible, your most preferred to least preferred type of shock: positive demand shock, negative demand shock, positive supply shock, negative supply shock. How would you rank them and why?

10. The most preferred shock would be a positive supply shock. The economy would have higher aggregate output without the danger of inflation. The government would not need to respond with a change in policy. The least preferred shock would be a negative supply shock. The economy would experience stagflation. There would be lower aggregate output and inflation. There is no good policy remedy for a negative supply shock: policies to counteract the slump in aggregate output would worsen inflation, and policies to counteract inflation would further depress aggregate output. It is unclear how economic policy makers would rank positive and negative demand shocks. A positive demand shock brings a higher level of aggregate output but at a higher aggregate price level. A negative demand shock brings a lower level of aggregate output but at a lower aggregate price level. With either a positive or negative demand shock, policy makers could try to use either monetary or fiscal policy to lessen the effects of the shock.

11. Explain whether the following government policies affect the aggregate demand curve or the short-run aggregate supply curve and how.

a. The government reduces the minimum nominal wage.

b. The government increases Temporary Assistance to Needy Families (TANF) payments, government transfers to families with dependent children.

c. To reduce the budget deficit, the government announces that households will pay much higher taxes beginning next year.

d. The government reduces military spending.

11. **a.** If the government reduces the minimum nominal wage, it is similar to a fall in nominal wages. Aggregate supply will increase, and the short-run aggregate supply curve will shift to the right.

b. If the government increases TANF, consumer spending will increase because disposable income increases (disposable income equals income plus government transfers, such as TANF payments, less taxes). Aggregate demand will increase, and the aggregate demand curve will shift to the right.

c. If the government announces a large increase in taxes on households for next year, consumer spending will fall this year. Since households base their spending in part on their expectations about the future, the anticipated increase in taxes will lower their spending this year. There will be a decrease in aggregate demand and the aggregate demand curve will shift to the left.

d. If the government reduces military spending, this will decrease aggregate demand. The amount of aggregate output demanded at any given aggregate price level will fall and the aggregate demand curve will shift to the left.

12. In Wageland, all workers sign an annual wage contract each year on January 1. In late January, a new computer operating system is introduced that increases labor productivity dramatically. Explain how Wageland will move from one short-run macroeconomic equilibrium to another. Illustrate with a diagram.

12. As labor productivity increases, producers will experience a reduction in production costs and profit per unit of output will increase. Producers will respond by increasing the quantity of aggregate output supplied at any given aggregate price level. The short-run aggregate supply curve will shift to the right. Beginning at short-run equilibrium, E_1 in the accompanying diagram, the short-run aggregate supply curve will shift from $SRAS_1$ to $SRAS_2$. The aggregate price level will fall, and real GDP will increase in the short run.

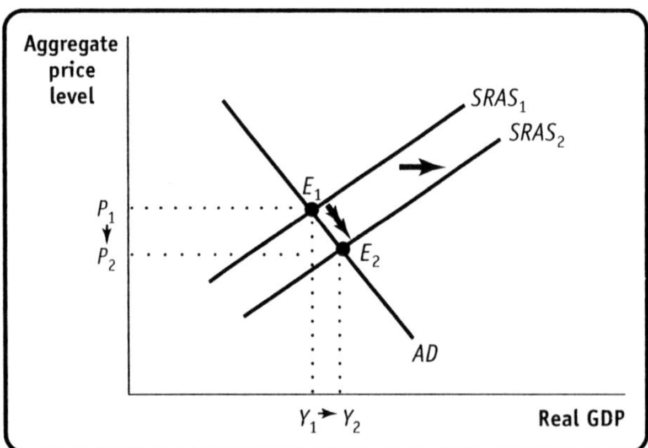

13. Using aggregate demand, short-run aggregate supply, and long-run aggregate supply curves, explain the process by which each of the following economic events will move the economy from one long-run macroeconomic equilibrium to another. Illustrate with diagrams. In each case, what are the short-run and long-run effects on the aggregate price level and aggregate output?

a. There is a decrease in households' wealth due to a decline in the stock market.

b. The government lowers taxes, leaving households with more disposable income, with no corresponding reduction in government purchases.

13. **a.** A decrease in households' wealth will reduce consumer spending. Beginning at long-run macroeconomic equilibrium, E_1 in the accompanying diagram, the aggregate demand curve will shift from AD_1 to AD_2. In the short run, nominal wages are sticky, and the economy will be in short-run macroeconomic equilibrium at point E_2. The aggregate price level will be lower than at E_1, and aggregate output will be lower than potential output. The economy faces a recessionary gap. As wage contracts are renegotiated, nominal wages will fall and the short-run aggregate supply curve will shift gradually to the right over time until it reaches $SRAS_2$ and intersects AD_2 at point E_3. At E_3, the economy is back at its potential output but at a much lower aggregate price level.

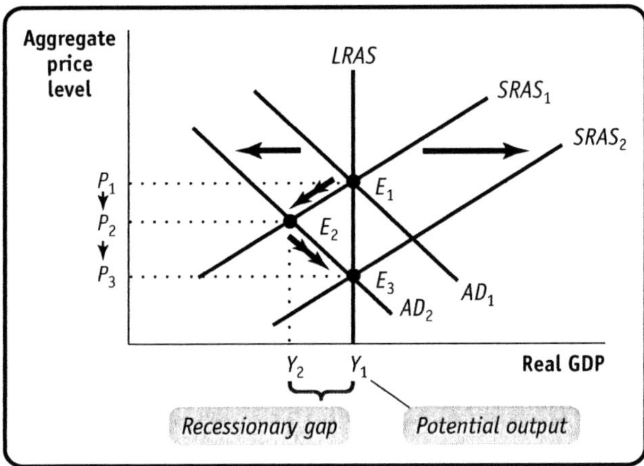

b. An increase in disposable income will increase consumer spending; at any given aggregate price level, the aggregate demand curve will shift to the right. Beginning at long-run macroeconomic equilibrium E_1 in the accompanying diagram, the aggregate demand curve will shift from AD_1 to AD_2. In the short run, nominal wages are sticky, and the economy will be in short-run macroeconomic equilibrium at point E_2. The aggregate price level is higher than at E_1, and aggregate output will be higher than potential output. The economy faces an inflationary gap. As wage contracts are renegotiated, nominal wages will rise and the short-run aggregate supply curve will shift gradually to the left over time until it reaches $SRAS_2$ and intersects AD_2 at point E_3. At E_3, the economy is back at its potential output but at a much higher aggregate price level.

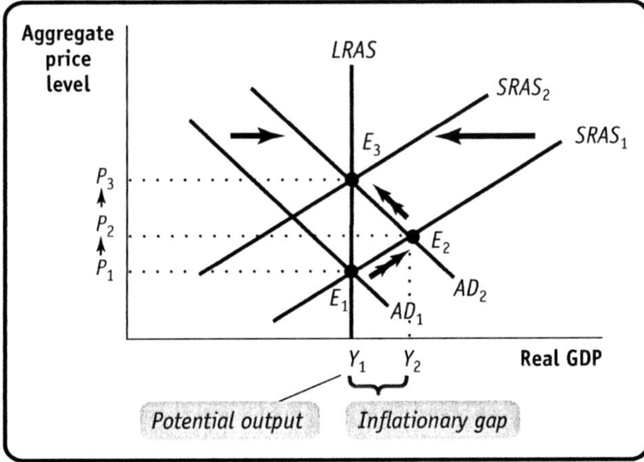

14. Using aggregate demand, short-run aggregate supply, and long-run aggregate supply curves, explain the process by which each of the following government policies will move the economy from one long-run macroeconomic equilibrium to another. Illustrate with diagrams. In each case, what are the short-run and long-run effects on the aggregate price level and aggregate output?

a. There is an increase in taxes on households.

b. There is an increase in the quantity of money.

c. There is an increase in government spending.

14. a. An increase in taxes will decrease consumer spending by households. Beginning at E_1 in the accompanying diagram, the aggregate demand curve will shift left from AD_1 to AD_2. In the short run, nominal wages are sticky, and the economy will be in short-run macroeconomic equilibrium at point E_2. The aggregate price level is lower than at E_1, and aggregate output is lower than potential output. The economy faces a recessionary gap. As wage contracts are renegotiated, nominal wages will fall and the short-run aggregate supply curve will shift gradually to the right over time until it reaches $SRAS_2$ and intersects AD_2 at point E_3. At E_3, the economy is back at its potential output but at a much lower aggregate price level.

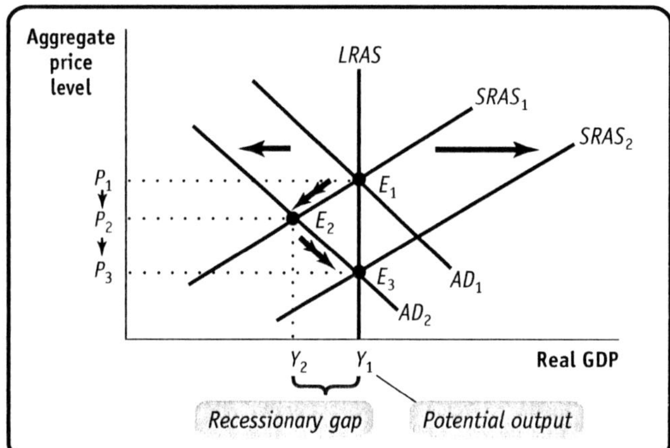

b. An increase in the quantity of money will encourage people to lend, lowering interest rates and increasing investment and consumer spending; at any given aggregate price level, the quantity of aggregate output demanded will be higher. Beginning at long-run macroeconomic equilibrium E_1 in the accompanying diagram, the aggregate demand curve will shift from AD_1 to AD_2. In the short run, nominal wages are sticky, and the economy will be in short-run macroeconomic equilibrium at point E_2. The aggregate price level is higher than at E_1, and aggregate output is higher than potential output. The economy faces an inflationary gap. As wage contracts are renegotiated, nominal wages will rise and the short-run aggregate supply curve will shift gradually to the left over time until it reaches $SRAS_2$ and intersects AD_2 at point E_3. At E_3, the economy is back at its potential output but at a much higher aggregate price level.

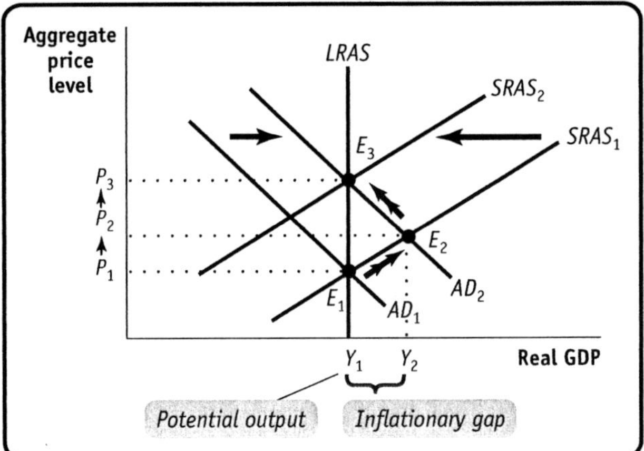

c. An increase in government spending will increase aggregate demand; at any given aggregate price level, the quantity of aggregate output demanded will be higher. Beginning at long-run macroeconomic equilibrium, E_1 in the accompanying diagram, the aggregate demand curve will shift from AD_1 to AD_2. In the short run, nominal wages are sticky, and the economy will be in short-run macroeconomic equilibrium at point E_2. The aggregate price level is higher than at E_1, and aggregate output is higher than potential output. The economy faces an inflationary gap. As wage contracts are renegotiated, nominal wages will rise and the short-run aggregate supply curve will shift gradually to the left over time until it reaches $SRAS_2$ and intersects AD_2 at point E_3. At E_3, the economy is back at its potential output but at a much higher aggregate price level.

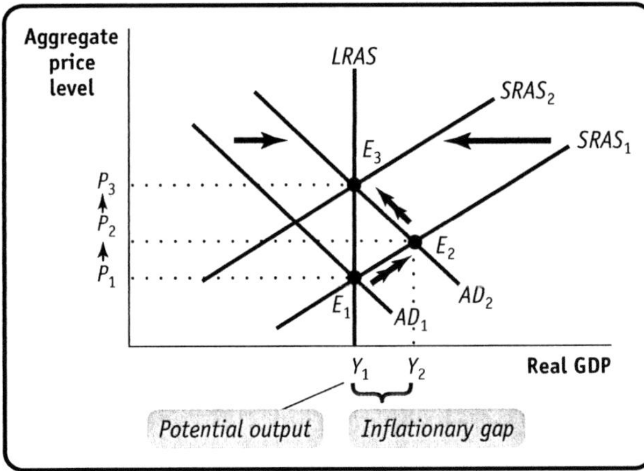

15. The economy is in short-run macroeconomic equilibrium at point E_1 in the accompanying diagram.

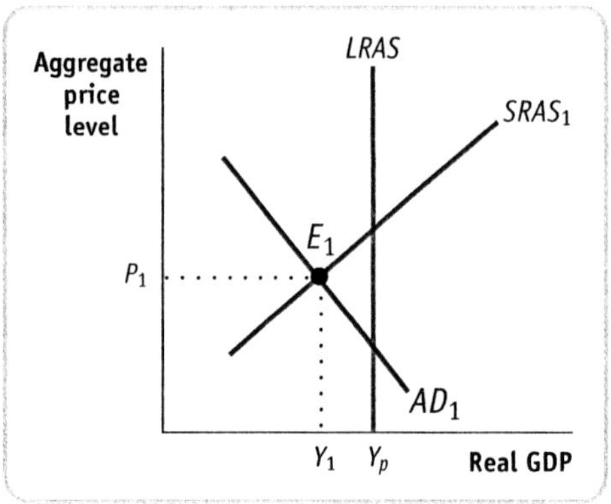

a. Is the economy facing an inflationary or a recessionary gap?

b. What policies can the government implement that might bring the economy back to long-run macroeconomic equilibrium? Illustrate with a diagram.

c. If the government did not intervene to close this gap, would the economy return to long-run macroeconomic equilibrium? Explain and illustrate with a diagram.

d. What are the advantages and disadvantages of the government's implementing policies to close the gap?

15. **a.** The economy is facing a recessionary gap because Y_1 is less than the potential output of the economy, Y_P.

b. The government could use either fiscal policy (increases in government spending or reductions in taxes) or monetary policy (increases in the quantity of money in circulation to reduce the interest rate) to move the aggregate demand curve from AD_1 to AD_2 in the accompanying diagram. This will move the economy back to potential output, and the aggregate price level will rise from P_1 to P_2.

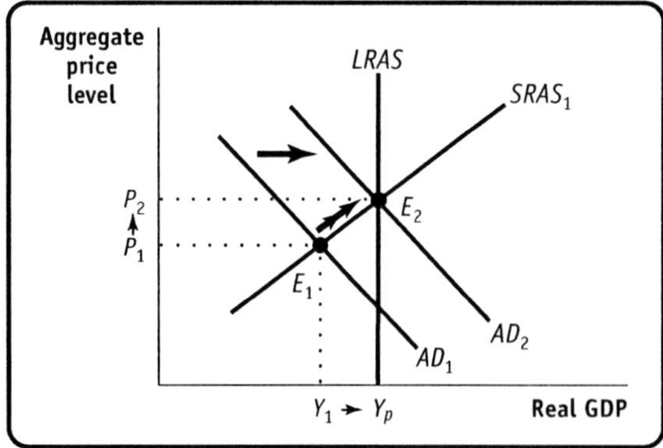

c. If the government did not intervene to close the recessionary gap, the economy would eventually self-correct and move back to potential output on its own. Due to unemployment, nominal wages will fall in the long run. The short-run aggregate supply curve will shift to the right, and eventually it will shift from $SRAS_1$ to $SRAS_2$ in the accompanying diagram. The economy will be back at potential output but at a lower aggregate price level.

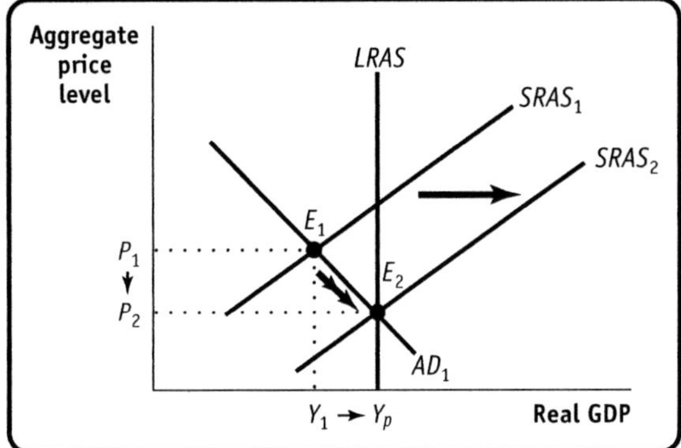

d. If the government implements fiscal or monetary policies to move the economy back to long-run macroeconomic equilibrium, the recessionary gap may be eliminated faster than if the economy were left to adjust on its own. However, because policy makers aren't perfectly informed and policy effects can be unpredictable, policies to close the recessionary gap can lead to greater macronomic instability. Furthermore, if the government uses fiscal or monetary policies, the price level will be higher than it will be if the economy is left to return to long-run macroeconomic equilibrium by itself. In addition, a policy that increases the budget deficit may lead to lower long-run growth through crowding-out.

16. In the accompanying diagram, the economy is in long-run macroeconomic equilibrium at point E_1 when an oil shock shifts the short-run aggregate supply curve to $SRAS_2$.

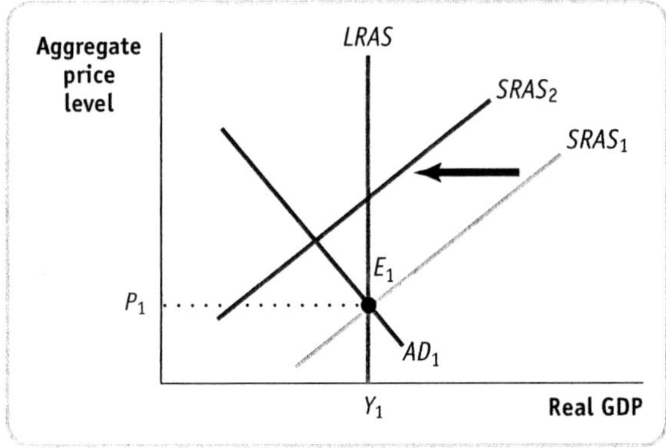

a. How do the aggregate price level and aggregate output change in the short run as a result of the oil shock? What is this phenomenon known as?

b. What fiscal or monetary policies can the government use to address the effects of the supply shock? Use a diagram that shows the effect of policies chosen to address the change in real GDP. Use another diagram to show the effect of policies chosen to address the change in the aggregate price level.

c. Why do supply shocks present a dilemma for government policy makers?

16. **a.** As a result of the increase in the price of oil and the shift to the left of the short-run aggregate supply curve, real GDP decreases to Y_2 (and with it unemployment rises) and the aggregate price level increases to P_2 as shown in the accompanying diagram. This combined problem of inflation and unemployment is known as stagflation.

b. The government can use fiscal and monetary policies to either increase real GDP or lower the aggregate price level, but not both. If the government increases government spending, decreases taxes, or increases the quantity of money in circulation, it can raise real GDP but it will also raise the aggregate price level. This is illustrated in the accompanying diagram by the rightward shift of AD_1 to AD_2.

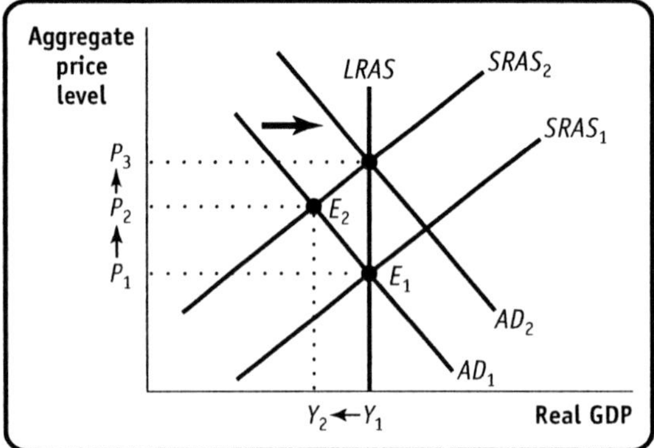

If the government decreases government spending, increases taxes, or decreases the quantity of money in circulation, it can lower the aggregate price level but it will also lower real GDP, worsening the recessionary gap. This is illustrated in the accompanying diagram by the leftward shift of AD_1 to AD_3.

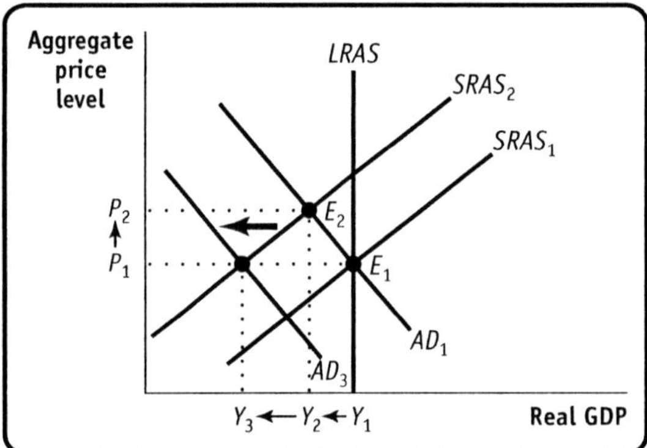

c. The government cannot use fiscal and monetary policies to correct for the lower real GDP and higher aggregate price level simultaneously. It can only use policies to alleviate one problem but at the expense of making the other worse.

17. The late 1990s in the United States were characterized by substantial economic growth with low inflation; that is, real GDP increased with little, if any, increase in the aggregate price level. Explain this experience using aggregate demand and aggregate supply curves. Illustrate with a diagram.

17. Increases in both long-run and short-run aggregate supply, along with increases in aggregate demand, can explain how real GDP grew with little if any increase in the aggregate price level. The accompanying diagram shows how the economy could move from one long-run macroeconomic equilibrium, point E_1, to another, point E_2, with an increase in real GDP and no increase in the aggregate price level. This may explain the U.S. experience during the late 1990s. During this time, increases in productivity due to increasing use of information technology may have shifted the long-run and short-run aggregate supply curves; simultaneously, increases in stock values may have led to increases in consumer spending and a shift to the right of the aggregate demand curve.

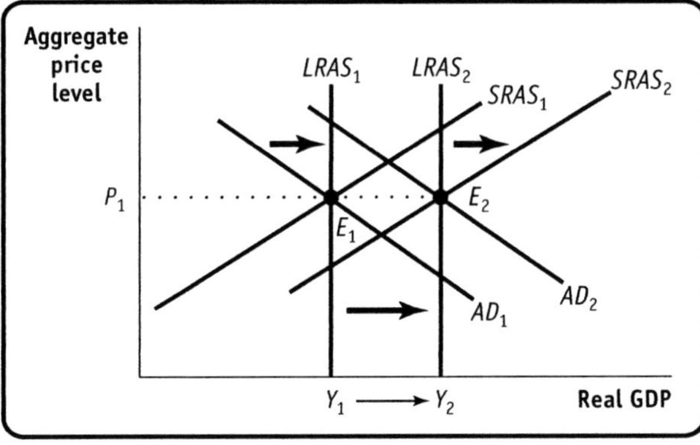

Income and Expenditure

1. Economists observed the only five residents of a very small economy and estimated each one's consumer spending at various levels of current disposable income. The accompanying table shows each resident's consumer spending at three income levels.

Individual consumer spending by	Individual current disposable income		
	$0	**$20,000**	**$40,000**
Andre	$1,000	$15,000	$29,000
Barbara	2,500	12,500	22,500
Casey	2,000	20,000	38,000
Declan	5,000	17,000	29,000
Elena	4,000	19,000	34,000

a. What is each resident's consumption function? What is the marginal propensity to consume for each resident?

b. What is the economy's aggregate consumption function? What is the marginal propensity to consume for the economy?

1. a. To determine autonomous consumer spending for each resident (the vertical intercept of his or her consumption function), we can look at each one's consumer spending when disposable income is zero. To calculate each resident's marginal propensity to consume (the slope of his or her consumption function), we can calculate the change in consumer spending when there is a change in disposable income. For example, Andre's marginal propensity to consume is equal to ($29,000 − $15,000)/($40,000 − $20,000) = 0.70.

	Autonomous consumption (a)	Marginal propensity to consume (MPC)	Consumption function (c)
Andre	$1,000	0.70	$1,000 + 0.70 \times yd$
Barbara	2,500	0.50	$2,500 + 0.50 \times yd$
Casey	2,000	0.90	$2,000 + 0.90 \times yd$
Declan	5,000	0.60	$5,000 + 0.60 \times yd$
Elena	4,000	0.75	$4,000 + 0.75 \times yd$

b. To find the economy's consumption function, we calculate total consumer spending at total disposable income:

- When each resident earns $0 in disposable income, total consumer spending is $14,500.

- When each resident earns $20,000 in disposable income, total disposable income is $100,000 and total consumer spending is $83,500.

- When each resident earns $40,000 in disposable income, total disposable income is $200,000 and total consumer spending is $152,500.

Total autonomous consumer spending is $14,500, and the marginal propensity to consume is 0.69 [= ($83,500 − $14,500)/($100,000 − $0)]. The aggregate consumption function is:

$$C = \$14,500 + 0.69 \times YD$$

2. From 2000 to 2005, Eastlandia experienced large fluctuations in both aggregate consumer spending and disposable income, but wealth, the interest rate, and expected future disposable income did not change. The accompanying table shows the level of aggregate consumer spending and disposable income in millions of dollars for each of these years. Use this information to answer the following questions.

Year	Disposable income (millions of dollars)	Consumer spending (millions of dollars)
2000	$100	$180
2001	350	380
2002	300	340
2003	400	420
2004	375	400
2005	500	500

a. Plot the aggregate consumption function for Eastlandia.

b. What is the aggregate consumption function?

c. What is the marginal propensity to consume? What is the marginal propensity to save?

2. a. The accompanying diagram shows the aggregate consumption function for Eastlandia.

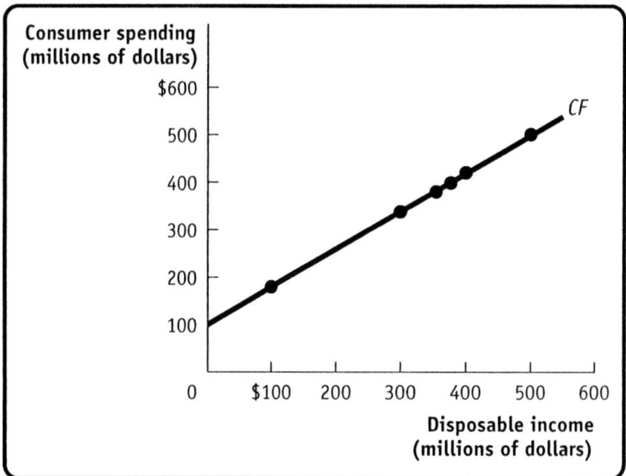

b. $C = \$100$ million $+ 0.8\ YD$

c. The marginal propensity to consume is 0.8, and the marginal propensity to save is 0.2.

3. How will each of the following actions affect the aggregate consumption function? Explain whether the event will result in a movement along or a shift of the aggregate consumption function and in which direction.

a. The government grants an unexpected and one-time tax cut to all households.

b. The government announces permanently higher tax rates beginning next year.

c. The Social Security Administration raises the age at which workers who are currently younger than 65 can qualify for Social Security benefits from age 65 to age 75.

3. **a.** If the government grants an unexpected and one-time tax cut, both disposable income and consumer spending will increase. It would be shown as a movement up and along the aggregate consumption function.

    b. If the government announces higher tax rates beginning next year, it represents a decrease in expected future disposable income. The aggregate consumption function will shift downward.

    c. If the government raises the age at which workers qualify for Social Security benefits from age 65 to 75, this can be seen as either a decrease in expected future disposable income (one source of expected future disposable income, Social Security benefits, will be delayed for 10 years) or a decrease in wealth (a decrease in the value of retirement benefits). In either case, the aggregate consumption function will shift downward.

4. From the end of 1995 to March 2000, the Standard and Poor's 500 (S&P 500) stock index, a broad measure of stock market prices, rose almost 150%, from 615.93 to a high of 1,527.46. From that time to September 10, 2001, the index fell 28.5% to 1,092.54. How do you think the movements in the stock index influenced both the growth in real GDP in the late 1990s and the concern about maintaining consumer spending after the terrorist attacks on September 11, 2001?

4. As the S&P 500 rose almost 150% from the end of 1995 to March 2000, stockholders experienced a large increase in the value of their wealth held in stocks. This increased consumer spending in the economy dramatically and added to the strong economic growth of the late 1990s. However, as the stock index fell 28.5% from its peak in March 2000 to the day before the terrorist attacks, other things equal, consumer spending should have fallen as stockholders' wealth decreased. There was great concern that the terrorist attacks would reduce consumer spending and worsen the recession that had begun earlier in 2001.

5. How will the interest rate and planned investment spending change as the following events occur?

    a. An increase in the quantity of money by the Federal Reserve increases the amount of money that people wish to lend at any interest rate.

    b. The U.S. Environmental Protection Agency decrees that corporations must adopt new technology that reduces their emissions of sulfur dioxide.

    c. Baby boomers begin to retire in large numbers and reduce their savings.

5. **a.** This results in an increase in the supply of loanable funds, a rightward shift of the supply curve for loanable funds, and a decrease in the interest rate. The lower interest rate leads to a rise in planned investment spending.

    b. Firms will need to replace older machinery with newer, less polluting, machinery. This will increase planned investment spending. As a result of this increase in the demand for loanable funds, the interest rate rises.

    c. As baby boomers begin to retire in large numbers and reduce their savings, there will be a decrease in the supply of loanable funds. The supply curve of loanable funds shifts leftward, the interest rate rises, and planned investment spending falls.

6. Explain how each of the following actions will affect the level of planned investment spending and unplanned inventory investment. Assume the economy is initially in income-expenditure equilibrium.

a. The Federal Reserve raises the interest rate.

b. There is a rise in the expected growth rate of real GDP.

c. A sizable inflow of foreign funds into the country lowers the interest rate.

6. a. A rise in the interest rate reduces planned investment spending. Planned aggregate spending will now be less than GDP, and inventories will accumulate. Hence unplanned inventory investment will be positive.

b. A rise in the expected growth rate of real GDP leads firms to increase their planned investment spending. Planned aggregate spending will now exceed GDP. Sales will exceed firms' expectations, firms will draw down inventories unexpectedly, and unplanned inventory investment will be negative.

c. A fall in the interest rate leads to an increase in planned investment spending. Planned aggregate spending will now exceed GDP. Sales will exceed firms' expectations, firms will draw down inventories unexpectedly, and unplanned inventory investment will be negative.

7. The accompanying table shows gross domestic product (GDP), disposable income (YD), consumer spending (C), and planned investment spending ($I_{Planned}$) in an economy. Assume there is no government or foreign sector in this economy. Complete the table by calculating planned aggregate spending ($AE_{Planned}$) and unplanned inventory investment ($I_{Unplanned}$).

GDP	YD	C	$I_{Planned}$	$AE_{Planned}$	$I_{Unplanned}$
		(billions of dollars)			
$0	$0	$100	$300	?	?
400	400	400	300	?	?
800	800	700	300	?	?
1,200	1,200	1,000	300	?	?
1,600	1,600	1,300	300	?	?
2,000	2,000	1,600	300	?	?
2,400	2,400	1,900	300	?	?
2,800	2,800	2,200	300	?	?
3,200	3,200	2,500	300	?	?

a. What is the aggregate consumption function?

b. What is Y*, income-expenditure equilibrium GDP?

c. What is the value of the multiplier?

d. If planned investment spending falls to $200 billion, what will be the new Y*?

e. If autonomous consumer spending rises to $200 billion, what will be the new Y*?

7.

GDP	YD	C	$I_{Planned}$	$AE_{Planned}$	$I_{Unplanned}$
			(billions of dollars)		
$0	$0	$100	$300	$400	−$400
400	400	400	300	700	−300
800	800	700	300	1,000	−200
1,200	1,200	1,000	300	1,300	−100
1,600	1,600	1,300	300	1,600	0
2,000	2,000	1,600	300	1,900	100
2,400	2,400	1,900	300	2,200	200
2,800	2,800	2,200	300	2,500	300
3,200	3,200	2,500	300	2,800	400

a. We can find the aggregate consumption function by calculating aggregate autonomous consumer spending and the marginal propensity to consume. Aggregate autonomous consumer spending equals aggregate consumer spending when disposable income is zero; in this case, aggregate autonomous consumer spending is $100 billion. The marginal propensity to consume is the change in aggregate consumer spending divided by the change in disposable income; in this case, it is 0.75 [= ($400 − $100)/($400 − $0)]. The aggregate consumption function is

$$C = \$100 \text{ billion} + 0.75 \times YD$$

b. Y^* is the level of GDP at which aggregate planned spending equals GDP. From the accompanying table, Y^* is $1,600 billion.

c. The multiplier equals $1/(1 − MPC)$; the value of the multiplier is $4 = 1/(1 − 0.75)$.

d. If planned investment spending falls to $200 billion, the new Y^* will equal $1,200 billion. If planned investment spending equals $200 billion, it has fallen by $100 billion. Since the multiplier is 4, Y^* will change by four times the change in planned investment spending, or decrease by $400 billion.

e. If autonomous consumer spending rises to $200 billion, the new Y^* will equal $2,000 billion. If autonomous consumer spending equals $200 billion, it has risen by $100 billion. Since the multiplier is 4, Y^* will change by four times the change in autonomous consumer spending, or increase by $400 billion.

8. In an economy with no government and no foreign sectors, autonomous consumer spending is $250 billion, planned investment spending is $350 billion, and the marginal propensity to consume is 2/3.

a. Plot the aggregate consumption function and planned aggregate spending.

b. What is unplanned inventory investment when real GDP equals $600 billion?

c. What is Y^*, income–expenditure equilibrium GDP?

d. What is the value of the multiplier?

e. If planned investment spending rises to $450 billion, what will be the new Y^*?

8. **a.** If autonomous consumer spending is $250 billion and the marginal propensity to consume is $\frac{2}{3}$, the aggregate consumption function is

$$C = \$250 \text{ billion} + \frac{2}{3} \times YD$$

Planned aggregate spending equals consumer spending plus planned investment spending:

$$AE_{Planned} = C + I_{Planned}$$
$$AE_{Planned} = (\$250 \text{ billion} + \tfrac{2}{3} \times YD) + \$350 \text{ billion}$$
$$AE_{Planned} = \$600 \text{ billion} + \tfrac{2}{3} \times YD$$

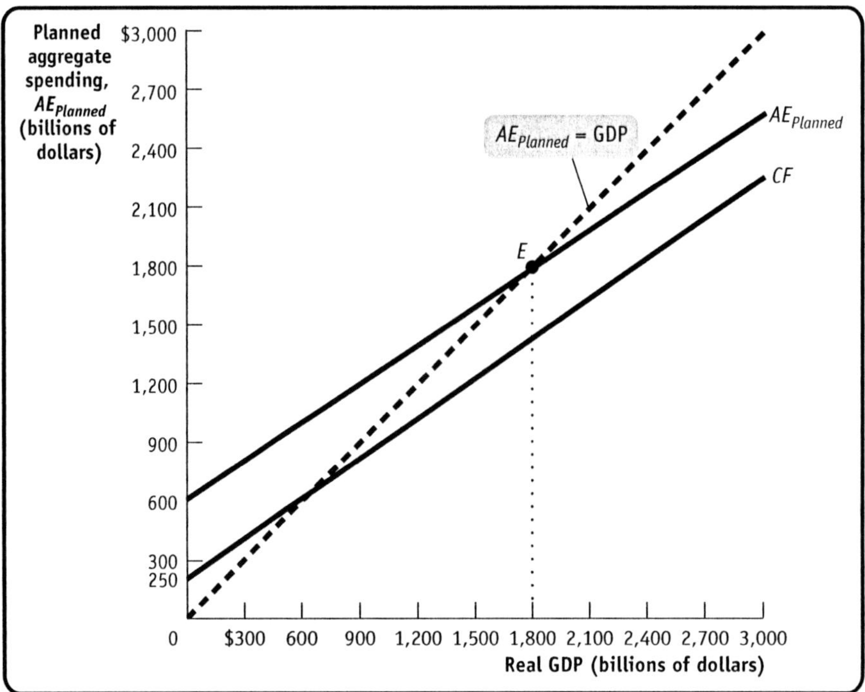

b. When GDP equals $600 billion, planned aggregate spending is $1,000 billion [= $600 billion + $\frac{2}{3}$ × $600 billion]. Unplanned inventory investment equals real GDP minus planned aggregate spending, or –$400 billion.

c. Y^* occurs where real GDP equals aggregate planned spending. From the accompanying diagram, we can see that this occurs at GDP equal to $1,800 billion.

d. The value of the multiplier is 3 [= $1/(1 - \frac{2}{3})$].

e. If planned investment spending rises to $450 billion, that will be an increase of $100 billion in planned investment spending. Given a multiplier of 3, Y^* will rise by $300 billion to $2,100 billion.

9. An economy has a marginal propensity to consume of 0.5 and Y^*, income-expenditure equilibrium GDP, equals $500 billion. Given an autonomous increase in planned investment of $10 billion, show the rounds of increased spending that take place by completing the accompanying table. The first and second rows are filled in for you. In the first row, the increase of planned investment spending of $10 billion raises real GDP and YD by $10 billion, leading to an increase in consumer spending of $5 billion ($MPC \times$ change in disposable income) in row 2.

Rounds	Change in $I_{Planned}$ or C	Change in real GDP	Change in YD
		(billions of dollars)	
1	$\Delta I_{Planned} = \$10.00$	$10.00	$10.00
2	$\Delta C = \$ 5.00$	$ 5.00	$ 5.00
3	$\Delta C = ?$	?	?
4	$\Delta C = ?$	?	?
5	$\Delta C = ?$	?	?
6	$\Delta C = ?$	?	?
7	$\Delta C = ?$	?	?
8	$\Delta C = ?$	?	?
9	$\Delta C = ?$	?	?
10	$\Delta C = ?$	?	?

a. What is the total change in real GDP after the 10 rounds? What is the value of the multiplier? What would you expect the total change in Y^* to be based on the multiplier formula? How do your answers to the first and third qestions compare?

b. Redo the table, assuming the marginal propensity to consume is 0.75. What is the total change in real GDP after 10 rounds? What is the value of the multiplier? As the marginal propensity to consume increases, what happens to the value of the multiplier?

9.

Rounds	Change in $I_{Planned}$ or C	Change in GDP	Change in YD
		(billions of dollars)	
1	$\Delta I_{Planned} = \$10.00$	$10.00	$10.00
2	$\Delta C = \$ 5.00$	5.00	5.00
3	$\Delta C = \$ 2.50$	2.50	2.50
4	$\Delta C = \$ 1.25$	1.25	1.25
5	$\Delta C = \$ 0.63$	0.63	0.63
6	$\Delta C = \$ 0.31$	0.31	0.31
7	$\Delta C = \$ 0.16$	0.16	0.16
8	$\Delta C = \$ 0.08$	0.08	0.08
9	$\Delta C = \$ 0.04$	0.04	0.04
10	$\Delta C = \$ 0.02$	0.02	0.02

a. The total change in GDP after the 10 rounds is $19.98 billion. The multiplier is 2 $[= (1/(1 - 0.5)]$. We would expect the total change in Y^* to be twice the change in planned investment spending. Since the autonomous change in planned investment spending was $10 billion, we would expect a change in Y^* of $20 billion. This is very similar to the change in GDP after 10 rounds ($19.98 billion).

Rounds	Change in $I_{Planned}$ or C	Change in real GDP (billions of dollars)	Change in YD
1	$\Delta I_{Planned} = \$10.00$	$10.00	$10.00
2	$\Delta C = \$\ 7.50$	7.50	7.50
3	$\Delta C = \$\ 5.63$	5.63	5.63
4	$\Delta C = \$\ 4.22$	4.22	4.22
5	$\Delta C = \$\ 3.16$	3.16	3.16
6	$\Delta C = \$\ 2.37$	2.37	2.37
7	$\Delta C = \$\ 1.78$	1.78	1.78
8	$\Delta C = \$\ 1.33$	1.33	1.33
9	$\Delta C = \$\ 1.00$	1.00	1.00
10	$\Delta C = \$\ 0.75$	0.75	0.75

b. The total change in GDP after 10 rounds is \$37.74 billion. The value of the multiplier is 4. As the marginal propensity to consume increases, so does the value of the multiplier.

10. Although the U.S. is one of the richest nations in the world, it is also the world's largest debtor nation. We often hear that the problem is the nation's low savings rate. Suppose policy makers attempt to rectify this by encouraging greater savings in the economy. What effect will their successful attempts have on real GDP?

10. If policy makers successfully encouraged greater savings, there would be a decrease in either consumer spending or planned investment spending. A drop in C or in $I_{Planned}$ would decrease the income–expenditure equilibrium GDP by several times the change in spending. This is the Paradox of Thrift. If households and producers decrease spending to reduce the nation's debt, these actions will depress the economy, leaving households and producers worse off than they were with the nation's large debt.

Deriving the Multiplier Algebraically

1. In an economy without government purchases, transfers, or taxes, aggregate autonomous consumer spending is \$500 billion, planned investment spending is \$250 billion, and the marginal propensity to consume is 0.5.

    a. Write the expression for planned aggregate spending as in Equation 11A-1.

    b. Solve for Y* algebraically.

    c. What is the value of the multiplier?

    d. How will Y* change if autonomous consumer spending falls to \$450 billion?

1. **a.** In an economy without government purchases, planned aggregate spending equals the aggregate consumption function plus planned investment spending:

$$AE_{Planned} = C + I_{Planned}$$
$$AE_{Planned} = \$500 \text{ billion} + 0.5 \times YD + \$250 \text{ billion}$$

    b. In an economy without taxes or government transfers, GDP equals disposable income. The economy will be in income–expenditure equilibrium when GDP equals planned aggregate spending:

$$Y^* = \$750 \text{ billion} + 0.5 \times Y^*$$
$$0.5 \times Y^* = \$750 \text{ billion}$$
$$Y^* = \$1,500 \text{ billion}$$

    c. The value of the multiplier is 2 $[= 1/(1 - 0.5)]$.

    d. If autonomous consumer spending falls to \$450 billion, it will have decreased by \$50 billion. Given a multiplier of 2, Y* will fall by \$100 billion when autonomous consumer spending falls by \$50 billion. The new Y* equals \$1,400 billion.

2. Complete the following table by calculating the value of the multiplier and identifiying the change in Y* due to the change in autonomous spending. How does the value of the multiplier change with the marginal propensity to consume?

MPC	Value of multiplier	Change in spending	Change in Y*
0.5	?	ΔC = + \$50 million	?
0.6	?	ΔI = − \$10 million	?
0.75	?	ΔC = − \$25 million	?
0.8	?	ΔI = + \$20 million	?
0.9	?	ΔC = − \$2.5 million	?

2. The value of the multiplier increases with an increase in the marginal propensity to consume.

MPC	Value of multiplier	Change in spending	Change in Y*
0.50	2 $(= 1/(1 - 0.5))$	ΔC = + \$50 million	+ \$100 million
0.60	2.5 $(= 1/(1 - 0.6))$	ΔI = − \$10 million	− \$25 million
0.75	4 $(= 1/(1 - 0.75))$	ΔC = − \$25 million	− \$100 million
0.80	5 $(= 1/(1 - 0.8))$	ΔI = + \$20 million	+ \$100 million
0.90	10 $(= 1/(1 - 0.9))$	ΔC = − \$2.5 million	− \$25 million

Fiscal Policy

1. The accompanying diagram shows the current macroeconomic situation for the economy of Albernia. You have been hired as an economic consultant to help the economy move to potential output, Y_P.

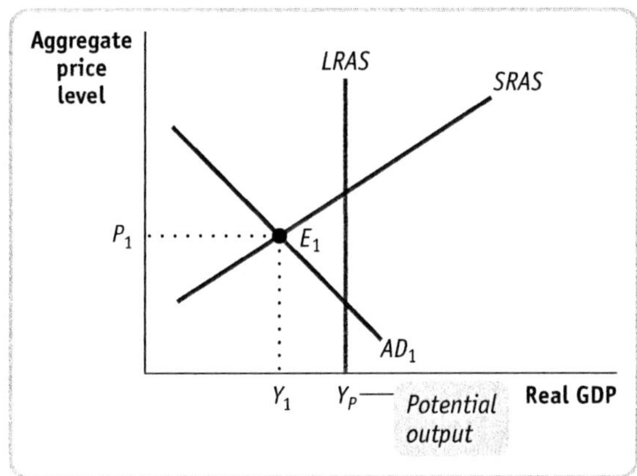

a. Is Albernia facing a recessionary or inflationary gap?

b. Which type of fiscal policy—expansionary or contractionary—would move the economy of Albernia to potential output, Y_E? What are some examples of such policies?

c. Illustrate the macroeconomic situation in Albernia with a diagram after the successful fiscal policy has been implemented.

1. a. Albernia is facing a recessionary gap; Y_1 is less than Y_P.

b. Albernia could use expansionary fiscal policies to move the economy to potential output. Such policies include increasing government purchases of goods and services, increasing government transfers, and reducing taxes.

c.

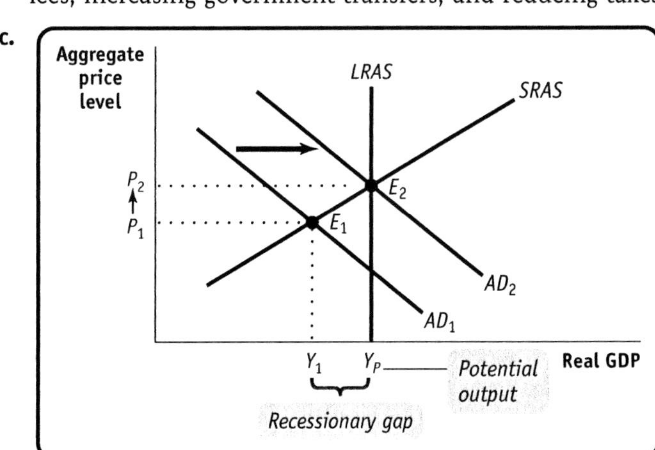

2. The accompanying diagram shows the current macroeconomic situation for the economy of Brittania; real GDP is Y_1 and the aggregate price level is P_1. You have been hired as an economic consultant to help the economy move to potential output, Y_P.

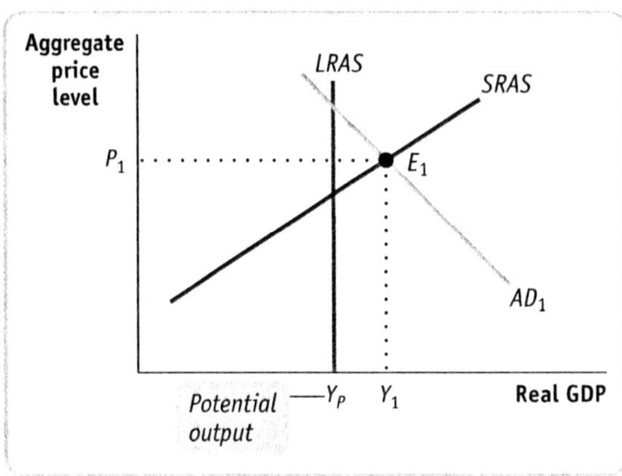

a. Is Brittania facing a recessionary or inflationary gap?

b. Which type of fiscal policy—expansionary or contractionary—would move the economy of Brittania to potential output, Y_P? What are some examples of such policies?

c. Illustrate the macroeconomic situation in Brittania with a diagram after the successful fiscal policy has been implemented.

2. **a.** Brittania is facing an inflationary gap; Y_1 is greater than Y_P.

b. Brittania could use contractionary fiscal policies to move the economy to potential output. Such policies include reducing government purchases of goods and services, lowering government transfers, and raising taxes.

c.

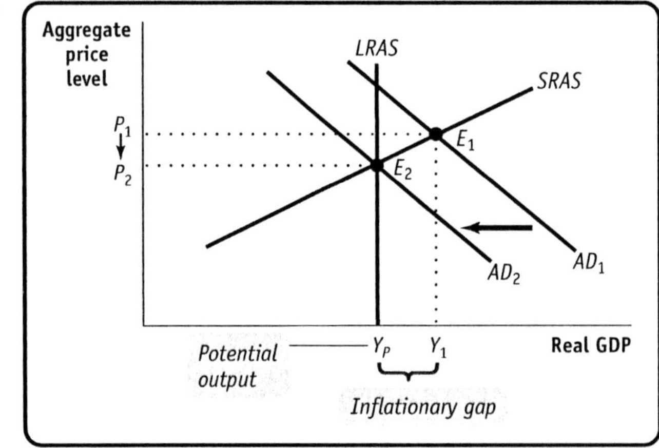

3. An economy is in long-run macroeconomic equilibrium when each of the following aggregate demand shocks occurs. What kind of gap—inflationary or recessionary—will the economy face after the shock, and what type of fiscal policies would help move the economy back to potential output?

a. A stock market boom increases the value of stocks held by households.

b. Firms come to believe that a recession in the near future is likely.

c. Anticipating the possibility of war, the government increases its purchases of military equipment.

d. The quantity of money in the economy declines and interest rates increase.

3.

a. As the stock market booms and the value of stocks held by households increases, there will be an increase in consumer spending; this will shift the aggregate demand curve to the right. The economy will face an inflationary gap. Policy makers could use contractionary fiscal policies to move the economy back to potential output.

b. If firms become concerned about a recession in the near future, they will decrease investment spending and aggregate demand will shift to the left. The economy will face a recessionary gap. Policy makers could use expansionary fiscal policies to move the economy back to potential output.

c. If the government increases its purchases of military equipment, the aggregate demand curve will shift to the right. The economy will face an inflationary gap. Policy makers could use contractionary fiscal policies to move the economy back to potential output. The government would need to reduce its purchases of nondefense goods and services, raise taxes or reduce transfers.

d. As interest rates rise, investment spending will decrease and the aggregate demand curve will shift to the left. The economy will face a recessionary gap. Policy makers could use expansionary fiscal policies to move the economy back to potential output.

4. Show why a $10 billion decrease in government purchases will have a larger effect on real GDP than a $10 billion reduction in government transfers by completing the table at the top of page 317 for an economy with a marginal propensity to consume (MPC) of 0.6. The first and second rows of the table are filled in for you: in the first row, the $10 billion decrease in government purchases decreases real GDP and disposable income, YD, by $10 billion, leading to a decrease in consumer spending of $6 billion ($MPC \times$ change in disposable income) in row 2. However, the $10 billion reduction in transfers has no effect on real GDP in round 1 but does lower YD by $10 billion, resulting in a decrease in consumer spending of $6 billion in round 2.

| | Decrease in G = −$10 billion | | | Decrease in TR = −$10 billion | | |
| | Billions of dollars | | | Billions of dollars | | |
Rounds	Change in G	Change in real GDP	Change in YD	Change in TR	Change in real GDP	Change in YD
1	ΔG = −$10.00	−$10.00	−$10.00	ΔTR = −$10.00	$0.00	−$10.00
2	ΔC = 6.00	−6.00	−6.00	ΔC = −6.00	−6.00	−6.00
3	ΔC = ?	?	?	ΔC = ?	?	?
4	ΔC = ?	?	?	ΔC = ?	?	?
5	ΔC = ?	?	?	ΔC = ?	?	?
6	ΔC = ?	?	?	ΔC = ?	?	?
7	ΔC = ?	?	?	ΔC = ?	?	?
8	ΔC = ?	?	?	ΔC = ?	?	?
9	ΔC = ?	?	?	ΔC = ?	?	?
10	ΔC = ?	?	?	ΔC = ?	?	?

a. When government purchases decrease by $10 billion, what is the sum of the changes in real GDP after the 10 rounds?

b. When the government reduces transfers by $10 billion, what is the sum of the changes in real GDP after the 10 rounds?

c. Using the formula for the multiplier for changes in government purchases and for changes in transfers, calculate the total change in real GDP due to the $10 billion decrease in government purchases and the $10 billion reduction in transfers. What explains the difference?

4. Here is the completed table:

	Decrease in G = -$10 billion billions of dollars			Decrease in TR = -$10 billion billions of dollars		
Rounds	**Change in G**	**Change in real GDP**	**Change in YD**	**Change in TR**	**Change in real GDP**	**Change in YD**
1	ΔG = -$10.00	-$10.00	-$10.00	ΔTR = -$10.00	$0.00	-$10.00
2	ΔC = -6.00	-6.00	-6.00	ΔC = -6.00	-6.00	-6.00
3	ΔC = -3.60	-3.60	-3.60	ΔC = -3.60	-3.60	-3.60
4	ΔC = -2.16	-2.16	-2.16	ΔC = -2.16	-2.16	-2.16
5	ΔC = -1.30	-1.30	-1.30	ΔC = -1.30	-1.30	-1.30
6	ΔC = -0.78	-0.78	-0.78	ΔC = -0.78	-0.78	-0.78
7	ΔC = -0.47	-0.47	-0.47	ΔC = -0.47	-0.47	-0.47
8	ΔC = -0.28	-0.28	-0.28	ΔC = -0.28	-0.28	-0.28
9	ΔC = -0.17	-0.17	-0.17	ΔC = -0.17	-0.17	-0.17
10	ΔC = -0.10	-0.10	-0.10	ΔC = -0.10	-0.10	-0.10
. . . .						
Sum for 10 rounds		-$24.86			-$14.86	

a. When government purchases decrease by $10 billion, the change in real GDP is -$24.86 billion after 10 rounds.

b. When transfers fall by $10 billion, the change in real GDP is -$14.86 billion after 10 rounds.

c. When the government decreases purchases by $10 billion, the total change in real GDP is -$25 billion $[(1/(1 - 0.6)) \times (-\$10 \text{ billion})]$. When transfers fall by $10 billion, the total change in real GDP is -$15 billion $[(-0.6/(1 - 0.6)) \times \$10 \text{ billion}]$. The difference is that the $10 billion fall in transfers does not directly affect real GDP. All rounds except the first are the same in the table for a decrease in government purchases and reduction in transfers; however, in the first round, real GDP falls by the same amount that government purchases declined but real GDP is initially unaffected when transfers fall by that amount.

5. In each of the following cases, either a recessionary or inflationary gap exists. Assume that the aggregate supply curve is horizontal so that the change in real GDP arising from a shift of the aggregate demand curve equals the size of the shift of the curve. Calculate both the change in government purchases of goods and services and the change in government transfers necessary to close the gap.

a. Real GDP equals $100 billion, potential output equals $160 billion, and the marginal propensity to consume is 0.75.

b. Real GDP equals $250 billion, potential output equals $200 billion, and the marginal propensity to consume is 0.5.

c. Real GDP equals $180 billion, potential output equals $100 billion, and the marginal propensity to consume is 0.8.

5. **a.** The economy is facing a recessionary gap; real GDP is less than potential output. Since the multiplier for a change in government purchases of goods and services is $1/(1 - 0.75) = 4$, an increase in government purchases of $15 billion will increase real GDP by $60 billion and close the recessionary gap. Each dollar of a transfer increase will increase real GDP by $MPC/(1 - MPC)$, or $0.75/(1 - 0.75) = 3. Since real GDP needs to increase by $60 billion, the government should increase transfers by $20 billion to close the recessionary gap.

b. The economy is facing an inflationary gap; real GDP is higher than potential output. Since the multiplier for a change in government purchases of goods and services is $1/(1 - 0.5) = 2, a decrease in government purchases of $25 billion will reduce real GDP by $50 billion and close the inflationary gap. Each dollar of a transfer reduction will decrease real GDP by $MPC/(1 - MPC)$, or $0.5/(1 - 0.5) = 1. Since real GDP needs to decrease by $50 billion, the government should increase transfers by $50 billion to close the inflationary gap.

c. The economy is facing an inflationary gap; real GDP is higher than potential output. Since the multiplier for a change in government purchases of goods and services is $1/(1 - 0.8) = 5$, a decrease in government purchases of $16 billion will reduce real GDP by $80 billion and close the inflationary gap. Each dollar of a transfer reduction will reduce real GDP by $MPC/(1 - MPC)$, or $0.8/(1 - 0.8) = 4. Since real GDP needs to decrease by $80 billion, the government should reduce transfer payments by $20 billion to close the inflationary gap.

6. Most macroeconomists believe it is a good thing that taxes act as automatic stabilizers and lower the size of the multiplier. However, a smaller multiplier means that the change in government purchases of goods and services, government transfers, or taxes necessary to close an inflationary or recessionary gap is larger. How can you explain this apparent inconsistency?

6. Automatic stabilizers, such as taxes, help to dampen the business cycle. As the economy expands, taxes increase; this increase acts as a contractionary fiscal policy. In this way any autonomous change in aggregate spending will have a smaller effect on real GDP than it would in the absence of taxes and result in a smaller inflationary or recessionary gap. Consequently, the need for discretionary fiscal policy is reduced. However, if a demand shock does occur and the government decides to use discretionary fiscal policy to help eliminate it, the smaller multiplier means that the change in government purchases of goods and services, government transfers, or taxes necessary to close the gap is larger.

7. The accompanying table shows how consumers' marginal propensities to consume in a particular economy are related to their level of income:

Income range	Marginal propensity to consume
$0–$20,000	0.9
$20,001–$40,000	0.8
$40,001–$60,000	0.7
$60,001–$80,000	0.6
Above $80,000	0.5

a. What is the "bang for the buck" in terms of the increase in real GDP for an additional $1 of income for consumers in each income range?

b. If the government needed to close a recessionary or inflationary gap, what types of fiscal policies would you recommend to close the gap with the smallest change in either government purchases of goods and services or taxes?

7. a. The accompanying table shows the "bang for the buck" for an additional $1 of income for a consumer in each income range. It is calculated as $1/(1 - MPC)$.

Income range	Marginal propensity to consume	"Bang for the buck"
$0–$20,000	0.9	10
$20,001–$40,000	0.8	5
$40,001–$60,000	0.7	3.33
$60,001–$80,000	0.6	2.5
Above $80,000	0.5	2

b. Since the "bang for the buck" is highest for the lowest income group, fiscal policies aimed at that income group would require the smallest change in government purchases of goods and services or the smallest change in taxes or transfers to close a recessionary or inflationary gap.

8. The government's budget surplus in Macroland has risen consistently over the past five years. Two government policy makers disagree as to why this has happened. One argues that a rising budget surplus indicates a growing economy; the other argues that it shows that the government is using contractionary fiscal policy. Can you determine which policy maker is correct? If not, why not?

8. It's impossible to determine which policy maker is correct given the information available. The government's budget surplus will rise either if real GDP is growing or if Macroland is using contractionary fiscal policy. When the economy grows, tax revenue rises and government transfers fall, leading to an increase in the government's budget surplus. However, if the government uses contractionary fiscal policy, then the government purchases fewer goods and services, increases taxes, or reduces government transfers. Any of those three changes will result in a temporary increase in the government's budget surplus, although the reduction in real GDP will eventually cause tax revenue to fall and government transfers to rise, which will reduce the budget surplus.

9. Figure 12-9 (Figure 29-9 in Economics) shows the actual budget deficit and the cyclically adjusted budget deficit as a percentage of real GDP in the United States since 1970. Assuming that potential output was unchanged, use this figure to determine in which years since 1992 the government used discretionary expansionary fiscal policy and in which years it used contractionary fiscal policy.

9. Since the cyclically adjusted budget balance is an estimate of what the budget balance would be if real GDP were exactly equal to potential output, the effect of changes in income on the budget are eliminated. And since we have assumed that there are no changes in potential output, any change in the cyclically adjusted budget balance represents changes in fiscal policies. When the cyclically adjusted budget deficit falls, the government must be engaging in contractionary fiscal policies: either government purchases and transfer payments are decreasing or taxes are increasing. When the cyclically adjusted budget deficit rises, the government must be engaging in expansionary fiscal policies: either government purchases and transfer payments are increasing or taxes are decreasing. From Figure 12-9 (Figure 29-9 in *Economics*), we see that from 1992 to 2001, the cyclically adjusted budget deficit was falling; this indicates that the government was pursuing contractionary fiscal policies during that period. From 2001 to 2004, the cyclically adjusted budget deficit was rising; this indicates that the government was pursuing expansionary fiscal policies during that period.

10. You are an economic adviser to a candidate for national office. She asks you for a summary of the economic consequences of a balanced-budget rule for the federal government and for your recommendation on whether she should support such a rule. How do you respond?

10. You might respond that balanced-budget rules are usually proposed because the government is running a budget deficit and many people think of deficits as bad. When the government runs a budget deficit, it adds to the public debt. If the government persists in running budget deficits, interest payments become an increasing part of government spending and the budget deficit itself. As a result, the debt–GDP ratio may rise. However, budget deficits themselves are not the problem; the problem arises when budget deficits become persistent. In the United States, there has been a strong relationship between the federal government's budget balance and the business cycle: when the economy expands, the budget moves toward surplus, and when the economy experiences a recession, the budget moves into deficit. The major disadvantage of a balanced-budget rule is that it would undermine the role of taxes and government transfers as automatic stabilizers and force the government to respond to an inflationary gap with expansionary fiscal policies and to a recessionary gap with contractionary fiscal policies. You might recommend, as most economists do, that rather than a balanced-budget rule, the government only balance its budget on average; it should run budget deficits during recessions and budget surpluses during expansions.

11. In 2005, the policy makers of the economy of Eastlandia projected the debt–GDP ratio and the deficit–GDP ratio for the economy for the next 10 years under different scenarios for growth in the government's deficit. Real GDP is currently $1,000 billion per year and is expected to grow by 3% per year, the public debt is $300 billion at the beginning of the year, and the deficit is $30 billion in 2005.

Year	Real GDP (billions of dollars)	Debt (billions of dollars)	Budget deficit (billions of dollars)	Debt (percent of real GDP)	Budget deficit (percent of real GDP)
2005	$1,000	$300	$30	?	?
2006	1,030	?	?	?	?
2007	1,061	?	?	?	?
2008	1,093	?	?	?	?
2009	1,126	?	?	?	?
2010	1,159	?	?	?	?
2011	1,194	?	?	?	?
2012	1,230	?	?	?	?
2013	1,267	?	?	?	?
2014	1,305	?	?	?	?
2015	1,344	?	?	?	?

a. Complete the accompanying table to show the debt–GDP ratio and the deficit–GDP ratio for the economy if the government's budget deficit remains constant at $30 billion over the next 10 years. (Remember that the government's debt will grow by the previous year's deficit.)

b. Redo the table to show the debt–GDP ratio and the deficit–GDP ratio for the economy if the government's budget deficit grows by 3% per year over the next 10 years.

c. Redo the table again to show the debt–GDP ratio and the deficit–GDP ratio for the economy if the government's budget deficit grows by 20% per year over the next 10 years.

d. What happens to the debt–GDP ratio and the deficit–GDP ratio for the economy over time under the three different scenarios?

11. a. Here is the completed table:

Year	Real GDP (billions of dollars)	Debt (billions of dollars)	Budget deficit (billions of dollars)	Debt (percent of real GDP)	Budget deficit (percent of real GDP)
2005	$1,000	$300	$30	30.0%	3.0%
2006	1,030	330	30	32.0	2.9
2007	1,061	360	30	33.9	2.8
2008	1,093	390	30	35.7	2.7
2009	1,126	420	30	37.3	2.7
2010	1,159	450	30	38.8	2.6
2011	1,194	480	30	40.2	2.5
2012	1,230	510	30	41.5	2.4
2013	1,267	540	30	42.6	2.4
2014	1,305	570	30	43.7	2.3
2015	1,344	600	30	44.6	2.2

b. Here is the table redone:

Year	Real GDP (billions of dollars)	Debt (billions of dollars)	Budget deficit (billions of dollars)	Debt (percent of real GDP)	Budget deficit (percent of real GDP)
2005	$1,000	$300	$30	30.0%	3.0%
2006	1,030	330	31	32.0	3.0
2007	1,061	361	32	34.0	3.0
2008	1,093	393	33	35.9	3.0
2009	1,126	426	34	37.8	3.0
2010	1,159	459	35	39.6	3.0
2011	1,194	494	36	41.4	3.0
2012	1,230	530	37	43.1	3.0
2013	1,267	567	38	44.7	3.0
2014	1,305	605	39	46.3	3.0
2015	1,344	644	40	47.9	3.0

c. And here is the table again:

Year	Real GDP (billions of dollars)	Debt (billions of dollars)	Budget deficit (billions of dollars)	Debt (percent of real GDP)	Budget deficit (percent of real GDP)
2005	$1,000	$300	$30	30.0%	3.0%
2006	1,030	330	36	32.0	3.5
2007	1,061	366	43	34.5	4.1
2008	1,093	409	52	37.4	4.7
2009	1,126	461	62	40.9	5.5
2010	1,159	523	75	45.1	6.4
2011	1,194	598	90	50.1	7.5
2012	1,230	687	107	55.9	8.7
2013	1,267	795	129	62.7	10.2
2014	1,305	924	155	70.8	11.9
2015	1,344	1,079	186	80.3	13.8

d. When the deficit remains constant at $30 billion, the deficit–GDP ratio declines but the debt–GDP ratio continues to increase because debt is rising faster than GDP. When the deficit grows by 3% per year, the same rate at which real GDP grows, the deficit–GDP ratio remains constant at 3% and the debt–GDP ratio continues to increase. When the deficit grows by 20% per year, the deficit–GDP ratio rises from 3.0% to 13.8% in 10 years and the debt–GDP ratio more than doubles from 30% to more than 80%.

12. Your study partner argues that the distinction between the government's budget deficit and debt is similar to the distinction between consumer savings and wealth. He also argues that if you have large budget deficits, you must have a large debt. In what ways is your study partner correct and in what ways is he incorrect?

12. Your study partner is correct that the distinction between the government's budget deficit and debt is similar to the distinction between consumer savings and wealth. Savings and deficits refer to actions that take place over time. When the government spends more than it receives in tax revenue in a particular time period, it is running a budget deficit. When consumers spend less than their disposable income in a particular time period, they are saving. However, both debt and wealth are measured at one point in time. When the government runs a budget deficit, the deficit is almost always financed by borrowing, which adds to its debt. Similarly, consumers accumulate wealth by saving. Your study partner is wrong in that the government can run a large budget deficit and have a small debt if it hasn't run large deficits in the past.

13. In which of the following cases does the size of the government's debt and the size of the budget deficit indicate potential problems for the economy?

a. The government's debt is relatively low, but the government is running a large budget deficit as it builds a high-speed rail system to connect the major cities of the nation.

b. The government's debt is relatively high due to a recently ended deficit-financed war, but the government is now running only a small budget deficit.

c. The government's debt is relatively low, but the government is running a budget deficit to finance the interest payments on the debt.

13. **a.** If the government has relatively little debt but is running a large budget deficit as it builds a high-speed rail system, this should not indicate potential problems for the economy. Like funding a war effort, it is difficult, if not impossible, to finance major improvements in a nation's infrastructure without borrowing. As long as the budget deficit ends with the building project, this should not create long-term problems.

b. If the government's debt is relatively high but the government has reduced its budget deficit, this should not indicate potential problems for the economy. However, the government needs to be careful that the deficits do not become persistent.

c. Even if the government's debt is relatively low, if it is running a budget deficit to finance the interest payments on that debt, this portends potential problems for the future. Without any changes, the government's debt will grow over time and with it the size of the government's budget deficit because of increasing interest payments.

14. How did or would the following affect the current public debt and implicit liabilities of the U.S. government?

a. In 2003, Congress passed and President Bush signed the Medicare Modernization Act, which provides seniors and individuals with disabilities with a prescription drug benefit. Some of the benefits under this law took effect immediately, but others will not begin until sometime in the future.

b. The age at which retired persons can receive full Social Security benefits is raised to age 70 for future retirees.

c. For future retirees, Social Security benefits are limited to those with low incomes.

d. Because the cost of health care is increasing faster than the overall inflation rate, annual increases in Social Security benefits are increased by the annual increase in health care costs rather than the overall inflation rate.

14. **a.** Because of its immediate impact on government spending, the Medicare Modernization Act increased the current public debt; implicit liabilities also rose because the act commits the government to a higher level of spending in the future.

b. If the age at which future retirees can receive full Social Security benefits is raised to age 70, implicit liabilities fall because government transfers will be lower in the future. There is no effect on the current public debt.

c. If Social Security benefits for future retirees are limited to those with low incomes, implicit liabilities fall because government transfers will be lower in the future. There is no effect on the current public debt because the change occurs in the future.

d. If annual increases in Social Security benefits are increased by the annual increase in health care costs rather than the overall inflation rate, implicit liabilities will rise. The current public debt will rise as soon as the rule is implemented.

Taxes and the Multiplier

1. An economy has a marginal propensity to consume of 0.6, real GDP equals $500 billion, and the government collects 20% of GDP in taxes. If government purchases increase by $10 billion, show the rounds of increased spending that take place by completing the accompanying table. The first and second rows are filled in for you. In the first row, the increase in government purchases of $10 billion raises real GDP by $10 billion, taxes increase by $2 billion, and YD increases by $8 billion; in the second row, the increase in YD of $8 billion increases consumer spending by $4.80 billion ($MPC \times$ change in disposable income).

Rounds	Change in G or C	Change in real GDP	Change in taxes	Change in YD
		(billions of dollars)		
1	$\Delta G = \$10.00$	$10.00	$2.00	$8.00
2	$\Delta C = \$4.80$	4.80	0.96	3.84
3	$\Delta C =$?	?	?	?
4	$\Delta C =$?	?	?	?
5	$\Delta C =$?	?	?	?
6	$\Delta C =$?	?	?	?
7	$\Delta C =$?	?	?	?
8	$\Delta C =$?	?	?	?
9	$\Delta C =$?	?	?	?
10	$\Delta C =$?	?	?	?

a. What is the total change in real GDP after the 10 rounds? What is the value of the multiplier? What would you expect the total change in real GDP to be, based on the multiplier formula? How do your two answers compare?

b. Redo the preceding table, assuming the marginal propensity to consume is 0.75 and the government collects 10% of the rise in real GDP in taxes. What is the total change in real GDP after 10 rounds? What is the value of the multiplier?

1. Here is the completed table.

Rounds	Change in G or C	Change in real GDP	Change in taxes	Change in YD
		(billions of dollars)		
1	$\Delta G = \$10.00$	$10.00	$2.00	$8.00
2	$\Delta C = 4.80$	4.80	0.96	3.84
3	$\Delta C = 2.30$	2.30	0.46	1.84
4	$\Delta C = 1.10$	1.10	0.22	0.88
5	$\Delta C = 0.53$	0.53	0.11	0.42
6	$\Delta C = 0.25$	0.25	0.05	0.20
7	$\Delta C = 0.12$	0.12	0.02	0.10
8	$\Delta C = 0.06$	0.06	0.01	0.05
9	$\Delta C = 0.03$	0.03	0.01	0.02
10	$\Delta C = 0.01$	0.01	0.00	0.01
. . .				
Sum for 10 rounds		$19.20		

a. The total change in real GDP after the 10 rounds is $19.20 billion. The multiplier is 1.923 $[1/(1 - (0.6 \times (1 - 0.2)))]$. We would expect the total change in real GDP to be 1.923 times the change in government purchases. Since the change in government purchases was $10 billion, we would expect a change in real GDP of $19.23 billion. This is very similar to the change in real GDP after 10 rounds ($19.20 billion).

b. Here is the table redone.

Rounds	Change in $I_{Planned}$ or C	Change in real GDP (billions of dollars)	Change in taxes	Change in YD
1	$\Delta G = \$10.00$	$10.00	$1.00	$9.00
2	$\Delta C = 6.75$	6.75	0.68	6.08
3	$\Delta C = 4.56$	4.56	0.46	4.10
4	$\Delta C = 3.08$	3.08	0.31	2.77
5	$\Delta C = 2.08$	2.08	0.21	1.87
6	$\Delta C = 1.40$	1.40	0.14	1.26
7	$\Delta C = 0.95$	0.95	0.09	0.85
8	$\Delta C = 0.64$	0.64	0.06	0.57
9	$\Delta C = 0.43$	0.43	0.04	0.39
10	$\Delta C = 0.29$	0.29	0.03	0.26
. . .				
Sum for 10 rounds		$30.18		

The total change in real GDP after the 10 rounds is $30.18 billion. The multiplier is 3.077 $[1/(1 - (0.75 \times (1 - 0.1)))]$. We would expect the total change in real GDP to be 3.077 times the change in government purchases. Since the change in government purchases was $10 billion, we would expect a change in real GDP of $30.77 billion. This is very similar to the change in real GDP after 10 rounds ($30.18 billion).

2. Calculate the change in government purchases of goods and services necessary to close the recessionary or inflationary gaps in the following cases. Assume that the aggregate supply curve is horizontal so that the change in real GDP arising from a shift of the aggregate demand curve equals the size of the shift of the curve.

a. Real GDP equals $100 billion, potential output equals $160 billion, the government collects 20% of any change in real GDP in the form of taxes, and the marginal propensity to consume is 0.75.

b. Real GDP equals $250 billion, potential output equals $200 billion, the government collects 10% of any change in real GDP in the form of taxes, and the marginal propensity to consume is 0.5.

c. Real GDP equals $180 billion, potential output equals $100 billion, the government collects 25% of any change in real GDP in the form of taxes, and the marginal propensity to consume is 0.8.

2. **a.** The economy is facing a recessionary gap; real GDP is less than potential output. Since the multiplier for a change in government purchases is 2.5 [$1/(1 - (0.75 \times (1 - 0.2)))$], an increase in government purchases of goods and services of $24 billion will increase real GDP by $60 billion and close the recessionary gap.

b. The economy is facing an inflationary gap; real GDP is higher than potential output. Since the multiplier for a change in government purchases is 1.82 [$1/(1 - (0.5 \times (1 - 0.1)))$], a decrease in government purchases of goods and services of $27.5 billion will reduce real GDP by $50 billion and close the inflationary gap.

c. The economy is facing an inflationary gap; real GDP is higher than potential output. Since the multiplier for a change in government purchases is 2.5 [$1/(1 - (0.8 \times (1 - 0.25)))$], a decrease in government purchases of goods and services of $32 billion will reduce real GDP by $80 billion and close the inflationary gap.

Money, Banking, and the Federal Reserve System

1. For each of the following transactions, what is the effect (increase or decrease) on M1? on M2?

a. You sell a few shares of stock and put the proceeds into your savings account.

b. You sell a few shares of stock and put the proceeds into your checking account.

c. You transfer money from your savings account to your checking account.

d. You discover $0.25 under the floor mat in your car and deposit it in your checking account.

e. You discover $0.25 under the floor mat in your car and deposit it in your savings account.

1. a. Shares of stock are not a component of either M1 or M2, so holding fewer shares does not decrease either M1 or M2. However, depositing the money into your savings account increases M2, since the savings account is part of M2 (but not part of M1). M1 does not change.

b. Shares of stock are not a component of either M1 or M2, and so holding fewer shares does not decrease either M1 or M2. However, depositing the money into your checking account increases M1, since checking accounts are part of M1. It also increases M2, since M1 is part of M2.

c. Moving money from savings to checking has no effect on M2, since both savings accounts and checking accounts are included in M2. However, since savings accounts are not part of M1, moving money from savings to checking does increase M1.

d. Depositing cash into a checking account does not change M1 or M2. You are simply transferring money from one component of M1 (currency in circulation) to another component of M1 (checkable deposits).

e. Depositing $0.25 into your savings account has no effect on M2, since both savings accounts and currency in circulation are in M2. However, since savings accounts are not part of M1, depositing the $0.25 into your savings account reduces M1.

2. There are three types of money: commodity money, commodity-backed money, and fiat money. Which type of money is used in each of the following situations?

a. Mother-of-pearl seashells were used to pay for goods in ancient China.

b. Salt was used in many European countries as a medium of exchange.

c. For a brief time, Germany used paper money (the "Rye Mark") that could be redeemed for a certain amount of grain rye.

d. The town of Ithaca, New York, prints its own currency, the Ithaca HOURS, which can be used to purchase local goods and services.

2. a. Mother-of-pearl is commodity money since the shells have other uses (for instance, for shirt buttons).

b. Salt is commodity money since it has other uses.

c. The "Rye Mark" is commodity-backed money since its ultimate value is guaranteed by a promise that it can be converted into valuable goods (grain rye).

d. Ithaca HOURS are fiat money because their value derives entirely from their status as a means of payment in Ithaca.

3. The table below shows the components of M1 and M2 in billions of dollars for the month of December in the years 1995 to 2004 as published in the *2005 Economic Report of the President.* Complete the table by calculating M1, M2, currency in circulation as a percentage of M1, and currency in circulation as a percentage of M2. What trends or patterns about M1, M2, currency in circulation as a percentage of M1, and currency in circulation as a percentage of M2 do you see? What might account for these trends?

Year	Currency in circulation	Traveler's checks	Checkable deposits	Money market funds	Time deposits smaller than $100,000	Savings deposits	M1	M2	Currency in circulation as a percentage of M1	Currency in circulation as a percentage of M2
1995	$372.1	$9.1	$745.9	$448.8	$931.4	$1,134.0	?	?	?	?
1996	394.1	8.8	676.5	517.4	946.8	1,273.1	?	?	?	?
1997	424.6	8.5	639.5	592.2	967.9	1,399.1	?	?	?	?
1998	459.9	8.5	627.7	732.7	951.5	1,603.6	?	?	?	?
1999	517.7	8.6	597.7	832.5	954.0	1,738.2	?	?	?	?
2000	531.6	8.3	548.1	924.2	1,044.2	1,876.2	?	?	?	?
2001	582.0	8.0	589.3	987.2	972.8	2,308.9	?	?	?	?
2002	627.4	7.8	582.0	915.5	892.1	2,769.5	?	?	?	?
2003	663.9	7.7	621.8	801.1	809.4	3,158.5	?	?	?	?
2004	699.3	7.6	656.2	714.7	814.0	3,505.9	?	?	?	?

3. Here is the completed table:

Year	Currency in circulation	Traveler's checks	Checkable bank deposits	Money market funds	Time deposits smaller than $100,000	Savings deposits	M1	M2	Currency in circulation as a percentage of M1	Currency in circulation as a percentage of M2
1995	$372.1	$9.1	$745.9	$448.8	$931.4	$1,134.0	$1,127.1	$3,641.3	33.0%	10.2%
1996	394.1	8.8	676.5	517.4	946.8	1,273.1	1,079.4	3,816.7	36.5%	10.3%
1997	424.6	8.5	639.5	592.2	967.9	1,399.1	1,072.6	4,031.8	39.6%	10.5%
1998	459.9	8.5	627.7	732.7	951.5	1,603.6	1,096.1	4,383.9	42.0%	10.5%
1999	517.7	8.6	597.7	832.5	954.0	1,738.2	1,124.0	4,648.7	46.1%	11.1%
2000	531.6	8.3	548.1	924.2	1,044.2	1,876.2	1,088.0	4,932.6	48.9%	10.8%
2001	582.0	8.0	589.3	987.2	972.8	2,308.9	1,179.3	5,448.2	49.4%	10.7%
2002	627.4	7.8	582.0	915.5	892.1	2,769.5	1,217.2	5,794.3	51.5%	10.8%
2003	663.9	7.7	621.8	801.1	809.4	3,158.5	1,293.4	6,062.4	51.3%	11.0%
2004	699.3	7.6	656.2	714.7	814.0	3,505.9	1,363.1	6,397.7	51.3%	10.9%

M1 consists of currency in circulation, traveler's checks, and checkable deposits. M2 consists of M1 plus money funds, time deposits, and savings deposits. From 1995 to 2004, there is no obvious trend in M1. M1 grew by $236 billion (or 21% from 1995 to 2004) but was essentially stable from 1995 to 2001; all of this growth occurred between 2002 and 2004. There is, however, a clear upward trend throughout the period for M2, which grew by $2,756.4 billion (or 76% from 1995 to 2004). Currency as a percentage of M1 grew from 33 percent to over 51 percent from 1995 to 2004, but currency as a percentage of M2 remained relatively constant, varying from a low of 10.2% in 1995 to a high of 11.1% in 1999. The increase in currency as a percentage of M1 could reflect increased use of credit cards, causing a reduction in the importance of traveler's checks and checkable deposits. Yet, since currency as a percentage of M2 did not change, it could also reflect a shift from checkable deposits to money funds, time deposits, and saving deposits.

4. Indicate whether each of the following is part of M1, M2, or neither:

   a. $95 on your campus meal card

   b. $0.55 in the change cup of your car

   c. $1,663 in your savings account

   d. $459 in your checking account

   e. 100 shares of stock worth $4,000

   f. A $1,000 line of credit on your Sears credit card

4. **a.** $95 on your campus meal card is similar to a gift certificate. Because it can only be used for one purpose, it is not part of either M1, M2.

   b. $0.55 in the change cup of your car is part of currency in circulation; it is part of both M1 and M2.

   c. $1,663 in your savings account isn't directly usable as a medium of exchange, so it is not part of M1; but because it can readily be converted into cash or checkable deposits, it is part of M2.

   d. A $459 balance in your checking account is part of M1 and M2; it represents a checkable deposit.

   e. 100 shares of stock are not part of either M1 or M2. Although an asset, stock is not a highly liquid asset.

   f. A $1,000 line of credit on your Sears credit card account is not part of either M1 or M2 because it does not represent an asset.

5. Tracy Williams deposits $500 that was in her sock drawer into a checking account at the local bank.

   a. How does the deposit initially change the T-account of the local bank? How does it change the money supply?

   b. If the bank maintains a reserve ratio of 10%, how will it respond to the new deposit?

   c. If every time the bank makes a loan, the loan results in a new checkable bank deposit in a different bank equal to the amount of the loan, by how much could the money supply in the economy expand in total?

   d. If every time the bank makes a loan, the loan results in a new checkable bank deposit in a different bank equal to the amount of the loan and the bank maintains a reserve ratio of 5%, by how much could the money supply expand in response to an initial cash deposit of $500?

5. a. Initially, the bank's reserves rise by $500, as do its checkable deposits. There is no initial change in the money supply; currency in circulation has fallen by $500 but checkable deposits have increased by $500.

Assets		Liabilities	
Reserves	+$500	Checkable Deposits	+$500

b. The bank will hold $50 as reserves against the new deposit and make additional loans equal to $450.

c. The money supply can expand by $4,500. Checkable deposits rise by $5,000—the initial $500 deposit of cash plus $4,500 in loans and deposits. Only $4,500 ($500/0.1 − $500) represents additions to the money supply. (Remember that $500 of the increase in deposits came at the expense of a reduction in currency in circulation when Tracy deposited $500 in her bank account.)

d. The money supply can expand by $9,500. Checkable deposits rise by $10,000 but because the first $500 was a deposit of cash, only $9,500 ($500/0.05 − $500) represents additions to the money supply.

6. Ryan Cozzens withdraws $400 from his checking account at the local bank and keeps it in his wallet.

a. How will the withdrawal change the T-account of the local bank and the money supply?

b. If the bank maintains a reserve ratio of 10%, how will the bank respond to the withdrawal?

c. If every time the bank decreases its loans, checkable bank deposits fall by the amount of the loan, by how much could the money supply in the economy contract in total?

d. If every time the bank decreases its loans, checkable bank deposits fall by the amount of the loan and the bank maintains a reserve ratio of 20%, by how much will the money supply contract in response to a withdrawal of $400?

6. a. Initially, the bank's reserves fall by $400, as do its checkable deposits. There is no initial change in the money supply; currency in circulation has risen by $400 but checkable deposits have decreased by $400.

Assets		Liabilities	
Reserves	−$400	Checkable Deposits	−$400

b. Assuming that the bank has other checkable deposits, the bank will be holding insufficient reserves. The bank was holding $40 of the $400 withdrawal as required reserves for the $400 deposit; however, the remaining $360 was being held as required reserves for other deposits. The bank will have to reduce its deposits by $3,600 (−$400/0.1 + $400) to reduce its required reserves by $360 (10% of $3,600). It will have to reduce deposits by calling in some of its loans.

c. The money supply will contract by $3,600 (−$400/0.1 + $400). Checkable deposits fall by $4,000, but only $3,600 represents a decrease in the money supply.

d. The money supply can decrease by $1,600 (−$400/0.2 + $400). Checkable deposits fall by $2,000, but only $1,600 represents a decrease in the money supply.

7. The government of Eastlandia uses measures of monetary aggregates similar to those used by the United States, and the central bank of Eastlandia imposes a required reserve ratio of 10%. Given the following information, answer the questions below.

Bank deposits at the central bank = $200 million
Currency held by public = $150 million
Currency in bank vaults = $100 million
Checkable bank deposits = $500 million
Traveler's checks = $10 million

a. What is M1?
b. What is the monetary base?
c. Are the commercial banks holding excess reserves?
d. Can the commercial banks increase checkable bank deposits? If yes, by how much can checkable bank deposits increase?

7. a. M1 equals the sum of currency held by the public ($150 million), checkable deposits ($500 million), and traveler's checks ($10 million) or $660.

b. The monetary base is the sum of currency held by the public ($150 million) and the reserves of the commercial banks (currency in bank vaults ($100 million) and bank deposits ($200 million) at the central bank). The monetary base is $450 million.

c. Required reserves are $50 million (10% of $500 million). Because total reserves are $300 million, the commercial banks are holding $250 million ($300 million − $50 million) in excess reserves.

d. Since the commercial banks are holding excess reserves, they can increase deposits. With a required reserve ratio of 10%, reserves of $300 million can support a total of $3,000 million ($300/0.1) in deposits. Commercial banks can increase deposits by an additional $2,500 million.

8. In Westlandia, the public holds 50% of M1 in the form of currency, and the required reserve ratio is 20%. Estimate how much the money supply will increase in response to a new cash deposit of $500 by completing the table below. (*Hint:* The first row shows that the bank must hold $100 in minimum reserves—20% of the $500 deposit—against this deposit, leaving $400 in excess reserves that can be loaned out. However, since the public wants to hold 50% of the loan in currency, only $400 × 0.5 = $200 of the loan will be deposited in round 2 from the loan granted in round 1.) How does your answer compare to an economy in which the total amount of the loan is deposited in the banking system and the public doesn't hold any of the loan in currency? What does this imply about the relationship between the public's desire for currency and the money multiplier?

Round	Deposits	Required reserves	Excess reserves	Loans	Held as currency
1	$500.00	$100.00	$400.00	$400.00	$200.00
2	200.00	?	?	?	?
3	?	?	?	?	?
4	?	?	?	?	?
5	?	?	?	?	?
6	?	?	?	?	?
7	?	?	?	?	?
8	?	?	?	?	?
9	?	?	?	?	?
10	?	?	?	?	?
Total after 10 rounds	?	?	?	?	?

8. Here is the completed table:

Round	Deposits	Required reserves	Excess reserves	Loans	Held as currency
1	$500.00	$100.00	$400.00	$400.00	$200.00
2	200.00	40.00	160.00	160.00	80.00
3	80.00	16.00	64.00	64.00	32.00
4	32.00	6.40	25.60	25.60	12.80
5	12.80	2.56	10.24	10.24	5.12
6	5.12	1.02	4.10	4.10	2.05
7	2.05	0.41	1.64	1.64	0.82
8	0.82	0.16	0.66	0.66	0.33
9	0.33	0.07	0.26	0.26	0.13
10	0.13	0.03	0.10	0.10	0.05
Total after 10 rounds	$833.25	$166.65	$666.60	$666.60	$333.30

After 10 rounds, loans can expand by $666.60; this is also the increase in the money supply at this point. (Although deposits increase by $833.25, currency held by the public falls by $166.70—it initially fell by $500 and eventually rose again by $333.30.) If the total amount of each loan is deposited in the banking system (that is, the public does not hold any of the loans in currency), the money supply would increase by $2,000 (500/0.2 − $500); deposits would increase by $2,500. The money multiplier decreases in size as the public holds a greater percentage of loans in currency.

9. What will happen to the money supply under the following circumstances?

a. The required reserve ratio is 25%, and a depositor withdraws $700 from his checkable bank deposit.

b. The required reserve ratio is 5%, and a depositor withdraws $700 from his checkable bank deposit.

c. The required reserve ratio is 20%, and a customer deposits $750 to her checkable bank deposit.

d. The required reserve ratio is 10%, and a customer deposits $600 to her checkable bank deposit.

9. **a.** Deposits contract by $2,800 but $700 is converted into currency held by the public. The money supply contracts by $2,100.

b. Deposits contract by $14,000 but $700 is converted into currency held by the public. The money supply contracts by $13,300.

c. Deposits expand by $3,750 but currency in circulation falls by $750. The money supply expands by $3,000.

d. Deposits expand by $6,000 but currency in circulation falls by $600. The money supply expands by $5,400.

10. Although the U.S. Federal Reserve doesn't use changes in reserve requirements to manage the money supply, the central bank of Albernia does. The commercial banks of Albernia have $100 million in reserves and $1,000 million in checkable deposits; the initial required reserve ratio is 10%. The commercial banks follow a policy of holding no excess reserves. The public holds a fixed amount of currency, so all loans create an equal amount of deposits in the banking system.

    a. How will the money supply change if the required reserve ratio falls to 5%?

    b. How will the money supply change if the minimum reserve ratio rises to 25%?

10. a. If the required reserve ratio falls to 5%, the commercial banks of Albernia will be holding $50 million in excess reserves. Since the banks follow a policy of holding no excess reserves, the banks will expand deposits by making loans. The banks' reserves of $100 million will support $2,000 million in deposits at a reserve ratio of 5%. The bank will expand loans and deposits by $1,000 million; so the money supply expands by $1,000 million.

    b. If the required reserve ratio rises to 25%, the commercial banks of Albernia will not be holding enough reserves to support $1,000 million in deposits. The banks' reserves will only support $400 million in deposits. The commercial banks will have to decrease loans and deposits by $600 million; so the money supply will contract by $600 million.

11. Using Figure 13-5, find the Federal Reserve district in which you live. Go to http://www.federalreserve.gov/bios/pres.htm and identify the president of that Federal Reserve Bank. Go to http://www.federalreserve.gov/fomc/and determine if the president of the Fed is currently a voting member of the Federal Open Market Committee (FOMC).

11. Answers will vary depending on where you live and when you look up your answer. If you live in Reedley, California, in July 2005, you were in the San Francisco district of the Federal Reserve system. Janet Yellen was the president of the Federal Reserve Bank of San Francisco and an alternate (nonvoting) member of the FOMC at that time.

12. Show the changes to the T-accounts for the Federal Reserve and for commercial banks when the Federal Reserve buys $50 million in U.S. Treasury bills. If the public holds a fixed amount of currency (so that all loans create an equal amount of deposits in the banking system), the minimum reserve ratio is 10%, and banks hold no excess reserves, by how much will deposits in the commercial banks change? By how much will the money supply change? Show the final changes to the T-account for commercial banks when the money supply changes by this amount.

12. When the Federal Reserve buys $50 million in Treasury bills from commercial banks, its assets increase by $50 million (it now owns $50 million in Treasury bills) but its liabilities also increase by $50 million as it credits the banks' account at the Federal Reserve, part of the monetary base. From the perspective of commercial banks, their assets fall by $50 million because they sell Treasury bills to the Fed but their assets also rise by $50 million when their deposits at the Fed (reserves) are credited with $50 million.

Initial changes to the T-account of the Federal Reserve immediately after Fed purchase of $50 million in Treasury bills:

Assets		Liabilities	
Treasury bills	+$50 million	Monetary base	+$50 million

Initial changes to the T-account of commercial banks immediately after Fed purchase of $50 million in Treasury bills:

Assets		Liabilities
Treasury bills	−$50 million	
Reserves	+$50 million	

After the Federal Reserve buys $50 million from commercial banks, the banks are holding $50 million in excess reserves. Since the banks do not want to hold any excess reserves, they will increase loans and deposits by $500 million, the maximum amount that $50 million in reserves can support. Therefore, the money supply will also increase by $500 million.

All changes to the T-account of commercial banks after the Fed purchase of $50 million in Treasury bills:

Assets		Liabilities	
Treasury bills	−$50 million	Checkable deposits	+$500 million
Reserves	+$50 million		
Loans	+$500 million		

13. Show the changes to the T-accounts for the Federal Reserve and for commercial banks when the Federal Reserve sells $30 million in U.S. Treasury bills. If the public holds a fixed amount of currency (so that all new loans create an equal amount of checkable bank deposits in the banking system) and the minimum reserve ratio is 5%, by how much will checkable bank deposits in the commercial banks change? By how much will the money supply change? Show the final changes to the T-account for the commercial banks when the money supply changes by this amount.

13. When the Federal Reserve sells $30 million in Treasury bills to commercial banks, its assets decrease by $30 million (it now owns $30 million less in Treasury bills) but its liabilities also decrease by $30 million as the banks pay the Federal Reserve for the Treasury bills from their accounts at the Fed (part of the monetary base). From the perspective of commercial banks, their assets rise by $30 million because they buy the Treasury bills from the Fed but their assets also fall by $30 million when they pay for the Treasury bills from their deposits at the Fed (their reserves).

Initial changes to the T-account of the Federal Reserve immediately after Fed sale of $30 million in Treasury bills:

Assets		Liabilities	
Treasury bills	−$30 million	Monetary base	−$30 million

Initial changes to the T-account of commercial banks immediately after Fed sale of $30 million in Treasury bills:

Assets		Liabilities
Treasury bills	+$30 million	
Reserves	−$30 million	

After the Federal Reserve sells $30 million in Treasury bills, the banks are no longer holding enough reserves to support their deposits. The banks will need to reduce loans and deposits by $600 million—the amount of deposits that were supported by the $30 million in reserves used to buy the Treasury bills. So the money supply will also decrease by $600 million.

All changes to the T-account of commercial banks after Fed sale of $30 million in Treasury bills:

Assets		**Liabilities**	
Treasury bills	+$30 million	Checkable deposits	−$600 million
Reserves	−$30 million		
Loans	−$600 million		

Monetary Policy

1. Go to the FOMC page of the Federal Reserve Board's website (http://www.
federalreserve.gov/FOMC/) to find the statement issued after the most recent FOMC
meeting. (Go to the bottom of the web page and click on the most recent statement
listed in the calendar.)

   a. What is the target federal funds rate?

   b. Is the target federal funds rate different from the target federal funds rate from
the previous FOMC statement? If yes, by how much does it differ?

   c. Does the statement comment on macroeconomic conditions in the United States?
How does it describe the U.S. economy?

1. Answers will vary depending on when you look up the information. As of July 2005,
the latest statement was issued June 30, after the June 29–30 FOMC meeting.

   a. On June 30, 2005, the Fed announced that it had raised its target for the federal
funds rate to 3¼%.

   b. Yes, the target federal funds rate is 25 basis points higher (the target had been 3%
before the June 29–30 FOMC meeting).

   c. It states that even with this increase in the federal funds rate, the committee
believes that "monetary policy remains accommodative." Coupled with the growth
in productivity, monetary policy is "providing ongoing support to economic activity." It also comments that "although energy prices have risen further, the expansion remains firm and labor market conditions continue to improve gradually."

2. How will the following events affect the nominal demand for money as defined by
M1? In each case, specify whether there is a shift of the demand curve or a movement along the demand curve and its direction.

   a. There is a fall in the interest rate from 12% to 10%.

   b. Thanksgiving arrives and, with it, the beginning of the holiday shopping season.

   c. McDonald's and other fast-food restaurants begin to accept credit cards.

   d. The Fed engages in an open-market purchase of U.S. Treasury bills.

2. **a.** Any decrease in the interest rate will lead to an increase in the quantity of money
demanded (a movement down the money demand curve) but no shift in the
money demand curve.

   b. When the holiday shopping season starts, consumers anticipate an increase in
expenditures and so, at each income level, increase the demand for money. The
money demand curve shifts to the right.

   c. As McDonald's and other fast-food restaurants begin to accept credit cards, it
reduces the demand for money, assuming that households put more money in
savings instead of holding currency. The money demand curve shifts to the left.

   d. When the Fed engages in open-market operations, it will change the money supply (the money supply curve will shift). This will affect the interest rate and consequently the quantity of money demanded. An open-market purchase of U.S.
Treasury bills by the Fed will increase the money supply, lowering the interest rate
and increasing the quantity of money demanded. This is a downward movement
along the money demand curve.

3. The accompanying table shows nominal GDP, M1, and M2 in billions of dollars in five-year increments from 1960 to 2000 as published in the *2005 Economic Report of the President*. Complete the table by calculating the velocity of money using both M1 and M2. What trends or patterns in the velocity of money do you see? What might account for these trends?

Year	Nominal GDP (billions of dollars)	M1 (billions of dollars)	M2 (billions of dollars)	Velocity using M1	Velocity using M2
1960	$526.4	$140.7	$312.4	?	?
1965	719.1	167.8	459.2	?	?
1970	1,038.5	214.4	626.5	?	?
1975	1,638.3	287.1	1,016.2	?	?
1980	2,789.5	408.5	1,599.8	?	?
1985	4,220.3	619.8	2,495.7	?	?
1990	5,803.1	824.8	3,279.2	?	?
1995	7,397.7	1,127.0	3,641.2	?	?
2000	9,817.0	1,087.9	4,932.5	?	?

3. The velocity is calculated as nominal GDP (from the second column of the table) divided by the nominal quantity of money (M1 or M2, from the third or fourth column of the table). The accompanying table shows that velocity using M1 increased dramatically (by 141%) from 1960 to 2000; velocity using M2 remained approximately constant from 1960 to 1990 and then increased by 15%. The increase in velocity using M1 coupled with the stability of velocity using M2 indicates people shifted from currency and checkable deposits to money market funds, time deposits, and savings deposits.

Year	GDP (billions of dollars)	M1 (billions of dollars)	M2 (billions of dollars)	Velocity using M1	Velocity using M2
1960	$526.4	$140.7	$312.4	3.74	1.69
1965	719.1	167.8	459.2	4.29	1.57
1970	1,038.5	214.4	626.5	4.84	1.66
1975	1,638.3	287.1	1,016.2	5.71	1.61
1980	2,789.5	408.5	1,599.8	6.83	1.74
1985	4,220.3	619.8	2,495.7	6.81	1.69
1990	5,803.1	824.8	3,279.2	7.04	1.77
1995	7,397.7	1,127.0	3,641.2	6.56	2.03
2000	9,817.0	1,087.9	4,932.5	9.02	1.99

4. The accompanying table shows the annual growth of M1 and nominal GDP in Japan during the early 2000s. What must have been happening to velocity during this time?

Year	M1 growth	Nominal GDP growth
2000	8.2%	2.9%
2001	8.5%	0.4%
2002	27.6%	−0.5%
2003	8.2%	2.5%

4. Since M1 was increasing substantially from 2000 to 2003 (and reached a growth rate of 27.6% in 2002) and nominal GDP growth was weak (and negative in 2002), velocity must have decreased dramatically. In Japan at this time, interest rates were very low, so the public held the increase in M1 in currency.

5. An economy is facing the recessionary gap shown in the accompanying diagram. To eliminate the gap, should the central bank use expansionary or contractionary monetary policy? How will the interest rate, investment spending, consumer spending, real GDP, and the aggregate price level change as the monetary policy closes the recessionary gap?

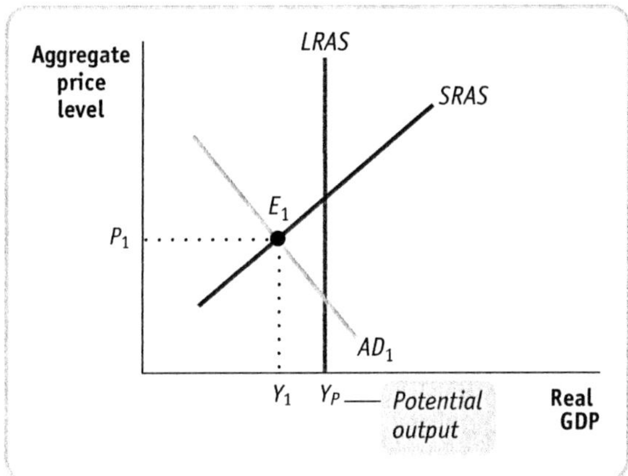

5. The central bank can use expansionary monetary policy to eliminate the recessionary gap. The central bank could engage in an open-market purchase of U.S. Treasury bills. This would increase the money supply, lowering the rate of interest and encouraging an increase in investment spending. The increase in investment spending will kick off the multiplier process, leading consumers to increase their spending. The final situation is illustrated in the accompanying diagram by the movement of the AD curve from its initial position, AD_1, to its new location, AD_2. Real GDP and the aggregate price level will rise.

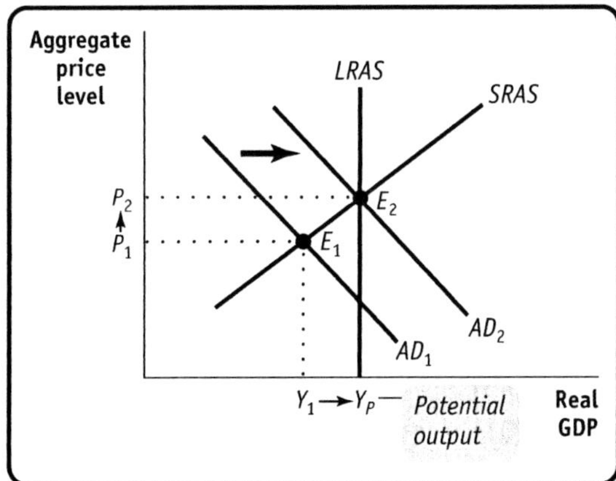

6. An economy is facing the inflationary gap shown in the accompanying diagram. To eliminate the gap, should the central bank use expansionary or contractionary monetary policy? How will the interest rate, investment spending, consumer spending, real GDP, and aggregate price level change as the monetary policy closes the inflationary gap?

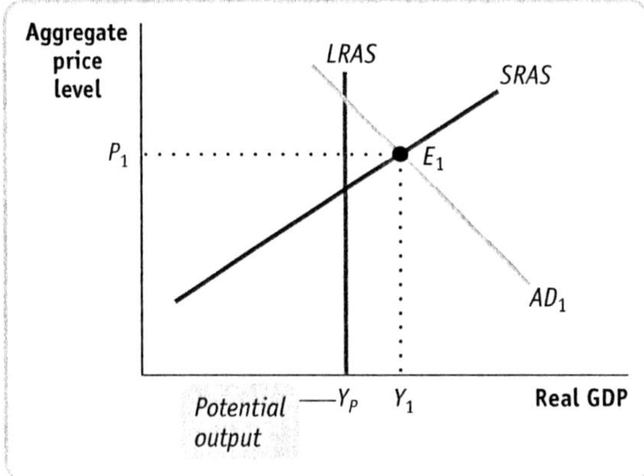

6. The central bank can use contractionary monetary policy to eliminate the inflationary gap. The central bank could engage in an open-market sale of U.S Treasury bills. This would decrease the supply of money, raising the interest rate and causing investment spending to fall. The decrease in investment spending will lead consumers to decrease their spending. The final situation is illustrated in the accompanying diagram by the movement of the AD curve from its initial position, AD_1, to its new location, AD_2. Real GDP and the aggregate price level will fall.

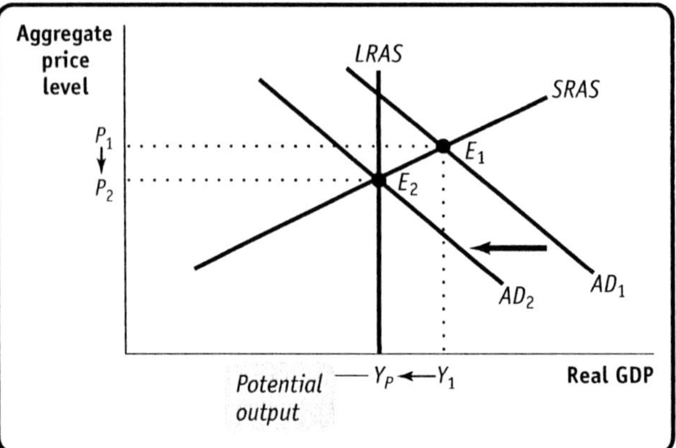

7. In the economy of Eastlandia, the money market is initially in equilibrium when the economy begins to slide into a recession.

    a. Using the accompanying diagram, explain what will happen to the interest rate if the central bank of Eastlandia keeps the money supply constant at M_1.

b. If the central bank is instead committed to maintaining an interest rate target of r_1, how should the central bank react as the economy slides into recession?

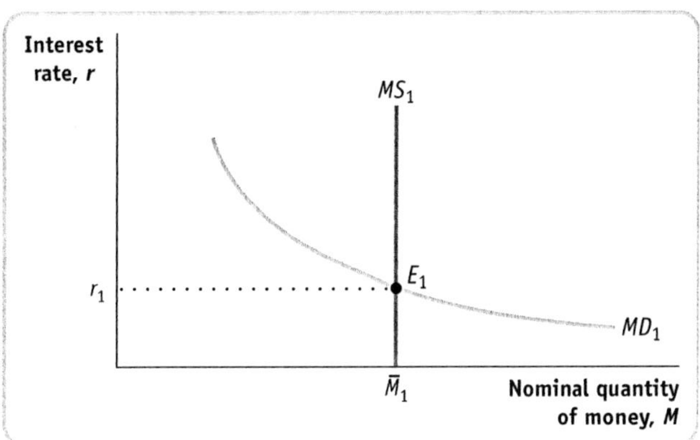

7. **a.** Beginning at equilibrium point E_1 in the accompanying money market diagram, when the economy of Eastlandia goes into recession, aggregate spending will fall and the money demand curve will shift to the left, from MD_1 to MD_2, moving the money market from its initial equilibrium, E_1, to a new equilibrium at E_2. If the central bank keeps the quantity of money constant, the interest rate will decrease to r_2, shown at the new equilibrium point, E_2. The decrease in the interest rate would encourage investment spending and would help close the recessionary gap.

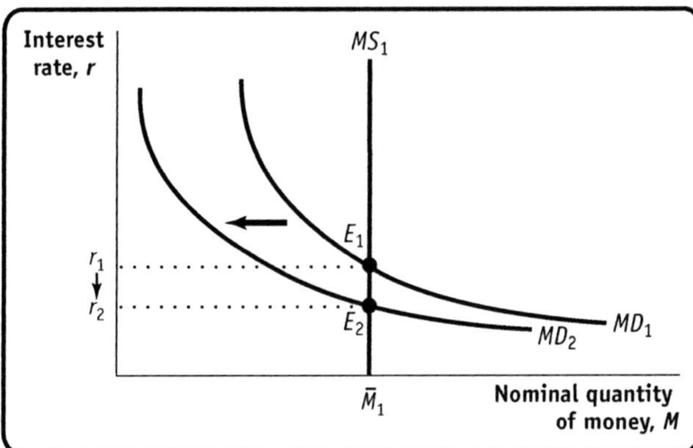

b. If the central bank is committed to maintaining an interest rate target of r_1, then the central bank will reduce the money supply as the economy goes into recession, from MS_1 to MS_2, in the accompanying diagram, eliminating the potential for interest rates to fall. The new equilibrium in the money market is at E_3, with the interest rate at its target rate, r_1.

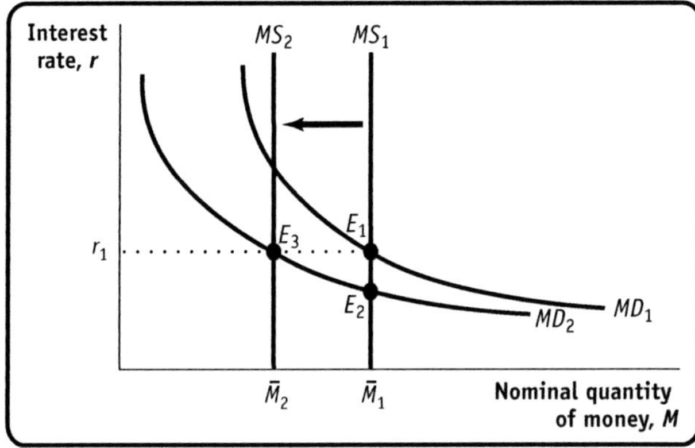

8. An economy is in long-run macroeconomic equilibrium with an unemployment rate of 5% when the government passes a law requiring the central bank to use monetary policy to lower the unemployment rate to 3% and keep it there. How could the central bank achieve this goal in the short run? What would happen in the long run? Illustrate with a diagram.

8. If the economy is in long-run macroeconomic equilibrium with an unemployment rate of 5%, then the long-run aggregate supply curve must be vertical at a real GDP that is associated with a 5% unemployment rate. This long-run macroeconomic equilibrium is E_1 in the accompanying diagram. In the short run, the central bank can engage in expansionary monetary policy to shift the aggregate demand curve to the right (from AD_1 to AD_2) and reduce the unemployment rate to 3%. Over time, because real GDP exceeds potential real GDP, the short-run aggregate supply curve will shift to the left (from $SRAS_1$ to $SRAS_2$). So to keep the unemployment rate at 3% in the short run, the central bank would have to engage in continuous increases in the money supply, shifting the aggregate demand curve to the right as the short-run aggregate supply curve shifts to the left, and the aggregate price level will go higher and higher. However, the central bank cannot keep the unemployment rate at 3% in the long run, since, in the long run, money is neutral. In the long run, output will return to its potential level and the unemployment rate will return to 5%.

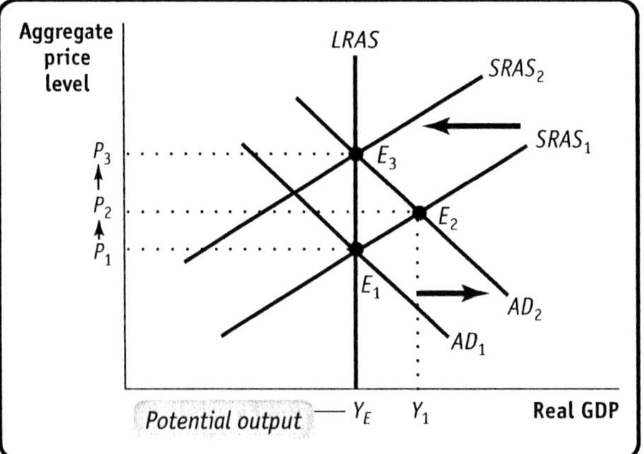

9. According to the European Central Bank website, the treaty establishing the European Community "makes clear that ensuring price stability is the most important contribution that monetary policy can make to achieve a favourable economic environment and a high level of employment." If price stability is the only goal of monetary policy, explain how monetary policy would be conducted during recessions. Analyze both the case of a recession that is the result of a demand shock and the case of a recession that is the result of a supply shock.

9. If price stability is the only goal of monetary policy, then during recessions resulting from a leftward shift in the aggregate demand curve, as the aggregate price level falls, the central bank would engage in expansionary monetary policy. This would lower interest rates, encourage investment spending, and eliminate the recessionary pressure while keeping prices constant. However, if the recession is the result of a leftward shift of the short-run aggregate supply curve, the recession would be accompanied by increases in the aggregate price level and the central bank would engage in contractionary monetary policy. The contractionary monetary policy would raise interest rates and discourage investment spending, shifting the aggregate demand curve to the left. Although the policy would keep prices constant, it would be at the expense of a deeper recession.

10. The effectiveness of monetary policy depends on how easy it is for changes in the money supply to change interest rates. By changing interest rates, monetary policy affects investment spending and the aggregate demand curve. The economies of Albernia and Brittania have very different money demand curves, as shown in the accompanying diagram. In which economy will changes in the money supply be a more effective policy tool? Why?

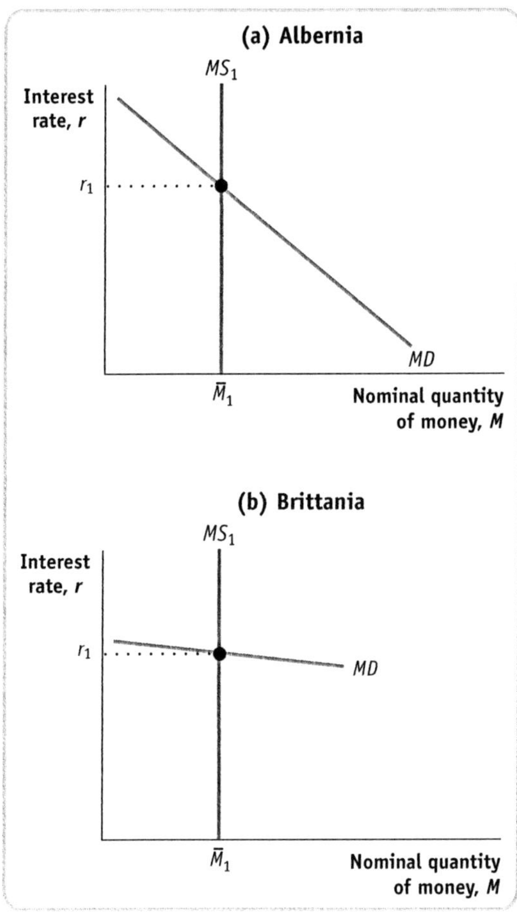

10. According to the accompanying diagram, monetary policy will be more effective in Albernia and less effective in Brittania. In Albernia a relatively small change in the money supply will lead to a large change in the interest rate, but in Brittania a relatively large change in the money supply will lead to only a small change in the interest rate.

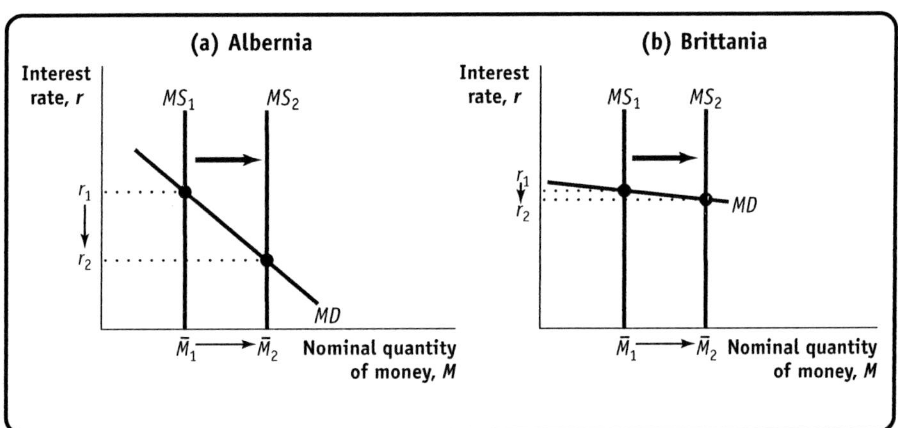

11. During the Great Depression, businesspeople in the United States were very pessimistic about the future of economic growth and reluctant to increase investment spending even when interest rates fell. How did this limit the potential for monetary policy to help alleviate the Depression?

11. Monetary policy is effective when changes in the money supply change the interest rate and, in turn, the change in the interest rate changes investment spending. If businesspeople are very pessimistic about the future of economic growth and reluctant to increase investment spending when interest rates decrease, monetary policy will not be very effective in shifting the aggregate demand curve to the right. Since this was the situation during the Great Depression, monetary policy had little to offer policy makers trying to promote economic growth.

12. Using a figure similar to Figure 14-11, explain how the money market and the loanable funds market react to a reduction in the money supply in the short run.

12. In the accompanying diagram, both the money market and the loanable funds market are initially in equilibrium at the same rate of interest, r_1. A decrease in the money supply shifts the money supply curve leftward to MS_2 and the equilibrium interest rate rises to r_2. The increase in the interest rate leads to a decrease in real GDP, which generates a decrease in savings through the multiplier process. This decrease in savings shifts the supply curve for loanable funds leftward to S_2. Consequently, the equilibrium interest rate in the loanable funds market rises. The new equilibrium interest rate in the loanable funds market equals the rate in the money market because savings fall by exactly enough to match the fall in investment spending.

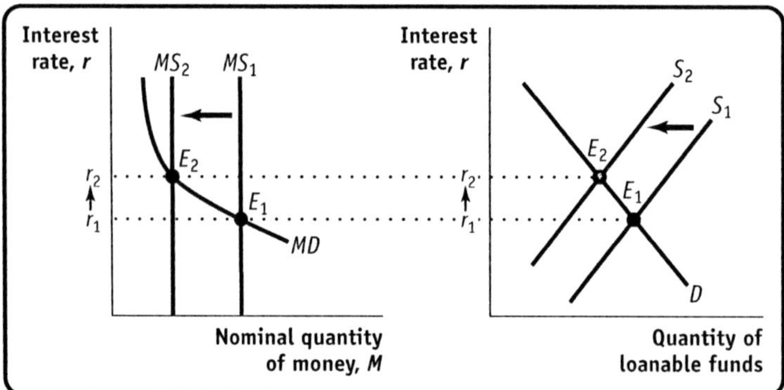

13. Contrast the short-run effects of an increase in the money supply on the interest rate to the long-run effects of an increase in the money supply on the interest rate. Which market determines the interest rate in the short run? Which market does so in the long run? What are the implications of your answers for the effectiveness of monetary policy in the short run and the long run in influencing real GDP?

13. In the short run, the interest rate is determined in the money market: the short-run equilibrium interest rate is determined where money demand equals money supply. Beginning with an economy in long-run macroeconomic equilibrium, an increase in the money supply will lead to a fall in the interest rate in the money market. The fall in the interest rate will lead to an increase in real GDP, followed by an increase in savings through the multiplier process. The increase in savings will increase the supply of loanable funds, leading to a fall in the interest rate in the loanable funds market as well. So in the short run an expansionary monetary policy will increase real GDP; similarly, a contractionary monetary policy will reduce real GDP in the short run.

In the long run, real GDP cannot differ from potential output. So in the long run, the interest rate is determined in the loanable funds market: the long-run equilibrium interest rate equalizes the supply of loanable funds and the demand for loanable funds that arises when aggregate output is equal to potential output. In the long run an increase in the money supply will ultimately result in an increase in nominal wages. The short-run aggregate supply curve will shift leftward and real GDP will fall. As real GDP falls, savings will fall as well, leading to a reduction in the supply of loanable funds and a rise in interest rate. This process will continue until aggregate output is equal to potential output. The interest rate in the money market will also rise, as a higher aggregate price level in the long run leads to an increase in the nominal demand for money. So in the long run the Fed cannot influence the interest rate and monetary policy will have no effect on real GDP.

Labor Markets, Unemployment, and Inflation

1. In each of the following situations, what type of unemployment is Melanie facing?

   a. After completing a complex programming project, Melanie is laid off. Her prospects for a new job requiring similar skills are good, and she has signed up with a programmer placement service. She has passed up low-paying job offers.

   b. When Melanie and her co-workers refused to accept pay cuts, her employer outsourced their programming tasks to workers in another country. This phenomenon is occurring throughout the programming industry.

   c. Due to the current slump in investment spending, Melanie has been laid off from her programming job. Her employer promises to re-hire her when business picks up.

1. **a.** Melanie is frictionally unemployed because she is refusing low-paying job offers in favor of searching for a higher-paying job.

   b. Melanie is structurally unemployed because she is demanding a higher wage than the current equilibrium wage in her industry. In this case, the equilibrium wage has been lowered by the outsourcing of work to other countries.

   c. Melanie is cyclically unemployed because her bout of unemployment is tied to the business cycle. It is likely she will be re-employed once the economy picks up.

2. Each month, usually on the first Friday of the month, the Bureau of Labor Statistics releases the Employment Situation Summary for the previous month. Part of the information released concerns how long individuals have been unemployed. Go to www.bls.gov to find the latest report. On the Bureau of Labor Statistics home page, click on the unemployment rate in the middle of the page, choose the Employment Situation Summary, and then click on the table titled "Unemployed persons by duration of unemployment." Use the seasonally adjusted numbers to answer the following questions.

   a. How many workers were unemployed less than 5 weeks? What percentage of all unemployed workers do these workers represent? How do these numbers compare to the previous month's data?

   b. How many workers were unemployed 27 or more weeks? What percentage of all unemployed workers do these workers represent? How do these numbers compare to the previous month's data?

   c. How long has the average worker been unemployed (average duration, in weeks)? How does this compare to the average for the previous month's data?

   d. Comparing the latest month for which there is data with the previous month, has the problem of long-term unemployment improved or deteriorated?

2. Answers will vary depending on when you look up the information.

   a. In June 2005, 2,666,000 workers had been unemployed less than 5 weeks. They represented 36.2% of all unemployed workers. The number was down from May 2005 when 2,699,000 workers had been unemployed less than 5 weeks, but the percentage of workers unemployed for less than 5 weeks was larger. In May 2005, workers unemployed less than 5 weeks represented 35.4% of the unemployed.

b. In June 2005, 1,310,000 workers had been unemployed 27 or more weeks. They represented 17.8% of all unemployed workers. The number was down from May 2005 when 1,534,000 workers had been unemployed 27 or more weeks, as was the percentage of workers unemployed for 27 or more weeks. In May 2005, workers unemployed 27 or more weeks represented 20.1% of the unemployed.

c. In June 2005, the average worker was unemployed 17.1 weeks, down from 18.8 weeks in May 2005.

d. The problem of long-term unemployment seems to be improving; the numbers for June 2005 were better than for May 2005.

3. There is only one labor market in Profunctia. All workers have the same skills and all firms hire workers with these skills. Use the accompanying diagram, which shows the supply of and demand for labor, to answer the following questions.

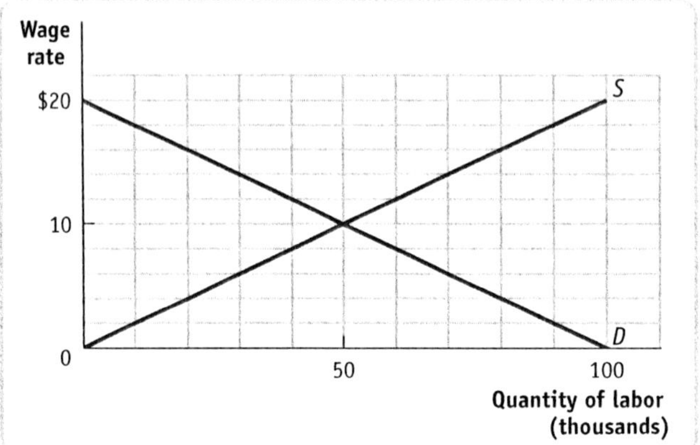

a. What is the equilibrium wage rate in Profunctia? At this wage rate, what is the level of employment, the size of the labor force, and the unemployment rate?

b. If the government of Profunctia sets a minimum wage equal to $12, what will be the level of employment, the size of the labor force, and the unemployment rate?

c. If unions bargain with the firms in Profunctia and set a wage rate equal to $14, what will be the level of employment, the size of the labor force, and the unemployment rate?

d. If the concern for retaining workers and encouraging high quality work leads firms to set a wage rate equal to $16, what will be the level of employment, the size of the labor force, and the unemployment rate?

3. a. The equilibrium wage rate is $10. At this wage rate, there will be 50,000 employed workers, no unemployed workers, a labor force of 50,000, and an unemployment rate of 0%.

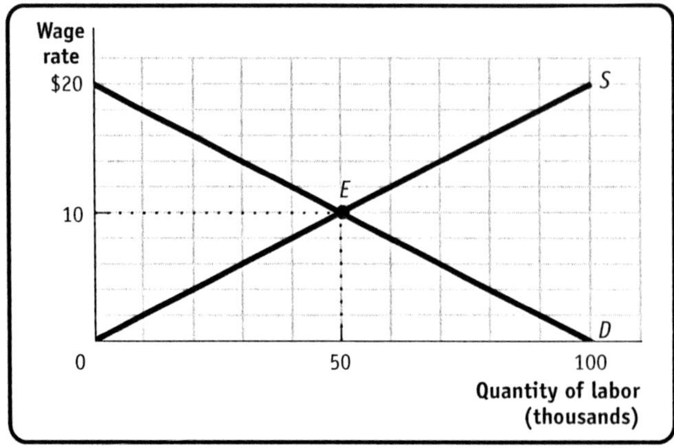

b. If the government of Profunctia sets a minimum wage equal to $12, 60,000 workers (the size of the labor force) will be looking for work but only 40,000 will find jobs. 20,000 will be unemployed and the unemployment rate will be 33.3% $(= (20,000/60,000) \times 100)$.

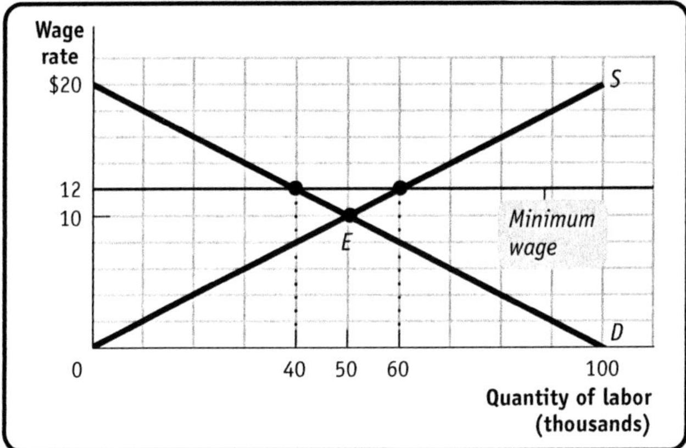

c. If unions bargain with the firms in Profunctia and set a wage rate equal to $14, 70,000 workers (the size of the labor force) will be looking for work but only 30,000 will find jobs. 40,000 will be unemployed and the unemployment rate will be 57.1% $(= (40,000/70,000) \times 100)$.

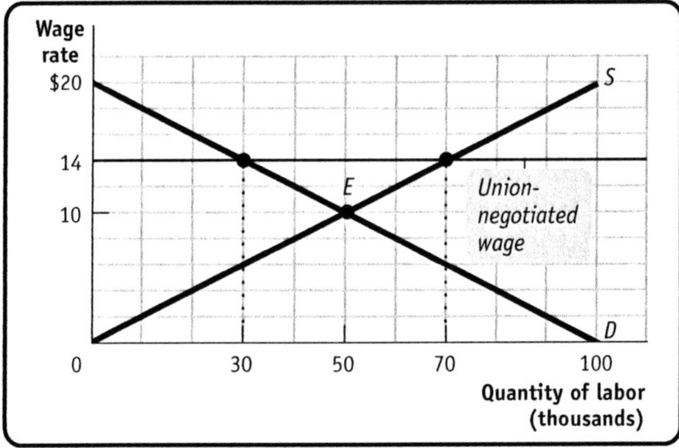

d. If the concern for retaining workers and encouraging high quality work leads firms to set a wage rate of $16, 80,000 workers (the size of the labor force) will be looking for work but only 20,000 will find jobs. 60,000 will be unemployed and the unemployment rate will be 75% $(= (60,000/80,000) \times 100)$.

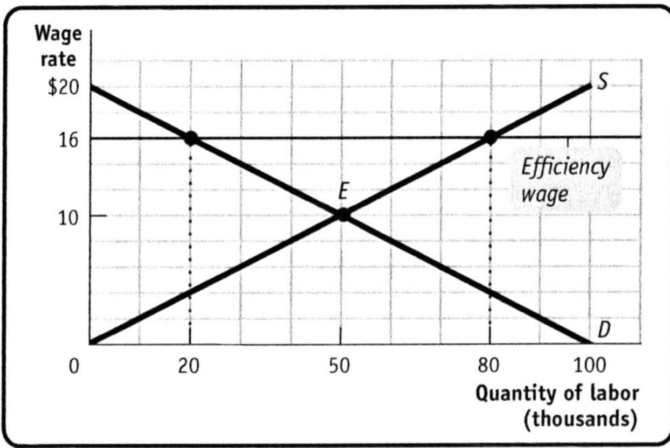

4. In Northlandia, there are no labor contracts; that is, wage rates can be renegotiated at any time. But in Southlandia, wage rates are set at the beginning of each odd year and last for two years. Why would equal-sized falls in aggregate output due to a fall in aggregate demand have different effects on the magnitude and duration of unemployment in these two economies?

4. The difference in effects on the magnitude and duration of unemployment in these two economies depends on how quickly wages can react to the change in aggregate output. When aggregate output falls, the demand for labor also falls, and firms will be willing to employ the same number of workers only if wages decline. In Northlandia where there are no labor contracts (wages can be renegotiated at any time), firms will quickly renegotiate wages and offer lower wages. Hence, the magnitude of the unemployment problem will be less and with a shorter duration in Northlandia. In Southlandia where wages are set at the beginning of each odd year and last for two years, employers will be unable to reduce wages for a period of time in the face of falling sales. Employers will lay people off rather than keep them at an unprofitably high wage. Hence, the magnitude and duration of unemployment will be larger in Southlandia until contracts can be renegotiated.

5. In which of the following cases is it more likely for efficiency wages to exist? Why?

a. Jane and her boss work as a team selling ice cream.

b. Jane sells ice cream without any direct supervision by her boss.

c. Jane speaks Korean and sells ice cream in a neighborhood in which Korean is the primary language. It is difficult to find another worker who speaks Korean.

5. a. If Jane and her boss work as a team selling ice cream, Jane will want her boss to see her doing a good job. The boss knows that the quality of her work will be high without an efficiency wage because he is there to observe her.

b. If Jane sells ice cream without any direct supervision, the boss is not certain that Jane will try her best to sell as much ice cream as she can. The boss may want to pay her an efficiency wage to encourage her to work harder.

c. Jane's boss will offer her an efficiency wage because he doesn't want to lose an employee with a skill (speaking Korean) who is not easily replaced.

6. How will the following changes affect the natural rate of unemployment?

a. The government reduces the time during which an unemployed worker can receive benefits.

b. More teenagers focus on their studies and do not look for jobs until after college.

c. Greater access to the Internet leads both potential employers and potential employees to use the Internet to list and find jobs.

d. Union membership declines.

6. a. If the government reduces the time during which an unemployed worker may obtain benefits, workers will be less willing to spend time searching for a job. This will reduce the amount of frictional unemployment and lower the natural rate of unemployment.

b. Since teenagers have a higher rate of frictional unemployment, this will lower the overall amount of frictional unemployment and lower the natural rate of unemployment.

c. Greater access to the Internet would facilitate job searches, reducing frictional unemployment, and lowering the natural rate of unemployment.

d. Since strong unions negotiate wages above the equilibrium level, they are a source of structural unemployment. A decline in union membership will reduce structural unemployment and, with it, the natural rate of unemployment.

7. With its tradition of a job for life for most citizens, Japan once had a much lower unemployment rate than that of the United States; from 1960 to 1995, the unemployment rate in Japan exceeded 3% only once. However, since the crash of its stock market in 1989 and slow economic growth in the 1990s, the job-for-life system has broken down and unemployment has risen to more than 5% in 2003. Explain the likely effect of these recent changes in Japan on the Japanese natural rate of unemployment.

7. The job-for-life system of employment in Japan led to a very low level of frictional unemployment. The only search for jobs occurred when workers first joined the labor force. The low level of frictional unemployment led to a low natural rate of unemployment. Since the stock market crash of 1989 and the slow economic growth of the 1990s, Japan has moved away from the job-for-life system. As some Japanese firms laid off workers who believed they had their jobs for life, it was difficult for many to find new jobs. Consequently, frictional unemployment has risen in Japan, leading to a higher natural rate of unemployment.

8. The accompanying scatter diagram shows the relationship between the unemployment rate and the output gap in the United States from 1990 to 2004. Draw a straight line through the scatter of dots in the figure. Assume that this line represents Okun's law:

$$\text{Unemployment rate} = b - (m \times \text{Output gap})$$
where b is the vertical intercept and m is the slope

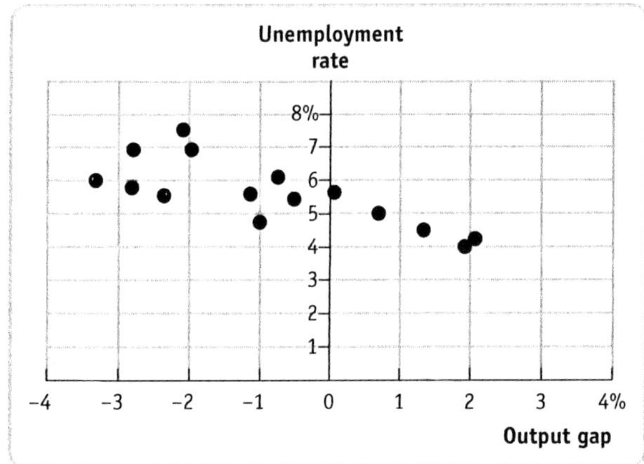

What is the unemployment rate when aggregate output equals potential output? What would the unemployment rate be if the output gap were 2%? What if the output gap were −3%? What do these results tell us about the coefficient m in Okun's law?

8. The figure below shows a line drawn through the dots relating the unemployment rate and the output gap for the U.S. from 1990 to 2004. Your line may be slightly different than the one drawn below. The line passes through the vertical axis at an unemployment rate of about 5.5%, as indicated by point A. So the unemployment rate when output equals potential output is 5.5%. At an output gap of 2%, the predicted unemployment rate is 4.5%, as shown by point B. At an output gap of −3%, the predicted unemployment rate is 7%, as shown by point C. The pattern of all three points fit Okun's law with a coefficient m equal to 0.5: Unemployment rate = 5.5% − (0.5 × Output gap).

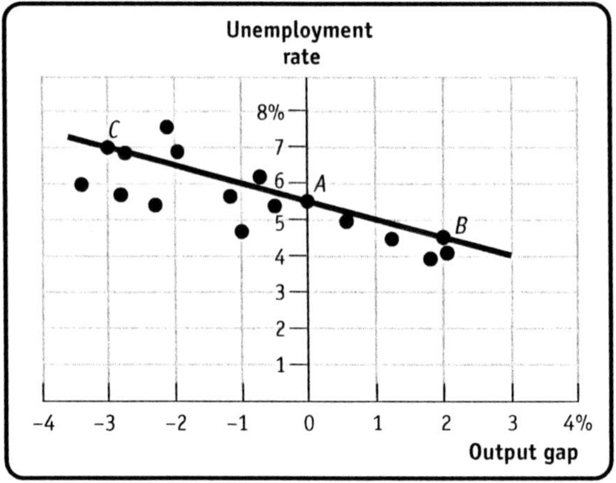

9. After experiencing a recession for the past two years, the residents of Albernia were looking forward to a decrease in the unemployment rate. Yet after six months of positive economic growth, the unemployment rate remains the same as it was at the end of the recession. How can you explain why the unemployment rate did not fall although the economy was experiencing economic growth?

9. Albernia is experiencing a jobless recovery. It must be that real GDP is growing in Albernia but at the same rate as potential output, so the output gap remains constant. According to Okun's law, the unemployment rate will remain constant as long as the output gap remains constant. For the unemployment rate to fall in Albernia, real GDP must grow at a higher rate than potential output.

10. Due to historical differences, countries often differ in how quickly a change in actual inflation is incorporated into a change in expected inflation. In a country such as Japan that has had very little inflation in recent memory, it will take longer for a change in the actual inflation rate to be reflected in a corresponding change in the expected inflation rate. In contrast, in a country such as Argentina, one that has recently had very high inflation, a change in the actual inflation rate will immediately be reflected in a corresponding change in the expected inflation rate. What does this imply about the short-run and long-run Phillips curves in these two types of countries? What does this imply about the effectiveness of monetary and fiscal policy to reduce the unemployment rate?

10. Countries such as Japan will find that they can sustain an unemployment rate lower than the NAIRU for longer periods of time before the expected inflation rate increases than countries such as Argentina. Hence, Japanese monetary and fiscal policy will be more effective than Argentinean monetary and fiscal policy in reducing unemployment below the NAIRU. However, given a sufficiently long period of higher-than-expected inflation, the Japanese people will revise their expected inflation rate upwards, and the

Japanese short-run Phillips curve will shift upwards. Hence, the long-run Japanese Phillips curve is still vertical. In contrast, Argentina will find that its short-run Phillips curve is practically vertical: because people are primed to quickly revise their inflationary expectations, an unemployment rate below the NAIRU will quickly cause an acceleration of inflation. Hence, Argentinean monetary and fiscal policy are largely ineffective even in the short run in reducing unemployment below the NAIRU.

11. The accompanying table shows data for the average annual rates of unemployment and inflation for the economy of Britannia from 1995 to 2004. Use it to construct a scatterplot similar to Figure 15-9 (Figure 32-9 in *Economics*).

Year	Unemployment rate	Inflation rate
1995	4.0%	2.5%
1996	2.0%	5.0%
1997	10.0%	1.0%
1998	8.0%	1.3%
1999	5.0%	2.0%
2000	2.5%	4.0%
2001	6.0%	1.7%
2002	1.0%	10.0%
2003	3.0%	3.0%
2004	7.0%	1.5%

Are the data consistent with a short-run Phillips curve? If the government pursues expansionary monetary policies in the future to keep the unemployment rate below the natural rate of unemployment, how effective will such a policy be?

11. As the figure below shows, the data are consistent with a short-run Phillips curve; there is a clear trade-off between the inflation rate and the unemployment rate. However, if the monetary authorities attempt to use the trade-off between inflation and unemployment to keep the unemployment rate below the natural rate, individuals will increase their expectation of inflation and the trade-off will no longer exist.

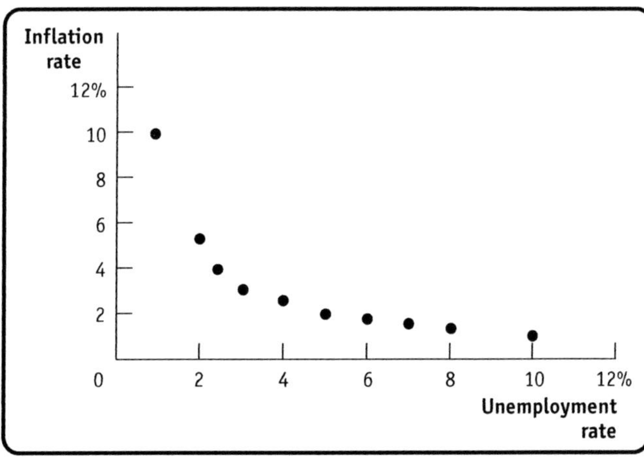

Inflation, Disinflation, and Deflation

1. In the economy of Scottopia, policy makers want to lower the unemployment rate and raise real GDP by using monetary policy. Using the accompanying diagram, show why this policy will ultimately result in a higher aggregate price level but no change in real GDP.

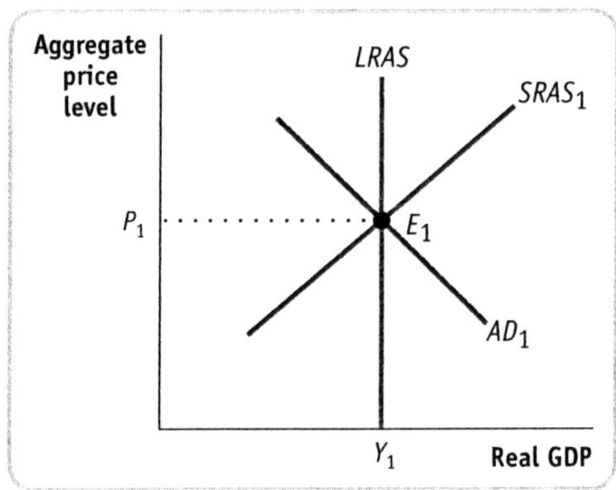

1. In the accompanying diagram, the economy of Scottopia is in long-run macroeconomic equilibrium at E_1. If policy makers want to lower the unemployment rate and raise real GDP, they will engage in expansionary monetary policy, which will shift AD_1 rightward to AD_2. In the short run, equilibrium moves to E_2; real GDP is higher and unemployment is lower. However, the aggregate price level has risen and over time, as workers are able to renegotiate wages, $SRAS_1$ will shift leftward to $SRAS_2$. In the long run, equilibrium moves to E_3 and the aggregate price level rises to P_3. The only result is that the increase in the money supply leads to an equal-percentage increase in the aggregate price level but no change in real GDP.

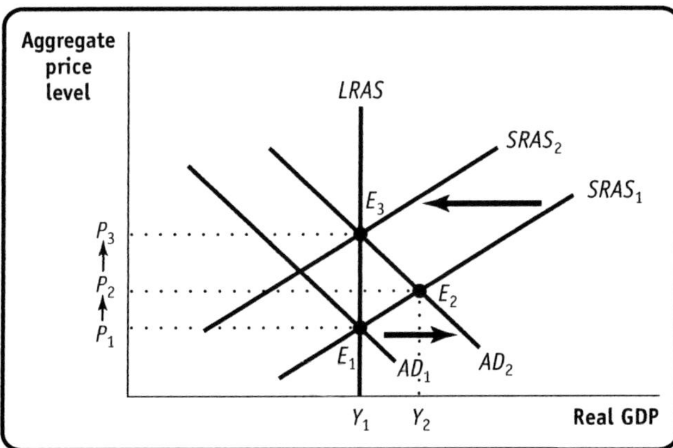

2. In the following examples, would the classical model of the price level be relevant?

a. There is a great deal of unemployment in the economy and no history of inflation.

b. The economy has just experienced five years of hyperinflation.

c. Although the economy experienced inflation in the 10% to 20% range 3 years ago, prices have recently been stable and the unemployment rate has approximated the natural rate of unemployment.

2. a. The classical model of the price level is not well suited to an economy with a great deal of unemployment and no history of inflation. Increases in aggregate output can occur without an immediate change in the aggregate price level because it takes some time for workers and firms to react to changes in the aggregate price level by increasing nominal wages and the prices of some intermediate goods.

b. When an economy has just experienced five years of hyperinflation, firms and workers will be very sensitive to any increase in the aggregate price level, so there would be little if any trade-off between inflation and unemployment. The classical model would be relevant.

c. If the economy has some history of inflation but prices have recently been stable and the unemployment rate has approximated the natural rate, there may be a trade-off between inflation and unemployment but it would be short lived because people would quickly adjust their expectations of inflation given their not-too-distant experiences of inflation. The classical model would be relevant.

3. The Federal Reserve regularly releases data on the U.S. monetary base. You can access that data at various websites, including the website for the Federal Reserve Bank of St. Louis. Go to _ http://research.stlouisfed.org/fred2/ and click on "Reserves and Monetary Base" and then on "Board of Governors Monetary Base, Adjusted for Changes in Reserve Requirements, Seasonally Adjusted (SA)" for the latest report.

a. How much did the monetary base grow in the last month?

b. How did this help in the government's efforts to finance its deficit?

c. Why is it important for the central bank to be independent from the part of the government responsible for spending?

3. Answers will vary depending on when you look up the information.

a. As of July 2005, the monetary base equaled $772.33 billion, up $0.66 billion from the previous month.

b. This $0.66 billion increase in the monetary base was created by the Fed and used to buy government securities—in effect paying off that amount of government debt by printing money.

c. It is important for the central bank to be independent from the part of the government responsible for spending because it might be too tempting to have the central bank print more money (creating inflation) whenever the government runs a budget deficit.

4. Answer the following questions about the (real) inflation tax, assuming that the price level starts at 1.

a. Maria Moneybags keeps $1,000 in her sock drawer for a year. Over the year, the inflation rate is 10%. What is the real inflation tax for this year?

b. Maria continues to keep the $1,000 in her drawer for a second year. What is the real value of this $1,000 at the beginning of the second year? Over the year, the inflation rate is again 10%. What is the real inflation tax for the second year?

c. For a third year, Maria keeps the $1,000 in the drawer. What is the real value of this $1,000 at the beginning of the third year. Over the year, the inflation rate is again 10%. What is the real inflation tax for the third year?

d. After three years, what is the cumulative real inflation tax?

e. Redo parts a through d with an inflation rate of 25%. Why is hyperinflation such a problem?

4. **a.** The real inflation tax is $100 ($1,000 × 0.10).

b. The price level at the end of the first year will be 1 × 1.10 = 1.10. The real value of $1,000 at the beginning of the second year is $1,000/(1.10) = $909.09. So the real inflation tax for the second year is $90.91 ($909.09 × 0.10).

c. The price level at the end of the second year will be 1.10 × 1.10 = 1.21 The real value of $1,000 at the beginning of the third year is $1,000/(1.21) = $826.45. So the real inflation tax for the second year is $82.64 ($826.45 × 0.10).

d. The cumulative real inflation tax for the three years is $100 + $90.91 + $82.64 = $273.55.

e. If the inflation rate is 25% and the aggregate price level equals 1 in year 1, the real inflation tax for the first year is $250.00 ($1,000 × 0.25). At the beginning of the second year, the real value of $1,000 is $1,000/1.25 = $800. For the second year, the real inflation tax is $200 ($800 × 0.25); and for the third year, it is $160 ([$1,000/(1.25)^2] × 0.25). The cumulative real inflation tax for the three years is $250 + $200 + $160 = $610. Hyperinflation is such a big problem because it can quickly erode the purchasing power of money. In our examples in just three years, an inflation rate of 10% created a real inflation tax of $273.55 on $1,000, while an inflation rate of 25% created a real inflation tax of $610 on $1,000.

5. Concerned about the crowding-out effects of government borrowing on private investment spending, a candidate for president argues that the United States should just print money to cover the government's budget deficit. What are the advantages and disadvantages of such a plan?

5. The main advantage to printing money to cover the deficit is to avoid the crowding-out effects—the reduction in private investment spending that occurs due to higher interest rates arising from government borrowing. However, the main disadvantage to printing money to cover the deficit is that it will result in inflation and individuals who currently hold money pay an inflation tax (a reduction in the value of money held by the public). Rather than financing the budget deficit with an increase in actual taxes, printing money imposes an inflation tax.

6. Boris Borrower and Lynn Lender agree that Lynn will lend Boris $10,000 and that Boris will repay the $10,000 with interest in one year. They agree to a nominal interest rate of 8%, reflecting a real interest rate of 3% on the loan and a commonly shared expected inflation rate of 5% over the next year.

a. If the inflation rate is actually 4% over the next year, how does that lower-than-expected inflation rate affect Boris and Lynn? Who is better off?

b. If the actual inflation rate is 7% over the next year, how does that affect Boris and Lynn? Who is better off?

6. **a.** If the actual inflation rate is 4%, Lynn is better off and Boris is worse off. Boris had expected to pay, and Lynn had expected to receive, a real interest rate of 3%. However, with an actual inflation rate of 4%, an 8% nominal interest rate yields a real interest rate of 4% (8% − 4% = 4%). So in real terms, Boris pays more, and Lynn receives more than was expected.

b. If the actual inflation rate is 7%, Boris is better off and Lynn is worse off. Boris had expected to pay, and Lynn had expected to receive, a real interest rate of 3%. However, with an actual inflation rate of 7%, an 8% nominal interest rate yields a real interest rate of 1% (8% − 7% = 1%). So in real terms, Boris pays less, and Lynn receives less than was expected.

7. Using the accompanying diagram, explain what will happen to the market for loanable funds when there is a fall of 2 percentage points in the expected future inflation rate. How will the change in the expected future inflation rate affect the equilibrium quantity of loanable funds?

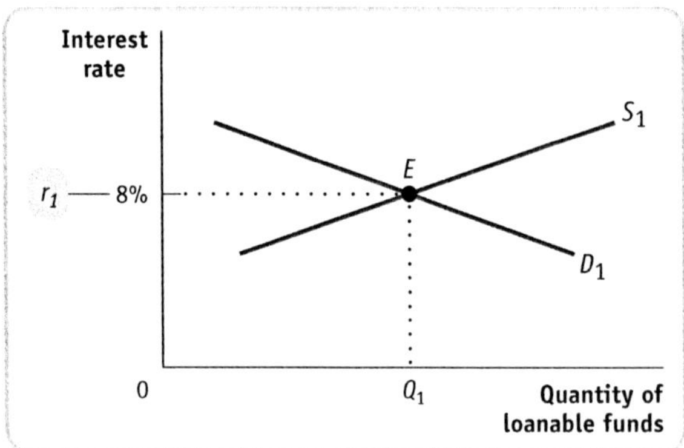

7. In the accompanying diagram, the market for loanable funds is initially in equilibrium at E_1, with a nominal interest rate of 8%. A fall of 2 percentage points in the expected future inflation rate leads, by the Fisher effect, to a fall of 2 percentage points in the nominal interest rate to 6%. The real interest rate and the equilibrium quantity of loanable funds remains unchanged. The change in expected inflation causes both a downward shift of the supply curve for loanable funds from S_1 to S_2 and a downward shift of the demand curve for loanable funds from D_1 to D_2.

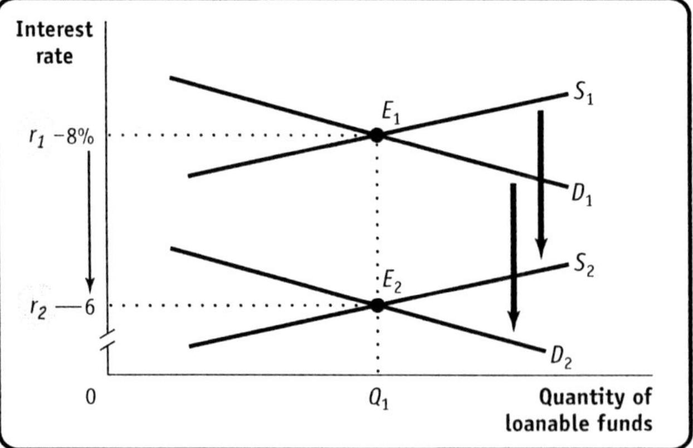

8. In the following examples, is inflation creating winners and losers at no net cost to the economy or is inflation imposing a net cost on the economy? If a net cost is being imposed, which type of cost is involved?

a. When inflation is expected to be high, workers get paid more frequently and make more trips to the bank.

b. Lanwei is reimbursed by her company for her work-related travel expenses. Sometimes, however, the company takes a long time to reimburse her. So when inflation is high, she is less willing to travel for her job.

   c. Hector Homeowner has a mortgage with a fixed nominal 6% interest rate that he took out five years ago. Over the years, the inflation rate has crept up unexpectedly to its present level of 7%.

   d. In response to unexpectedly high inflation, the manager of Cozy Cottages of Cape Cod must reprint and resend expensive color brochures correcting the price of rentals this season.

8. **a.** This is an example of the effect of shoe-leather costs, a net cost of inflation to the economy. Workers spend valuable resources going to the bank more frequently, and firms spend valuable resources (such as bookkeepers' time) in paying workers more frequently.

   b. This is an example of unit-of-account costs. A dollar when Lanwei spends it on a work-related expense is worth more than a dollar she receives much later in reimbursement from her company. Because she is less willing to travel for her job, there is a net cost to the economy of her forgone output.

   c. This is an example of inflation creating winners and losers. As the inflation rate creeps up unexpectedly, the real value of the funds that Hector pays to the mortgage company falls. So Hector is better off as inflation increases and the lender of his mortgage is worse off. At present, the real interest rate on his mortgage is negative: $6\% - 7\% = -1\%$. So he is now financing his house virtually cost-free.

   d. This is an example of menu costs, a net cost of inflation to the economy. The manager of Cozy Cottages of Cape Cod must reprint and resend an expensive brochure because it is necessary to raise the price of rentals due to unexpectedly high inflation.

9. The accompanying diagram shows mortgage interest rates and inflation during 1990–2005 in the economy of Albernia. When would home mortgages have been especially attractive and why?

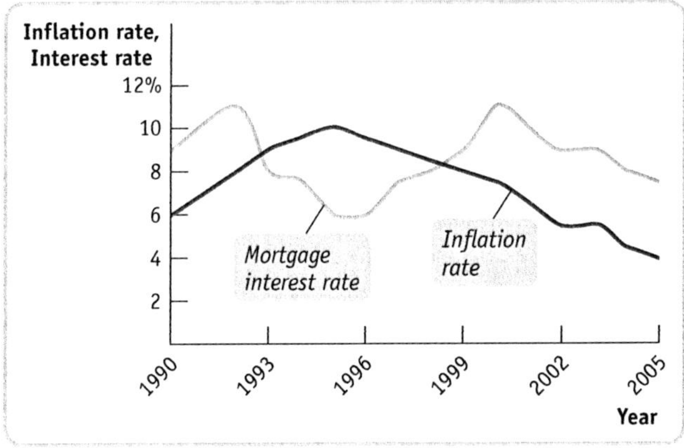

9. Home mortgages in Albernia would have been especially attractive from about 1993 to 1998. During this time, inflation was higher than mortgage interest rates, making real interest rates negative. Whenever nominal interest rates are lower than inflation, borrowers are better off and lenders are worse off.

10. The accompanying diagram shows data for the short-term (three-month) nominal interest rate as reported by the European Central Bank and inflation for the euro area for 1996 through mid-2005. How would you describe the relationship between the two? How does the pattern compare to that of the United States in Figure 16-5 (Figure 33-5 in *Economics*)?

10. The short-term nominal interest rate and the inflation rate moved somewhat together (both moving up or down) from the beginning of 1996 to the end of 2000. From 2001 to mid-2005, there doesn't seem to be an obvious pattern. From the beginning of 2002 to the beginning of 2005, inflation was higher than the short-term nominal interest rate, indicating that the real short-term nominal interest rate was negative. The pattern is similar to that of the United States shown in Figure 16-5 (Figure 33-5 in *Economics*).

11. The economy of Brittania has been suffering from high inflation with an unemployment rate equal to its natural rate. Policy makers would like to disinflate the economy with the lowest economic cost possible. Assume that the state of the economy is not the result of a negative supply shock. How can they try to minimize the unemployment cost of disinflation? Is it possible for there to be no cost of disinflation?

11. A major obstacle to achieving disinflation is that the public has come to expect continuing inflation. To reduce inflation, it is often necessary to keep the unemployment rate above the natural rate for an extended period of time so that the public can adjust its expectations to a lower inflation rate. The harder it is to change the public's expectations, the higher will be the unemployment cost associated with disinflation. To minimize the cost of disinflation, the public must believe that policy makers are committed to a lower inflation rate and will do what is necessary to achieve a lower rate. Policy makers in Brittania can announce their policy to reduce inflation in advance, in time for firms and workers to build lower inflation expectations into their wage contracts. As long as policy makers are perceived as credible, the cost of disinflation will be minimized. It is possible but unlikely for policy makers to reduce inflation without unemployment; it would require that they be seen as absolutely committed and able to disinflate the economy. If this were the case, expectations would adjust and inflation would fall immediately upon announcement of the policy.

12. Who are the winners and losers when a mortgage company lends $100,000 to the Miller family to buy a house worth $105,000 and during the first year prices unexpectedly fall by 10%? What would you expect to happen if the deflation continued over the next few years? How would continuing deflation affect the economy as a whole?

12. Over the first year, as prices fall 10%, the value of the Millers' house will fall from $105,000 to $94,500. Since they borrowed $100,000 to buy it, the value of the house is now less than the amount they owe. If they sold the house, they would not be able to pay off their mortgage. The Millers are worse off. The mortgage company is better off because as the Millers pay off their mortgage, the mortgage company will be able to lend to more potential homeowners. As the deflation continues, it will become harder and harder for the Millers to pay off their mortgage. Assuming wages are falling with deflation, the Millers will have to work more hours to pay off the mortgage. The Millers will cut back on their consumer spending. At some point, the Millers will decide to walk away from the house and default on the mortgage. Both the Millers and the mortgage company will lose, as will the economy. The Millers will find it difficult to borrow at all because they defaulted on the mortgage, and the mortgage company will be reluctant to lend in fear that the borrower will default. Continuing deflation would be extremely detrimental to the economy. Individuals and firms will be reluctant to borrow, fearing that the value of their assets will fall even though the value of their debt remains fixed, and lenders will be reluctant to lend, fearing that the borrowers will default and they will own assets whose value is less than the amount they lent.

The Making of Modern Macroeconomics

1. Since the crash of its stock market in 1989, the Japanese economy has seen little economic growth and some deflation. The accompanying table from the Organization for Economic Cooperation and Development (OECD) shows some key macroeconomic data for Japan for 1991 (a "normal" year) and 1995–2003. How did Japan's policy makers try to promote growth in the economy during this time? How does this fit in with the Keynesian and classical models of the macroeconomy?

Year	Real GDP annual growth rate	Short-term interest rate	Government debt (percent of GDP)	Government budget deficit (percent of GDP)
1991	3.4%	7.38%	64.8%	−1.81%
1995	1.9	1.23	87.1	4.71
1996	3.4	0.59	93.9	5.07
1997	1.9	0.6	100.3	3.79
1998	−1.1	0.72	112.2	5.51
1999	0.1	0.25	125.7	7.23
2000	2.8	0.25	134.1	7.48
2001	0.4	0.12	142.3	6.13
2002	−0.3	0.06	149.3	7.88
2003	2.5	0.04	157.5	7.67

1. From the annual real GDP growth rate, we can see the slow growth of the Japanese economy; the economy actually contracted in 1998 and 2002, with minimal growth in 1999 and 2001. We can also see that policy makers used expansionary monetary policy to spur the economy: short-term interest rates fell from 7.38% in 1991 to 0.04% in 2003. Finally, since government debt as a percentage of GDP rose from 64.8% in 1991 to 157.5% in 2003 but the government deficit as a percentage of GDP rose from −1.81% to 7.67%, we can conclude that they were also using expansionary fiscal policy. These monetary and fiscal policies are consistent with the Keynesian model. When the economy is facing a recessionary gap, the government should try to stimulate the economy using fiscal and monetary policies. We also see the limits of monetary policy (another Keynesian belief)—once we use expansionary monetary policy and interest rates are low, little is gained by pursuing additional expansionary monetary policy. The Japanese economy faced a liquidity trap. According to the classical model, policy makers should not have intervened in the economy because any deviation from full employment would be temporary.

2. The National Bureau of Economic Research (NBER) maintains the official chronology of past U.S. business cycles. Go to its website at http://www.nber.org/cycles/cyclesmain.html to answer the following questions.

a. How many business cycles have occurred since the end of World War II in 1945?

b. What was the average duration of a business cycle when measured from the end of one expansion (its peak) to the end of the next? That is, what was the average duration of a business cycle in the period from 1945 to the present?

c. When and what was the last announcement by the NBER's Business Cycle Dating Committee?

2. **a.** As of July 2005, there had been 10 business cycles since the end of 1945.

b. As of July 2005, the average duration of a business cycle for the period 1945–2005, when measured from the beginning of one recession (peak) to the next, was 67 months.

c. As of July 2005, the last NBER Business Cycle Dating Committee announcement was of the November 2001 trough (bottom of recession) on July 17, 2003.

3. The fall of the Soviet Union in 1989 and the subsequent reduction in U.S. defense spending helped ease some of the inflationary pressure in the United States that could have occurred during the strong economic growth of the late 1990s. Using the data in the accompanying table from the *Economic Report of the President*, replicate Figure 17-3 (Figure 34-3 in *Economics*) for the 1990–2000 period. Why would a Keynesian see the decrease in defense spending as fortunate?

Year	Budget deficit (percent of GDP)	Unemployment rate
1990	3.90%	5.60%
1991	4.5	6.8
1992	4.7	7.5
1993	3.9	6.9
1994	2.9	6.1
1995	2.2	5.6
1996	1.4	5.4
1997	0.3	4.9
1998	−0.8	4.5
1999	−1.4	4.2
2000	−2.4	4.0

3. The accompanying diagram replicates Figure 17–3 (Figure 34-3 in *Economics*) for the 1990–2000 period. It was fortunate that defense spending fell and the budget deficit declined during this period because additional spending at a time of strong growth (and low unemployment rates) could have caused inflationary pressure.

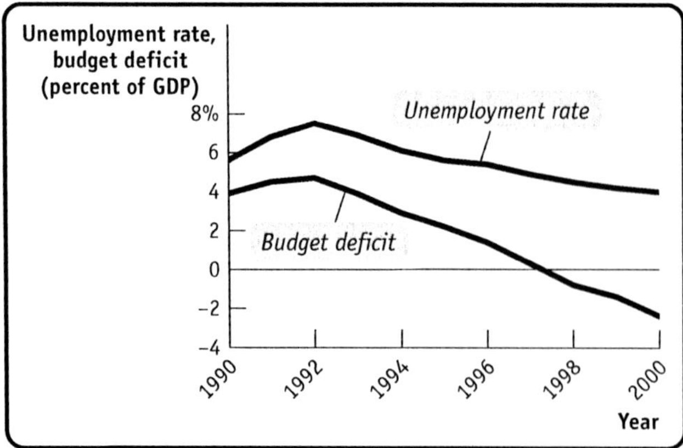

4. In the modern world, central banks are free to increase or reduce the money supply as they see fit. However, some people harken back to the "good old days" of the gold standard. Under the gold standard, the money supply could only expand when the amount of available gold increased.

   a. Under the gold standard, if the velocity of money was stable when the economy was expanding, what would have had to happen to keep prices stable?

   b. John Maynard Keynes once dismissed the gold standard as a "barbarous relic." Why would he have considered it a bad idea?

4. **a.** For prices to remain stable when the economy was expanding and the velocity of money was stable, the stock of gold would have had to grow at the same rate as real GDP.

   b. Under the gold standard there is no room for activist monetary policy, which Keynes favored.

5. The chapter explains that Kenneth Rogoff proclaimed Richard Nixon "the all-time hero of political business cycles." Using the accompanying table of data from the *Economic Report of the President,* explain why Nixon may have earned that title. (*Note:* Nixon entered office in January 1969 and was reelected in November 1972. He resigned in August 1974.)

Year	Government receipts (billions of dollars)	Government outlays (billions of dollars)	Government budget balance (billions of dollars)	M1 growth	M2 growth	3-month Treasury bill rate
1969	$186.9%	$183.6	3.2	3.3%	3.7%	6.68%
1970	192.8	195.6	−2.8	5.1	6.6	6.46
1971	187.1	210.2	−23.0	6.5	13.4	4.35
1972	207.3	230.7	−23.4	9.2	13.0	4.07
1973	230.8	245.7	−14.9	5.5	6.6	7.04

5. The data indicate that President Nixon may have used fiscal and monetary policy to aid his reelection efforts. From his first year in office, 1969, to his reelection year, 1972, federal spending grew by 27% but federal receipts grew by only 11%. Overall, the federal budget balance went from a $3.2 billion surplus to a $23.4 billion deficit as a result of these expansionary fiscal policies. Nixon also used expansionary monetary policy to increase his popularity. M1 grew 179% from 1969 to 1972, and M2 grew 251%. In response, the three-month Treasury bill rate (a short-term interest rate) fell from 6.68% to 4.07% during this same time period. After his reelection, these expansionary policies were reversed and the budget deficit shrank by $8.5 billion, or by more than a third; while the growth of M1 fell 3.7 percentage points, the growth of M2 fell 6.4 percentage points, and the three-month Treasury bill rate rose to 7.04%.

6. The economy of Albernia is facing a recessionary gap, and the leader of that nation calls together four of its best economists representing the classical, Keynesian, monetarist, and modern consensus views of the macroeconomy. Explain what policies each economist would recommend and why.

6. In response to a recessionary gap in Albernia, the economists representing the different views of the macroeconomy would make the following suggestions.

Classical: Do nothing. The recessionary gap will exist only in the short run, and the only focus for policy makers is the long run.

Keynesian: The best policies to alleviate the recessionary gap are fiscal policies. Although expansionary monetary policies can be effective in promoting economic growth, they will not be very effective when the economy is in a deep recession or depression. Also, the economy may face a liquidity trap.

Monetarist: The government should not engage in discretionary fiscal or monetary policies because such policies can worsen economic fluctutations. GDP will grow steadily without inflationary pressure if the money supply grows steadily.

Modern consensus: Both monetary and fiscal policies can reduce a recessionary gap, although if a liquidity trap exists, it will reduce or eliminate the effectiveness of monetary policy. Discretionary monetary policy is preferred over discretionary fiscal policy.

7. Which of the following policy recommendations are consistent with the classical, Keynesian, monetarist, and/or modern consensus views of the macroeconomy?

a. Since the long-run growth of real GDP is 2%, the money supply should grow at 2%.

b. Decrease government spending in order to decrease inflationary pressure.

c. Increase the money supply in order to alleviate a recessionary gap.

d. Always maintain a balanced budget.

e. Decrease the budget deficit as a percent of GDP when facing a recessionary gap.

7. **a.** Monetarists would support such a policy; they believe in a monetary policy rule that allows the money supply to grow at the same rate as real GDP. Since classical economists focus on long-term policies, they would also recommend such a policy. Keynesians and followers of the modern consensus believe that monetary policy can be useful in addressing short-run problems and would not recommend a monetary policy rule.

b. Classical economists would see the inflationary pressure as a short-run problem and would not advocate any policy; their view would be that the inflationary pressure will not exist in the long run. Monetarists would also be reluctant to endorse fiscal policy in the short run; they believe discretionary fiscal policy actually makes the economy worse. Contractionary fiscal policy, such as a decrease in government spending, would definitely be recommended by Keynesians and, *only* in very unusual circumstances, by followers of the modern consensus.

c. Classical economists would see a recessionary gap as a short-run problem and would not advocate any policy; their view would be that the recessionary gap will not exist in the long run. Monetarists would also be reluctant to endorse a short-run monetary policy because they believe it will make the economy worse. Expansionary monetary policy, such as an increase in the money supply, would be recommended by Keynesians and by followers of the modern consensus if the economy is not suffering from a liquidity trap.

d. Keynesians and followers of the modern consensus would disagree with this policy recommendation. A balanced-budget rule would eliminate the possibility of using discretionary fiscal policy whenever a recessionary or expansionary gap exists. In fact, a balanced-budget rule would require that the government employ contractionary fiscal policy during recessions (making the recession worse) and expansionary fiscal policy during expansions (creating additional inflationary pressure). Monetarists would be sympathetic to a balanced-budget rule because of the problem of crowding out. Given classical economists' focus on the long run, they would probably favor such fiscal conservatism.

e. No one would agree with this policy recommendation. Decreasing the budget deficit as a percent of GDP when facing a recessionary gap would be using contractionary fiscal policy (a decrease in government spending or an increase in taxes)—and that would make the recession worse.

International Trade

1. Assume Saudi Arabia and the United States face the production possibilities for oil and cars shown in the accompanying table.

Saudi Arabia		United States	
Quantity of oil (millions of barrels)	Quantity of cars (millions)	Quantity of oil (millions of barrels)	Quantity of cars (millions)
0	4	0	10.0
200	3	100	7.5
400	2	200	5.0
600	1	300	2.5
800	0	400	0

a. What is the opportunity cost of producing a car in Saudi Arabia? In the United States? What is the opportunity cost of producing a barrel of oil in Saudi Arabia? In the United States?

b. Which country has the comparative advantage in producing oil? In producing cars?

c. Suppose that in autarky, Saudi Arabia produces 200 million barrels of oil and 3 million cars; and that the United States produces 300 million barrels of oil and 2.5 million cars. Without trade, can Saudi Arabia produce more oil *and* more cars? Without trade, can the United States produce more oil *and* more cars?

1. a. In Saudi Arabia, 1 car can be produced by giving up production of 200 barrels of oil. So the opportunity cost of 1 car in Saudi Arabia is 200 barrels of oil. The opportunity cost of 2.5 cars in the United States is 100 barrels of oil, making the opportunity cost of 1 car equal to $100/2.5 = 40$ barrels of oil. The opportunity cost of 1 barrel of oil in Saudi Arabia is 0.005 of a car. The opportunity cost of 1 barrel of oil in the United States is 0.025 of a car.

b. Since the opportunity cost of producing oil is lower in Saudi Arabia, it has the comparative advantage in oil production. And since the opportunity cost of producing cars is lower in the United States, it has the comparative advantage in car production.

c. In autarky, Saudi Arabia cannot produce both more oil *and* more cars. If Saudi Arabia produces 200 million barrels of oil and 3 million cars, it is on its production possibility frontier. This means that it can produce more oil only if it produces fewer cars. The same is true for the United States.

2. The production possibilities for the United States and Saudi Arabia are given in Problem 1. Suppose now that each country specializes in the good in which it has the comparative advantage, and the two countries trade. Also assume that for each country the value of imports must equal the value of exports.

a. What is the total quantity of oil produced? What is the total quantity of cars produced?

b. Is it possible for Saudi Arabia to consume 400 million barrels of oil and 5 million cars, and for the United States to consume 400 million barrels of oil and 5 million cars?

c. Suppose that, in fact, Saudi Arabia consumes 300 million barrels of oil and 4 million cars and the United States consumes 500 million barrels of oil and 6 million cars. How many barrels of oil does the United States import? How many cars does the United States export? Suppose a car costs $10,000 on the world market. How much, then, does a barrel of oil cost on the world market?

2. **a.** If each country specializes, Saudi Arabia will produce 800 million barrels of oil and the United States will produce 10 million cars.

b. It is possible for Saudi Arabia to consume 400 million barrels of oil and for the United States to consume 400 million barrels of oil (for a total of 800 million barrels). And it is possible for Saudi Arabia to consume 5 million cars and for the United States to consume 5 million cars (for a total of 10 million cars).

c. The United States imports 500 million barrels of oil and exports 4 million cars. That is, each car trades for 125 barrels of oil. If a car costs $10,000 on the world market, then a barrel of oil costs $10,000/125 = $80.

3. Both Canada and the United States produce lumber and music CDs with constant opportunity costs. The United States can produce either 10 tons of lumber and no CDs, or 1,000 CDs and no lumber, or any combination in between. Canada can produce either 8 tons of lumber and no CDs, or 400 CDs and no lumber, or any combination in between.

a. Draw the U.S. and Canadian production possibility frontiers in two separate diagrams, with CDs on the horizontal axis and lumber on the vertical axis.

b. In autarky, if the United States wants to consume 500 CDs, how much lumber can it consume at most? Label this point A in your diagram. Similarly, if Canada wants to consume 1 ton of lumber, how many CDs can it consume in autarky? Label this point C in your diagram.

c. Which country has the absolute advantage in lumber production?

d. Which country has the comparative advantage in lumber production?

Suppose each country specializes in the good in which it has the comparative advantage, and there is trade.

e. How many CDs does the United States produce? How much lumber does Canada produce?

f. Is it possible for the United States to consume 500 CDs and 7 tons of lumber? Label this point B in your diagram. Is it possible for Canada at the same time to consume 500 CDs and 1 ton of lumber? Label this point D in your diagram.

3. **a.** The two accompanying diagrams illustrate the U.S. and Canadian production possibility frontiers.

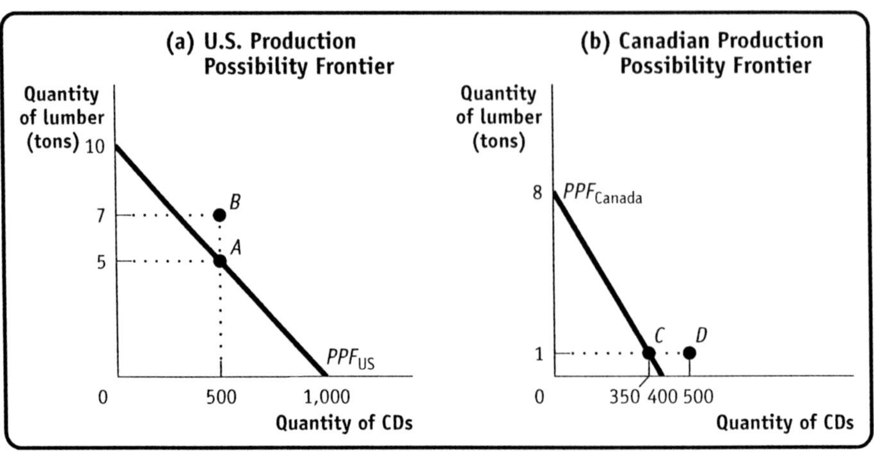

b. If the United States wants to consume 500 CDs, in autarky it can at most consume 5 tons of lumber, as indicated by point *A* in panel (a) of the diagram. And if Canada wants to consume 1 ton of lumber, it can at most consume 350 CDs in autarky, as shown by point *C* in panel (b).

c. The United States can produce at most 10 tons of lumber, and Canada can produce at most 8 tons. Therefore, the United States has the absolute advantage in lumber production.

d. In the United States, producing 1 additional ton of lumber means forgoing production of 100 CDs: the opportunity cost of 1 ton of lumber is 100 CDs. In Canada, the opportunity cost of 1 ton of lumber is 50 CDs. Since the opportunity cost of lumber production in Canada is lower, Canada has the comparative advantage in lumber production.

e. If there is trade, the United States will specialize in the production of CDs and so produce 1,000 CDs. Canada will specialize in lumber production and produce 8 tons of lumber.

f. With trade, it is possible for the United States to consume 500 CDs and 7 tons of lumber. This is shown by point *B* in the diagram. That leaves exactly 500 CDs and 1 ton of lumber to be consumed by Canada, shown by point *D*.

4. For each of the following trade relationships, explain the likely source of the comparative advantage of each of the exporting countries.

    a. The United States exports software to Venezuela, and Venezuela exports oil to the United States.

    b. The United States exports airplanes to China, and China exports clothing to the United States.

    c. The United States exports wheat to Colombia, and Colombia exports coffee to the United States.

4. a. The United States has the comparative advantage in software production because of a factor endowment: a relatively large supply of human capital. Venezuela has the comparative advantage in oil production because of a factor endowment: large oil reserves.

    b. The United States has the comparative advantage in airplane production because of an advantage in human capital: it has the human capital needed to produce airplanes. China has the comparative advantage in clothing production because of a factor endowment: it has a relatively large supply of unskilled labor.

    c. The United States has the comparative advantage in wheat production because of an advantage in climate: it has a climate suitable for growing wheat. Colombia has the comparative advantage in coffee production because of an advantage in climate: it has a climate suitable for growing coffee.

5. Shoes are labor-intensive and satellites are capital-intensive to produce. The United States has abundant capital. China has abundant labor. According to the Heckscher–Ohlin model, which good will China export? Which good will the United States export? In the United States, what will happen to the price of labor (the wage) and to the price of capital?

5. The Heckscher–Ohlin model predicts that a country will have a comparative advantage in the good whose production is intensive in the factor the country has abundantly available: the United States has the comparative advantage in satellite production, and China has the comparative advantage in shoe production. So the United States will export satellites, and China will export shoes. In the United States, demand for capital increases, raising the price of capital, but the demand for labor decreases, lowering the wage.

6. Before the North American Free Trade Agreement (NAFTA) gradually eliminated import tariffs on goods, the autarky price of tomatoes in Mexico was below the world price and in the United States was above the world price. Similarly, the autarky price of poultry in Mexico was above the world price and in the United States was below the world price. Draw diagrams with domestic supply and demand curves for each country and each of the two goods. As a result of NAFTA, the United States now imports tomatoes from Mexico and the United States now exports poultry to Mexico. How would you expect the following groups to be affected?

a. Mexican and U.S. consumers of tomatoes. Illustrate the effect on consumer surplus in your diagram.

b. Mexican and U.S. producers of tomatoes. Illustrate the effect on producer surplus in your diagram.

c. Mexican and U.S. tomato workers.

d. Mexican and U.S. consumers of poultry. Illustrate the effect on consumer surplus in your diagram.

e. Mexican and U.S. producers of poultry. Illustrate the effect on producer surplus in your diagram.

f. Mexican and U.S. poultry workers.

6. The four accompanying diagrams illustrate the U.S. and Mexican domestic demand and supply curves.

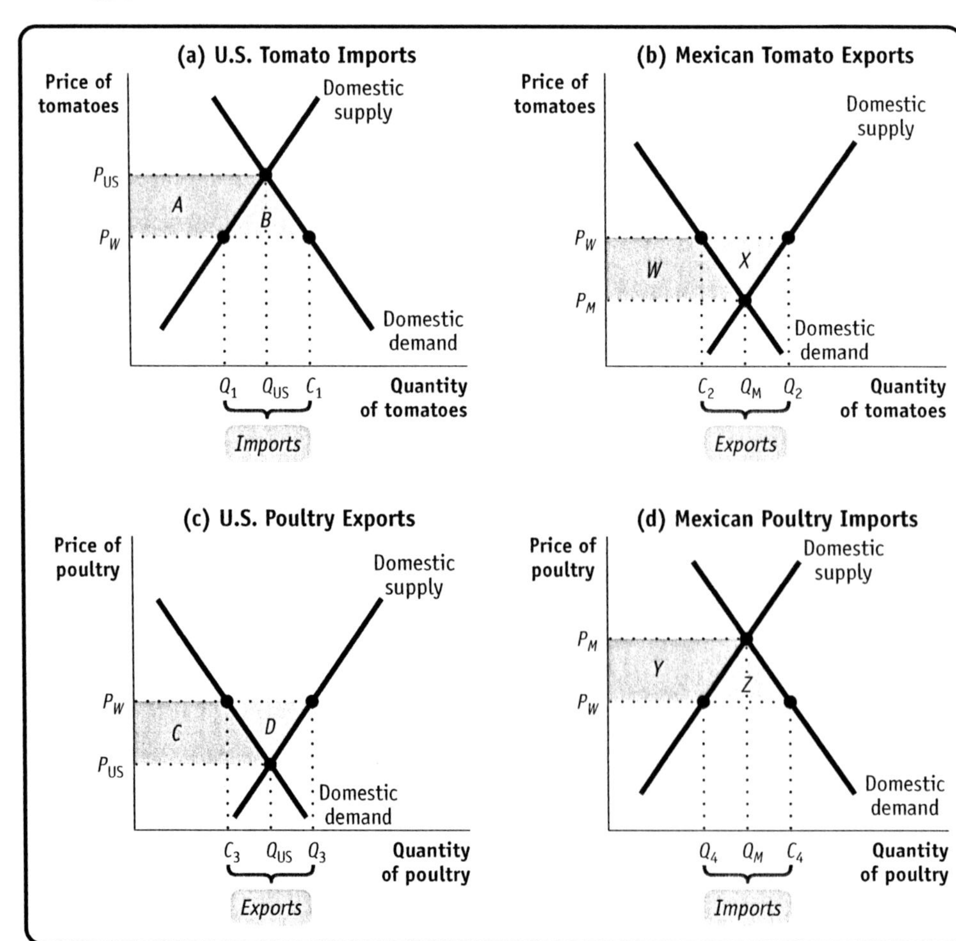

a. As shown in panel (b), consumer surplus of Mexican tomato consumers decreases by the size of area W as the price rises from P_M to P_W. As shown in panel (a), consumer surplus of U.S. tomato consumers increases by the size of the area $A + B$ as the price falls from P_{US} to P_W.

b. As shown in panel (a), production of tomatoes decreases in the United States from Q_{US} to Q_1; producer surplus decreases by the area A. As shown in panel (b), in Mexico, production of tomatoes increases from Q_M to Q_2, so producer surplus increases by the area $W + X$.

c. As production of tomatoes decreases in the United States, the demand for U.S. tomato workers falls and so the wages of U.S. tomato workers fall. In Mexico, as the production of tomatoes increases, the wages of Mexican tomato workers rise.

d. As shown in panel (d), consumer surplus increases in Mexico by the size of the area $Y + Z$ as the price falls from P_M to P_W. As shown in panel (c), consumer surplus decreases in the United States by the size of area C as the price rises from P_{US} to P_W.

e. As shown in panel (d), production of poultry decreases in Mexico, from Q_M to Q_4; therefore producer surplus in Mexico decreases by area Y. As shown in panel (c), U.S. production of poultry increases from Q_{US} to Q_3; therefore producer surplus in the United States increases by the area $C + D$.

f. As production of poultry increases in the United States, the demand for poultry workers rises and therefore the wages of poultry workers rise. In Mexico, as the production of poultry decreases, the wages of poultry workers fall.

7. The accompanying table indicates the U.S. domestic demand schedule and domestic supply schedule for commercial jet airplanes. Suppose that the world price of a commercial jet airplane is $100 million.

Price of jet (millions)	Quantity of jets demanded	Quantity of jets supplied
$120	100	1,000
110	150	900
100	200	800
90	250	700
80	300	600
70	350	500
60	400	400
50	450	300
40	500	200

a. In autarky, how many commercial jet airplanes does the United States produce, and at what price are they bought and sold?

b. With trade, what will the price for commercial jet airplanes be? Will the United States import or export airplanes? How many?

7. **a.** In autarky, the equilibrium price will be $60 million, and 400 airplanes will be bought and sold at that price.

b. When there is trade, the price rises to the world price of $100 million. At that price, the domestic quantity supplied is 800, and the domestic quantity demanded is 200. So 600 airplanes are exported.

8. The accompanying table shows the U.S. domestic demand schedule and domestic supply schedule for oranges. Suppose that the world price of oranges is $0.30 per orange.

Price of orange	Quantity of oranges demanded (thousands)	Quantity of oranges supplied (thousands)
$1.00	2	11
0.90	4	10
0.80	6	9
0.70	8	8
0.60	10	7
0.50	12	6
0.40	14	5
0.30	16	4
0.20	18	3

a. Draw the U.S. domestic supply curve and domestic demand curve.

b. With free trade, how many oranges will the United States import or export?

Suppose that the U.S. government imposes a tariff on oranges of $0.20 per orange.

c. How many oranges will the United States import or export after introduction of the tariff?

d. In your diagram, shade the gain or loss to the economy as a whole from the introduction of this tariff.

8. a. The U.S. domestic supply and demand curves are illustrated in the accompanying diagram.

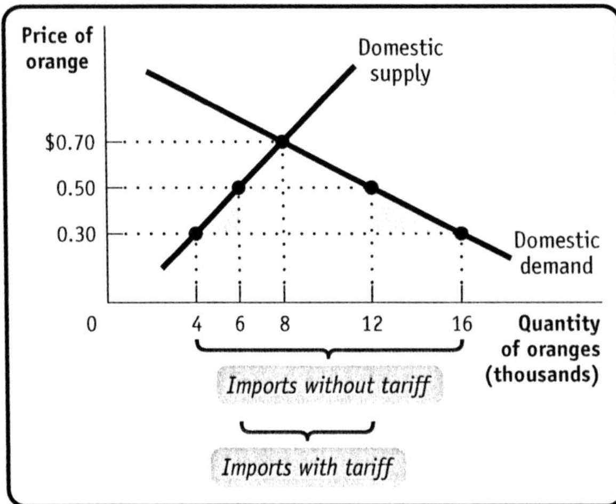

b. With free trade, the price will be the world price, $0.30, the domestic quantity demanded will be 16,000 oranges, and the domestic quantity supplied will be 4,000 oranges. The United States therefore imports 12,000 oranges.

    c. With the tariff, the domestic price rises to $0.50. At that price, the domestic quantity demanded exceeds the domestic quantity supplied by 6,000. The United States imports 6,000 oranges.

    d. The shaded areas indicate the deadweight loss to the economy as a whole due to the tariff.

9. The U.S. domestic demand schedule and domestic supply schedule for oranges was given in Problem 8. Suppose that the world price of oranges is $0.30. The United States introduces an import quota of 3,000 oranges. Draw the domestic demand and supply curves and answer the following questions.

    a. What will the domestic price of oranges be after introduction of the quota?

    b. What is the value of the quota rents that importers of oranges receive?

9. The domestic demand and domestic supply curves are shown in the accompanying diagram.

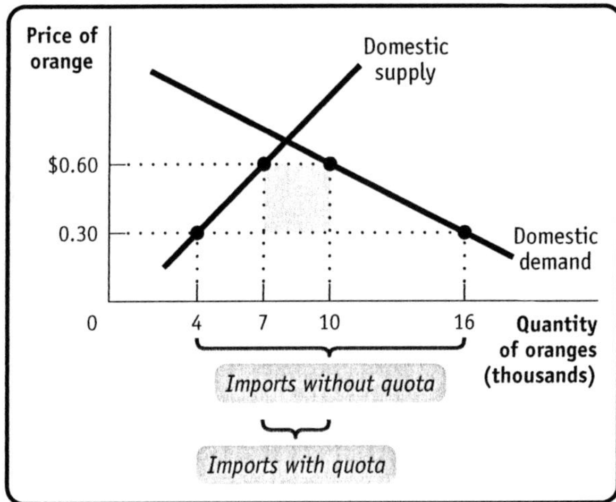

    a. After imposition of the quota, instead of importing 16,000 − 4,000 = 12,000 oranges, the United States imports only 3,000 oranges. The price rises to $0.60.

    b. The importers of oranges receive quota rent of $0.30 × 3,000 = $900.

10. The accompanying diagram illustrates the U.S. domestic demand curve and domestic supply curve for beef.

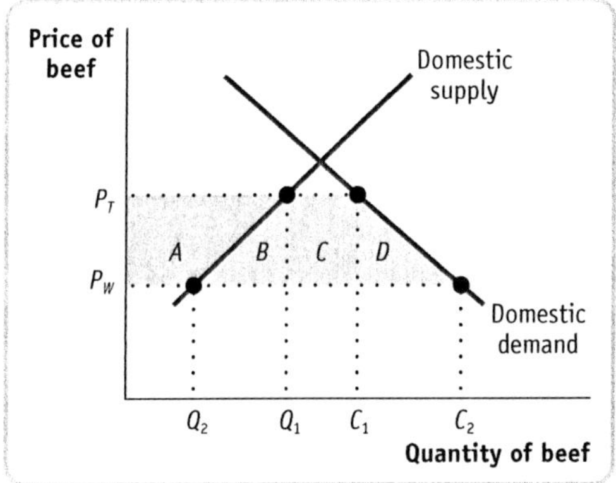

The world price of beef is P_W. The United States currently imposes an import tariff on beef, so the price of beef is P_T. Congress decides to eliminate the tariff. In terms of the areas marked in the diagram, answer the following questions.

a. What is the gain/loss in consumer surplus?

b. What is the gain/loss in producer surplus?

c. What is the gain/loss to the government?

d. What is the gain/loss to the economy as a whole?

10. **a.** As the price falls from P_T to P_W, consumer surplus increases by the area $A + B + C + D$.

b. As the price falls, producer surplus decreases by the area A.

c. As the tariff is eliminated, the government loses revenue of area C, which is the amount of imports under the tariff $(C_1 - Q_1)$ times the tariff.

d. The gain to the economy as a whole is the gain to consumers minus the loss to producers minus the loss to the government: $A + B + C + D - A - C = B + D$.

11. As the United States has opened up to trade, it has lost many of its low-skill manufacturing jobs, but it has gained jobs in high-skill industries, such as the software industry. Explain whether the United States as a whole has been made better off by trade.

11. As the United States has opened up to trade, it has specialized in producing goods that use high-skill labor (such as software design) in which it has a comparative advantage, and it has allowed other countries to specialize in producing low-skill manufactured goods in which they have the comparative advantage. As a result, the country has lost low-skill manufacturing jobs (and the wage to low-skill workers has fallen), and it has gained jobs in high-skill industries (and the wage to high-skill workers has risen). That is, demand for labor in exporting industries has risen, and demand for labor in the import-competing industries has fallen, as the Heckscher–Ohlin model predicts. But as a result of trade, the United States can now consume more of all goods than before. That is, overall the economy is better off: so the gains to highly skilled workers outweigh the losses to low-skill workers.

12. The United States is highly protective of its agricultural industry, imposing import tariffs, and sometimes quotas, on imports of agricultural goods. The chapter has presented three arguments for trade protection. For each argument, discuss whether it is a valid justification for trade protection of U.S. agricultural products.

12. The three arguments for trade protection are the national security, job creation, and infant industry arguments. Agriculture is not an infant industry, so this argument does not apply. Some argument can be made that agricultural products are necessary for national security: if we depended completely on imports for our agricultural goods, we would be vulnerable if our trading partners cut off our imports. And protecting agriculture does not create jobs. It does protect farming jobs; but it is likely that if agriculture lost its protection from imports, those workers could find other jobs in industries that expand due to lower food costs (such as the restaurant industry). The rationale for protecting agricultural markets from imports must lie elsewhere—in the political power of the farm lobby.

13. In World Trade Organization (WTO) negotiations, if a country agrees to reduce trade barriers (tariffs or quotas), it usually refers to this as a *concession* to other countries. Do you think that this terminology is appropriate?

13. The word *concession* implies that when a country lowers its trade barriers, it is giving up something to other countries. As discussed in this chapter, free trade is beneficial to all countries, including the country that lowers its trade barriers. In fact, even if no other country reduces its trade barriers, the country that does lower its trade barriers still benefits from trade. By allowing more international trade, each country's economy simply gains overall.

14. Producers in import-competing industries often make the following argument: "Other countries have an advantage in production of certain goods purely because workers abroad are paid lower wages. In fact, American workers are much more productive than foreign workers. So import-competing industries need to be protected." Is this a valid argument? Explain your answer.

14. Even if American workers are better at everything than are foreign workers (that is, even if America has the absolute advantage in everything), this does not mean that the United States should restrict trade. What matters for trade is who has the comparative advantage. In fact, other countries will have a comparative advantage in some good or service, and specialization and trade will mean welfare improvements for both countries. Claiming that other countries have an advantage only because labor is so cheap relies on the pauper labor fallacy.

Open-Economy Macroeconomics

1. How would the following transactions be categorized in the U.S. balance of payments accounts? Would they be entered in the current account (as a payment to or from a foreigner) or the financial account (as a sale to or purchase of assets from a foreigner)? How will the balance of payments on the current and financial accounts change?

  a. A French importer buys a case of California wine for $500.

  b. An American who works for a French company deposits her paycheck, drawn on a Paris bank, into her San Francisco bank.

  c. An American buys a bond from a Japanese company for $10,000.

  d. An American charity sends $100,000 to Africa to help local residents buy food after a harvest shortfall.

1. a. When the French importer buys the California wine, the transaction is entered as a payment from foreigners in the current account. The balance of payments on the U.S. current account will rise.

  b. When the American is paid by the French company, she is receiving factor income in exchange for export of her labor sevices. It is entered in the U.S. current account as an export. The balance of payments on the U.S. current account will rise.

  c. When an American buys a Japanese bond, the transaction is entered in the U.S. financial account as a purchase of a Japanese asset from an American. The balance of payments on the U.S. financial account will fall.

  d. When an American charity sends a gift to Africa, it is entered as a transfer payment to a foreigner in the U.S. current account. The balance on the U.S. current account will fall.

2. In the economy of Scottopia in 2005, exports equaled $400 billion of goods and $300 billion of services, imports equaled $500 billion of goods and $350 billion of services, and the rest of the world purchased $250 billion of Scottopia's assets. What was the merchandise trade balance for Scottopia? What was the balance of payments on current account in Scottopia? What was the balance of payments on financial account? What was the value of Scottopia's purchases of assets from the rest of the world?

2. In 2005, the merchandise trade balance was −$100 billion ($400 billion − $500 billion). The balance of payments on current account was −$150 billion [($400 billion + $300 billion) − ($500 billion + $350 billion)]. Since the balance of payments on financial account plus the balance of payments on current account must sum to zero, the balance of payments on financial account must have been +$150 billion. If the rest of the world bought $250 billion of Scottopia's assets, Scottopia must have bought $100 billion of assets from the rest of the world.

3. In the economy of Popania in 2005, total Popanian purchases of assets in the rest of the world equaled $300 billion, purchases of Popanian assets by the rest of the world equaled $400 billion, and Popania exported goods and services equal to $350 billion. What was Popania's balance of payments on financial account in 2005? What was its balance of payments on current account? What was the value of its imports?

3. In 2005, Popania's balance of payments on financial account was +$100 billion ($400 billion − $300 billion). Since the balance of payments on financial account plus the balance of payments on current account must sum to zero, the balance of payments on current account must have been −$100 billion. If Popania exported $350 billion of goods and services, it must have imported $450 billion of goods and services.

4. Suppose that Northlandia and Southlandia are the only two trading countries in the world, that each nation runs a balance of payments on both current and financial accounts equal to zero, and that each nation sees the other's assets as identical to its own. Using the accompanying diagrams, explain how the demand and supply of loanable funds, the interest rate, and the balance of payments on current and financial accounts will change in each country if international capital flows are possible.

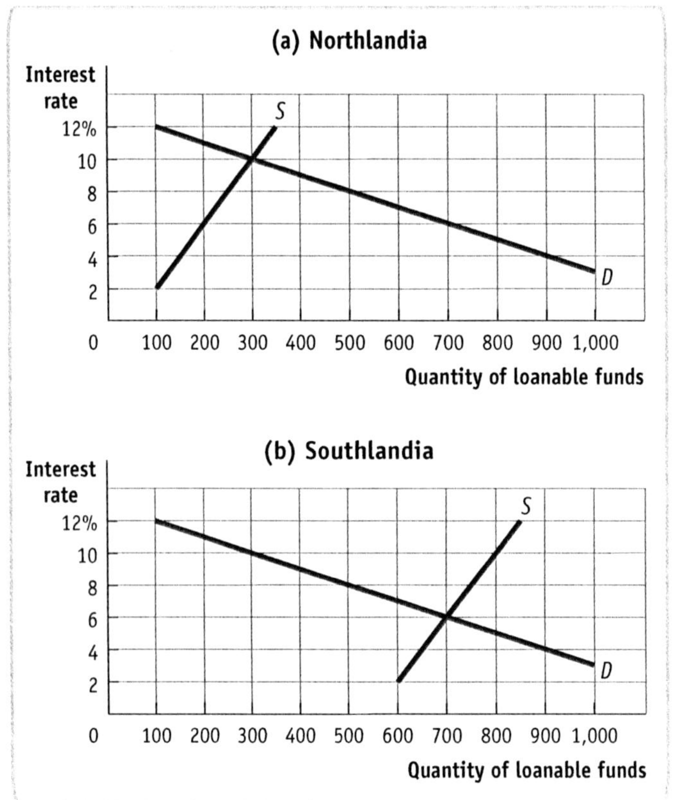

4. Since the interest rate is 10% in Northlandia and 6% in Southlandia, demanders of loanable funds in Northlandia will want to borrow in Southlandia and suppliers of loanable funds in Southlandia will want to lend in Northlandia. As the supply of loanable funds falls in Southlandia, the interest rate in Southlandia will rise; as the supply of loanable funds rises in Northlandia, the interest rate in Northlandia will fall. This will narrow the gap between interest rates in the two countries. Since no one distinguishes between the assets in the two countries, interest rates will change in both countries until they are equal, so that there is no additional incentive for suppliers of loanable funds in Southlandia to lend in Northlandia and for demanders of loanable funds in Northlandia to borrow in Southlandia. In the accompanying diagrams, you can see that at an interest rate of 8% there is an excess supply of loanable funds in Southlandia equal to 250 and an excess demand for loanable funds in Northlandia equal to 250. So the two countries will both end up with an interest rate of 8%.

end up with an interest rate of 8%. Northlandia will run a surplus of 250 in the financial account and a deficit of 250 in the current account; Southlandia will run a deficit of 250 in the financial account and a surplus of 250 in the current account.

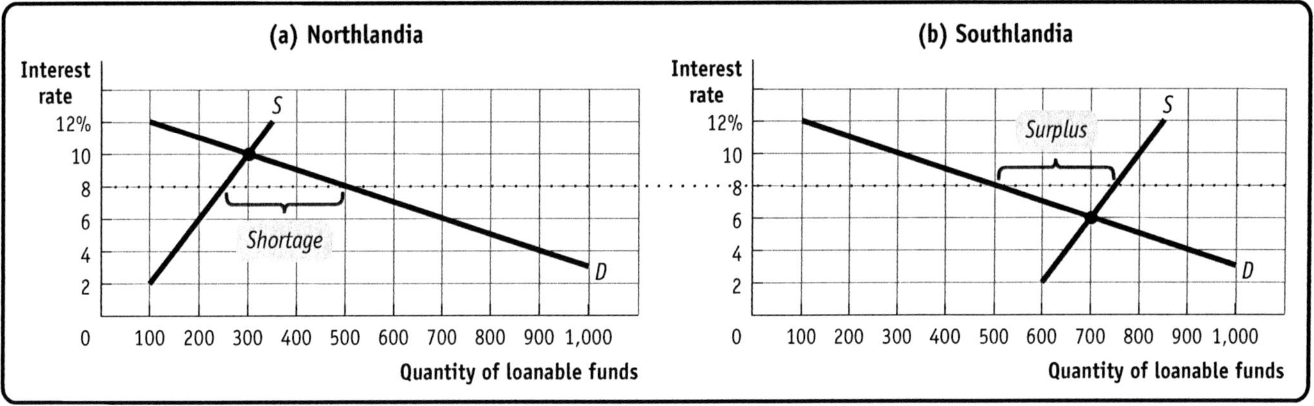

5. Based on the exchange rates for the first trading days of 2004 and 2005 shown in the accompanying table, did the U.S. dollar appreciate or depreciate during 2004? Did the movement in the value of the U.S. dollar make American goods and services more or less attractive to foreigners?

January 2, 2004	January 3, 2005
US$1.79 to buy 1 British pound sterling	US$1.91 to buy 1 British pound sterling
33.98 Taiwan dollars to buy US$1	31.71 Taiwan dollars to buy US$1
US$0.78 to buy 1 Canadian dollar	US$0.83 to buy 1 Canadian dollar
104.27 Japanese yen to buy US$1	106.95 Japanese yen to buy US$1
US$1.26 to buy 1 euro	US$1.38 to buy 1 euro
1.24 Swiss francs to buy US$1	1.15 Swiss francs to buy US$1

5. For each of the exchange rates shown except for the U.S. dollar–Japanese yen exchange rate, the U.S. dollar depreciated. When the U.S. dollar depreciates, it is less attractive for Americans to buy foreign goods and more attractive for foreigners to buy American goods, other things equal.

6. Suppose the United States and Japan are the only two trading countries in the world. What will happen to the value of the U.S. dollar if the following occur, other things equal?

a. Japan relaxes some of its import restrictions.

b. The United States imposes some import tariffs on Japanese goods.

c. Interest rates in the United States rise dramatically.

d. A report indicates that Japanese cars last much longer than previously thought, especially compared with American cars.

6. **a.** If Japan relaxes import restrictions, Japanese residents will demand more U.S. goods and more U.S. dollars to buy those goods. The U.S. dollar will appreciate due to the increase in the demand for U.S. dollars.

b. If the United States imposes import restrictions, Americans will buy fewer Japanese goods. Americans will want to exchange fewer U.S. dollars for yen, so the supply of U.S. dollars will decrease and the U.S. dollar will appreciate.

c. A dramatic rise in U.S. interest rates will attract Japanese buyers of American assets as well as discourage Americans from buying Japanese assets. There will be an increase in the demand for U.S. dollars and a decrease in the supply of U.S. dollars; the U.S. dollar will appreciate.

d. A report indicating that Japanese cars last much longer than previously thought, especially when compared with American cars, will increase the demand for Japanese cars and the demand for Japanese yen. The yen will appreciate and the U.S. dollar will depreciate.

7. In each of the following scenarios, suppose that the two nations are the only trading nations in the world. Given inflation and the change in the nominal exchange rate, which nation's goods become more attractive?

a. Inflation is 10% in the United States and 5% in Japan; the U.S. dollar–Japanese yen exchange rate remains the same.

b. Inflation is 3% in the United States and 8% in Mexico; the price of the U.S. dollar falls from 12.50 to 10.25 Mexican pesos.

c. Inflation is 5% in the United States and 3% in the Euro-area; the price of the euro falls from $1.30 to $1.20.

d. Inflation is 8% in the United States and 4% in Canada; the price of the Canadian dollar rises from US$0.60 to US$0.75.

7. **a.** If inflation is 10% in the United States and 5% in Japan, and the U.S. dollar–Japanese yen nominal exchange rate remains the same, Japanese goods and services will be more attractive than U.S. ones.

b. If inflation is 3% in the United States and 8% in Mexico, and the price of the U.S. dollar falls from 12.50 to 10.25 Mexican pesos, both the lower inflation and the depreciation of the dollar (appreciation of the peso) make American goods more attractive.

c. If inflation is 5% in the United States and 3% in the Euro-area, and the price of the euro falls from $1.30 to $1.20, both the lower inflation in the Euro-area and the appreciation of the dollar (depreciation of the euro) make Euro-area goods more attractive.

d. If inflation in the United States is higher than in Canada, this makes Canadian goods more attractive. However, if the U.S. dollar depreciates against the Canadian dollar, this makes American goods more attractive. In this case, the depreciation of the U.S. dollar is so dramatic that it overwhelms the difference in inflation rates. American goods are more attractive.

8. Starting from a position of equilibrium in the foreign exchange market under a fixed exchange rate system, how must a government react to an increase in the demand for the nation's goods and services by the rest of the world to keep the exchange rate at its fixed value?

8. If there is an increase in the demand for that nation's goods and services, there will also be an increase in the demand for its currency, putting upward pressure on the value of the currency. There are three ways in which the central bank can keep the exchange rate at its fixed value. First, it can increase supply of the domestic currency by purchasing foreign assets. Second, it could decrease interest rates, which would discourage foreign investors from buying domestic assets (decreasing the demand for the domestic currency) and encourage domestic residents to buy foreign assets (increasing the supply of the domestic currency). Third, it can impose foreign exchange controls that limit the ability of foreigners to buy the domestic currency.

9. Suppose that Albernia's central bank has fixed the value of its currency, the bern, to the U.S. dollar (at a rate of US$1.50 to 1 bern) and is committed to that exchange rate. Initially, the foreign exchange market for the bern is also in equilibrium, as shown in the accompanying diagram. However, both Albernians and Americans begin to believe that there are big risks in holding Albernian assets; and as a result, they become unwilling to hold Albernian assets unless they receive a higher rate of return on them than they do on U.S. assets. How would this affect the diagram? If the Albernian central bank tries to keep the exchange rate fixed using monetary policy, how will this affect the Albernian economy?

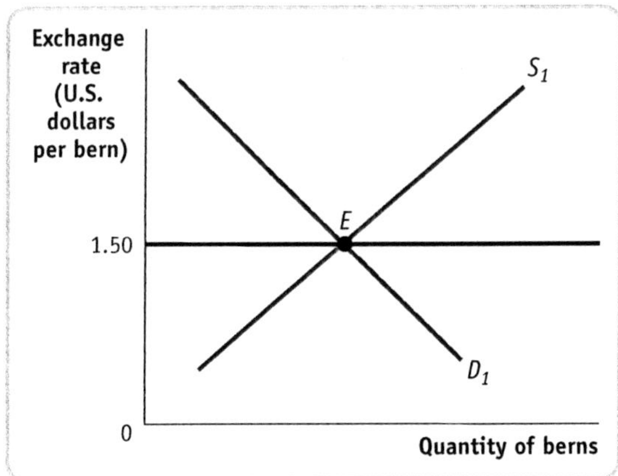

9. If both Albernians and Americans begin to believe that the Albernian assets are risky, this will reduce the demand for the bern (from D_1 to D_2 in the accompanying figure), as Americans become less willing to buy Albernian assets, and increase the supply of the bern (from S_1 to S_2), as Albernians become more willing to buy American assets. Both the decrease in demand and the increase in supply will put downward pressure on the bern; in the diagram, the equilibrium value of the bern falls to $1.00. Since the central bank is committed to a value of $1.50 for the bern, it must

act to make Albernian assets more attractive by raising the interest rate. This will
have a contractionary effect on the Albernian economy.

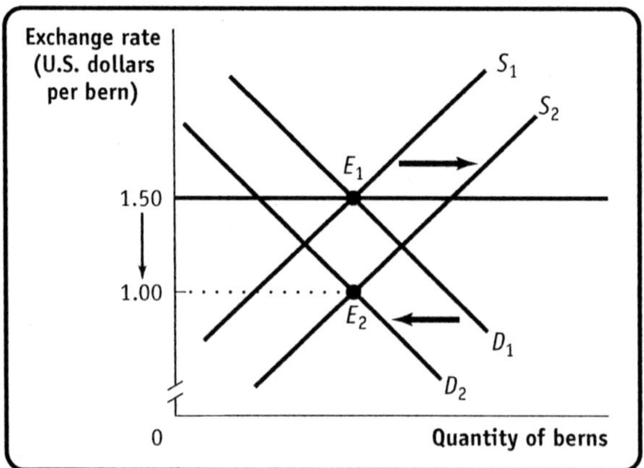

10. Your study partner asks you, "If central banks lose the ability to use discretionary
monetary policy under fixed exchange rates, why would nations agree to a fixed
exchange rate system?" How do you respond?

10. You would respond by explaining the advantages of a fixed exchange rate. First, it
reduces some uncertainty that might make businesses reluctant to undertake international transactions. In particular, it eliminates any uncertainty about the value of
the currency. When businesses enter into a contract that calls for payment in a foreign currency at some time in the future, they know exactly how much it will cost
them in the domestic currency. Also, by committing to a fixed exchange rate, the
country eliminates any possibility that it will engage in inflationary policies.